A Shell Guide

Cambridgeshire

inscribed for Gwen for Christmas
with the author's very
best wishes.

A Shell Guide

Faber and Faber   3 Queen Square   London

Cambridgeshire

by Norman Scarfe

First published in 1983
by Faber and Faber Limited
3 Queen Square London WC1N 3AU
Printed in Great Britain by
BAS Printers Ltd, Over Wallop,
Hampshire
All rights reserved

*The Isle of Ely and Cambridgeshire
were two separate counties from the
early Middle Ages until the year
1965, when they became one county
known as 'Cambridgeshire and the
Isle of Ely'. This is the county described here.*
*—In 1974, Huntingdonshire was
added, and the amalgam is officially
called Cambridgeshire. Nevertheless,
a shell Guide to Huntingdonshire is
being prepared.*

*British Library Cataloguing in
Publication Data*

Scarfe, Norman
   Cambridgeshire—(A Shell
Guide)
   1. Cambridgeshire—Description
and travel—Guide-books
   I. Title   II. Series
   914.26'50485   DA670 C2

   ISBN 0–571–09817–7
   ISBN 0–571–13250–2 Pbk

Contents

Under the Trinity College Library,
Cambridge

**To William Hoskins,
interpreter of the English landscape,
and Nigel Hamilton,
interpreter of Monty.**

CAMBRIDGE, known the world over and
visited by some 2½ million people every year,
lies at the heart of a little-known, richly interesting county. What Cambridge is is not at all shire
obvious, and its gradual discovery is all the
more rewarding. Looking at each of its parishes, at its boundaries and its patterns of
building, I have satisfied much of my own
curiosity, and I hope that by doing so I may
have met many of the needs of readers sightseeing in Cambridgeshire.

I have run up heavy debts to generous
scholars and friends: Tony Baggs, Kathleen
Burall, Colin Forbes, Julia Hedgecoe,
Dorothy Owen and Denys Spittle. Olive
Cook's friendship, and her writing, are an
unfailing inspiration. A. K. Astbury's *The
Black Fens* and Jack Ravensdale's *Liable to
Floods* are both books of revelation. The standard sources are naturally indispensable: I've
largely relied on the volumes of the Royal
Commission on Historical Monuments, of the
Victoria County History, the Cambridge
Antiquarian Society and Sir Nikolaus
Pevsner. George Coulson shared countless
parish explorations with me, and both I and
the reader owe a lot to his acute and sympathetic observation. Frank Collieson's vigilant
eyes have checked the proofs, and I'm deeply
grateful to him and his colleagues at Heffers
for their friendly welcome and frequent hospitality in the lunch-break behind their magic
galleries of books. Ted Sheppard, of Shell
U.K. Oil, has been most kindly encouraging.
So has John Piper: with him and Edward
Piper, and Sandie Boccacci at Faber, it is truly
a pleasure to work.

Woodbridge, Suffolk.   N.S.
March, 1983.

The Backs in autumn at King's College, **Cambridge**

Illustrations

Note: Captions to the photographs include place names in **bold type**. These refer to entries in the gazetteer, pages 37–218.

Burwell: Nave roof-cornice, Annunciation and Assumption

9

Wicken Fen

Cambridge Frontiers

The Bridge

The only bridge built into the name of a shire is the main one in Cambridge, across the Cam. Lately strengthened, not much to look at, and long called, very parochially, Magdalene Bridge (after the adjacent college), it was the Great Bridge till Tudor times. With none of the dignity and proclamation of Oxford's Magdalen Bridge, the Cam bridge nevertheless spans a river-line in the ancient frontier-zone between the Midlands and East Anglia. The town grew up as a port and trading-post beside a river-crossing, and only centuries later a settlement of scholars, a frontier-town for minds.

Until the Fens were drained, this was the lowest reliable place for crossing the Cam. The Roman road from Colchester, sweeping round from Haverhill to the Gog Magog Hills, crossed the river here on the way to Godmanchester and beyond. It was called the Via Devana by antiquaries who supposed it to be heading for Deva (Chester), but its older name, used occasionally in this book, is Wool Street, which began as Wolvestreet, infested by wolves. Just west of the Cam, the Roman precursor of the present administrative headquarters of Cambridgeshire was called *Duroliponte* but the toponymist experts will not allow *ponte* to refer to a Roman bridge. *Duro* means 'walled town', and *uliponti*, they say, means 'by a swampy river'. Not improbably.

The first English bridge here is thought to have been built by King Offa of Mercia (757–96), better remembered for his Dyke. He had trade and diplomatic links with Charlemagne. One begins to form a picture of the struggling cart-horse forerunners of the juggernaut lorries that until recently ran through Cambridge on their way between Birmingham and the East Anglian ports. For years the visitor drove over Magdalene Bridge noticing only the traffic congestion. Busy though it still is, it is the best place to start looking at the town, and thinking about the county.

Whether or not it was built by Offa, the English name for it was Grontabridge, or Grantabridge, meaning, again, 'swampy-river bridge', and the name was attached to the settlements at either side of the bridge. Then, in 874, five years after the Danes slew Edmund, king of East Anglia, making him Saint Edmund, three of their own 'kings', including Guthrum, settled for a year at Grantabridge with 'a great army'. They recognized the strategic value of the place, plain to Iron Age people as to Cromwell, a major river-crossing with good lateral movement and excellent defences: the fen in the rear, and, by Anglo-Saxon times, a series of enormous ramparts and ditches blocking the great chalk prehistoric highway from the south. In 920, the Grantabridge 'host' accepted the overlordship of King Alfred's son, Edward the Elder, and one detects the beginnings of an Anglo-Danish *Grantabridgeshire*. In 1010, at the epic battle of Ringmere (Norfolk), its men proudly stood and fought the intolerable new Viking invaders before whom the Anglo-Danes of East Anglia broke and fled (q.v. Balsham). Cambridgeshire had been brought into being: more, it had established an identity to be proud of. Half a century later, the French Normans took over, and recorded the whole contents of the county in Domesday Book, though not until Hereward the Wake had put up a last fight against them in the Ely fens. Cambridgeshire kept its identity under the Normans and down the centuries till 1974. It was administratively separate from the Isle of Ely until 1965; both were then sudenly merged with Huntingdonshire, which naturally retains its people's loyalty and, with its own qualities of upland and riverside, is covered in another Guide.*

The Norman-French quickly turned the name Grantabridge into Cantabridge, which by the 14th century had become Caumbridge. In that change, you see how the confusion arises, whether we are to call the river Granta or Cam. The people of Cambridge now tend to resolve it irrationally, changing it from Granta to Cam as it flows under Silver Street, the first road-bridge upstream from Magdalene. I follow those who call the whole river the Cam, distinguishing its main tributaries by their places of origin: Linton Cam, Essex (or Saffron Walden) Cam, Ashwell Cam (and Bourn Brook). The name Grantchester perplexes similarly and needs explaining. It was used by Bede and the Anglo-Saxons to describe the 'chester' (the 'walled town') beside the Granta that the Romans had called Duroliponte and that gave its name also to Chesterton (a parish devised so as to take in Cambridge castle and much of the site of the Roman town). Once that original Grantchester's name was supplanted by Grantabridge and Cambridge, it was adopted, misguidedly, by the charming village upstream that began life as *Granteseta* ('settlers on the Granta'), with no suspicion of Roman urbanity, nor trace of a town wall.

* In this series, it is being prepared by David Lloyd. The Soke of Peterborough, also now merged with Cambridgeshire, is already described in the Northamptonshire Guide.

Boundaries

If East Anglia pushed its political and cultural boundaries as far west as the river at Cambridge, the king most likely to have done that is Raedwald, 599–624, whose magnificence was uncovered in the burial-ship at Sutton Hoo, and who established his supremacy over the other English kingdoms. It may have been towards the end of the seventh century, when the East Anglian diocese was divided between two bishops, that the southern one fixed his western boundary along the great earthwork defences 8 miles back from the river-line at Cambridge. Throughout the Middle Ages and down to 1836, the boundary of the Norwich diocese lay along Devil's Dyke (or Ditch). The most skilful excavations have not forced the Dyke to yield the secrets of its age. Whether it was built during the dissolution of the Roman empire or the creation of the English kingdoms, its service as an early episcopal boundary certainly demonstrates its value to those East Anglian kings. So, incidentally, does the birth of one of their daughters at Exning, close to the Dyke: she was Etheldreda (Audrey), foundress of the great church at Ely (q.v.).

The Devil's Dyke is one of a famous series of parallel defensive earthworks barring approaches up the bare chalk corridor. We visit them all in the Gazetteer of parishes, several of which set their boundaries by them. But notice here how this great series of 'anti-tank ditches', anti-warrior-from-the-south obstacles, reveals another aspect of Cambridge's 'frontier' character. It is important, in understanding Cambridge, to clamber up on to the Dyke and feel its purpose—perhaps at its W extremity, where it meets the fen beside the little medieval inland port at Reach (q.v.), or as it crosses Newmarket Heath in the presence of very unwarlike horses and riders.

Devil's Dyke, summer, from above ▷

Devil's Dyke, winter, from below ▽

The shire's identity had emerged under the Danes. Its components were detailed in Domesday Book. In 1109, the diocese of Ely was created in order to reduce the formidable extent of the Lincoln bishopric, stretching to the upper Thames. Ely's diocesan perimeter coincided almost precisely with that of the shire of Cambridge as set out in Domesday Book—but excluded fifteen Cambridgeshire parishes lying immediately north of Devil's Dyke. They remained in the Norwich bishopric—a clear indication that the boundaries of the early East Anglian church and state coincided along the line of that great earthwork, and were fixed in pre-Danish times. Then, when political power passed to the kingdom of England, the East Anglian diocese continued to operate within the unaltered domain of the former East Anglian kings.

Landscapes

The Boulder-clay Woodland, running from Ashley and Cheveley through Westley and Brinkley to Balsham: the -ley names suggest English settling in aboriginal wildwood (ley = clearing). This is part of the heavy carpet of boulder clay laid across Suffolk and NW Essex by glaciers. Here it is defined roughly by the 100-m/330-ft contour and by surviving woodland-green blobs on the map and shade on the ground. The villages were planted along a spring-line, and the streams run (surprisingly, so near the Cam) east to the sea (indeed the Essex/Suffolk Stour is one of them).

These particular boulder-clay parishes are distinguished by elongated, strip shapes—prominent on most maps—the long, parallel boundaries designed to take in the dry chalk grazing slopes to the W and combine them with the heavier woodland-cornland in the E. Wood Ditton is one of these, running alongside Devil's Dyke as far as the

Steeplechase Course and the A11 crossing, and overlapping.

The Chalk Downland Corridor. How strikingly arid this band of chalk is, the line of the A11 shows on the map and on the ground: not an old village in sight till you reach Babraham and the Abingtons, snug beside the Linton Cam (in my fifth landscape). Driving along, you notice an exhilarating sense of space, interrupted only by clumps of beeches or by monumental earthworks—Devil's Dyke, Fleam Dyke, Brent Ditch, Heydon Ditch. It was a natural line for a great prehistoric route, the Icknield Way. Two other major prehistoric defence-works rose partly in relation to it—Wandlebury on the Gog Magog Hills (see Stapleford) and the War Ditches at Cherry Hinton: both of the Iron Age and worth climbing to see. The next constructive defenders, the Normans, built their major castle in Cambridge (more precisely Chesterton) itself.

The Fen-edge. Along the line where the chalk meets the fen, some of the most richly rewarding Cambridgeshire villages stand, each with its spring bubbling up through the chalk. *Burwell* is a delightful example (q.v.), its eponymous spring recalling those rising among the roots of ash trees in Ashwell, just across the border in Hertfordshire: the appropriately pretty source of the Ashwell Cam. Villages on the fen-edge enjoyed such advantages as the fertile fen offered without the fen-dwellers' worst drawbacks of instability (from floods and swelling and shrinkage of peat), poor communications, absence of spring water, etc. Soham, till the 17th-century drainage of the Bedford Level, was a narrow-necked peninsula jutting right out into the fen and dependent for its first occupation upon the large mere, or lake, that gave the settlement its

Chalk landscape near **Royston** ▷

Eponymous stream at **Burwell**: earthworks of fort in background

name, 'lake-farm' (*sae* is Old English for lake). Soham (or Saham, as it was) in the days of St Felix, conjures up a picture not unlike that of Wilfred Thesiger's marsh Arabs of Southern Iraq, where Tigris and Euphrates wander like Ouse and Cam, larger scale of course, and in much warmer weather, but equally doomed by progress.

Moving west along the fen-edge, as far as Willingham and Swavesey, we find subtle differences: there is no longer a 50-ft chalk edge to anchor on, the accepted level of dwelling is down to the 24-ft and even 17-ft contour (Over manages 48 ft!). In his fine study of Waterbeach and Landbeach and Cottenham (*Liable to Floods*, CUP, 1974), J.R. Ravensdale showed that medieval Waterbeach was a true fen-island, indeed an archipelago linked by causeways—much as with parts of Soham. Drinking water was supplied, presumably, not by springs but neighbouring brooks. These little brooks descending from the clay plateau of the SW corner of Cambridgeshire are what, in village-siting terms, chiefly distinguish this old clay-woodland from its eastern counterpart.

The Cambridgeshire Heights. The earliest English inhabitants, and indeed their predecessors, enjoyed these wooded slopes, and almost invariably settled on the spring-line (corresponding almost exactly with the 100-ft contour)—Elsworth, Knapwell, Boxworth, Lolworth, Dry Drayton, Madingley and Coton, along the N edge, then round to Comberton, Toft and Bourn, the Eversdens, Harlton, Haslingfield and Orwell. If you look at the map of the old county you immediately notice that the villages are closer together and more numerous to the S and W of Cambridge.

Here the structure of clays is slightly more complicated than the simple boulder clay that lies over the eastern edge. The main plateau

Near **Grantchester**

(rising to about 100 ft) is built of older clays and rocks, supplying a few building materials. On top of this plateau, two E–W ridges, mainly of boulder clay, rise to about 200 ft: the ridges themselves support no villages, but form well-known eastward-looking spurs. The northern one cradles the American Cemetery, near Madingley. The other ridge, farther S, supports the Mare Way, a very ancient boundary-way, passing Maypole Farm on the Harlton–Orwell boundary en route to the spur at Chapel Hill, Haslingfield, a splendid vantage-point (almost comparable with Wandlebury, opposite) overlooking the broad main valley of the Cam. One of the Cam feeders, Bourn Brook, rises above Bourn and divides the two spurs.

The Cam Valleys provide a fifth distinctive kind of Cambridgeshire village—in some ways the most attractive of all. Wendy, Barrington and Grantchester make a good start along the Ashwell Cam. Ickleton, Hinxton, Duxford, Whittlesford, Sawston, the Shelfords and Hauxton add to the pleasure of the Essex Cam. Linton, Hildersham, the Abingtons, Babraham and Stapleford complete the series: Cam-valley villages that lead you towards the life-stream of Cambridge itself.

That stream emerges, beyond Cambridge, into one of the strangest parts of England. The Fenland is too often thought to be the only scenery Cambridgeshire offers, but it is undeniably fundamental to her character.

Ickleton ▷

◁ **Newton** Fen

◁ Near **Leverington**

△ **Stretham** Old Engine

▽ Near **Chatteris**

Black fen near **Reach**

The Cambridgeshire Fens and the Isle of Ely. To enjoy travelling in these broad fertile lands, ideally beneath a peculiarly brilliant broad sky, it is wise to remember that it was all once wet and sedgy, fit only for monks and nuns, fish and fowl (and fishermen and fowlers). The story goes back to the very old, Jurassic clays that formed the plateau of the Cambridgeshire heights and run in a belt to face the North Sea at the Wash. Long ago the Jurassic clays and gravels had a shield: the chalk ridge running from Dorset up the W side of Norfolk veered round the Wash and continued northward as the Lincolnshire Wolds. Over thousands of years, most of the rivers of the E Midlands and western E Anglia poured down into the Jurassic clay-belt and broke through the chalk barrier on their way to join the Rhine. The last ice age came to an end, the North Sea filled with water, and beside it the land has proved unsteady, rising sometimes but subsiding more over centuries. Those of us who have lived beside the North Sea know its potential for aggression, but no one knows it better than the Fenlanders. They may be living miles inland, but inundation may be their experience any winter when spring tides coincide with NE gales. Great tides flow in from the Wash, creating a temporary inland sea and bottling up the mouths and lower reaches of the rivers, and thus the freshwater floods. In these conditions, the Fens were made.

At the bottom, a layer of (vegetable) peat was left by the freshwater floods; then marine clay. Then in the N silt was dumped by the salt tides; in the south, more peat was formed from fresh waters. Both show the phenomenal fertility we associate with deltas. But there is a fundamental difference. The even richer, silted, soil of the northern fens, north of about Wisbech, is expanding at the expense of the Wash. In the 17th century a Dutch engineer called Cornelius Vermuyden came and organized the draining of the Fens. Since then the vegetable, soft but soot-black peat soil to the south has inexorably contracted, shrunk and subsided—its surface dropping as much as 12 ft in a century. The result has been unsteady buildings (the leaning Victorian church tower of Friday Bridge, in Elm, for instance, recalling campaniles in Venice, if not Pisa). What is more serious is that ultimately the peat will all vanish.

Meanwhile, how are we to view it? Below the peat, remains of great trees, known by old Fenmen as 'bog oaks', have occasionally come to light, giving sensational glimpses of earlier very ancient landscapes. In his book, *Fenland: its Ancient Past and Future* (1978), Sir Harry Godwin illustrates a prodigious rooted yew, $14\frac{1}{2}$ft in girth and still impenetrably hard, uncovered in 1935 in Isleham Fen. But there are less accidental and more permanent ocular demonstrations of the way time has moulded these deceptive plains.

I suppose most of us know of estuaries in which the river's outflow is checked and reversed by a rising tide. Now look at the very flatness of the Fens and imagine the result of even a normal rising tide. Rivers can flow backwards here and easily change course. The first book that brought this home to me was A.K. Astbury's *The Black Fens* (1958), in which I learned that 'neither the Ouse, nor its tributaries, nor indeed any river which flows through the peat fens now follows its original channel, or even one of its original channels, for more than a small part of its course.' The heart sinks. It is hard enough learning which river flows where now: do we need to know all this? Yes. I think it is no use looking at Upwell or Wisbech, or Chatteris or Ely, without knowing that, in their natural state before centuries of human diversionary cuttings and drainings, *all* the rivers in this Cambridgeshire fenland flowed through the 'Well Stream', i.e. past Upwell and Outwell, and entered the Wash at Wisbech, which stood at the head of an estuary. There was only one exception, a minor stream entering the Wash at Lynn!

I have put some relevant parts of this detailed story into the gazetteer. Here I need to explain what 'roddons', or 'rodhams', are and how they help us to see the ancient history of fen waterways with our own eyes. The relatively swift incoming salt tides, because of the low natural fall (only a few feet), brought large deposits of silt right up the rivers and watercourses. These silt banks, gradually built up within the peat of centuries of fresh-water flooding, clogged the streams and encouraged their change of course. Then by hardening and fossilizing they left their mark in a way that we can see for ourselves. For the surrounding peat has shrunk and left these defunct silt sea-serpents with their spines raised, sometimes as much as 8ft above the black fields. These are the roddons. The gazetteer marks some places where they are easily seen—on the Shippea Hill to Littleport road, notably, and at Prickwillow nearby.

Next the Romans: what on earth were they doing here? Naturally the antiquary William Stukeley, born at Holbeach (Lincs.) in 1687, soon noticed traces of Roman activity in the neighbouring siltlands. But the extraordinary uncovering of something like the full story had to wait until the Great Drainage of the 17th century had had time to take effect, shrinking the peat and exposing the results to the aerial photographers of our generation. In 1970, Charles Phillips in *The Fenland in Roman Times* was able to describe it as 'one of the most completely recognizable ancient landscapes in Western Europe'. Aerial cameras have pieced together an astonishing jig-saw of enclosures, drove-roads and hamlets. At first the antiquaries thought they had uncovered the great granary of the Province, and Stukeley thought the Romans constructed the Car Dyke (see Waterbeach) as a canal to move

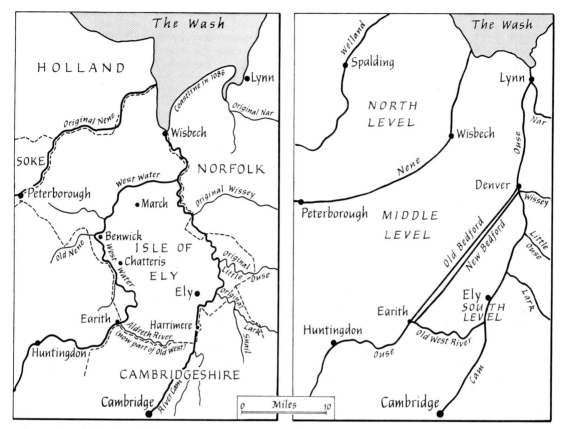

Map 1. The main fen rivers *before* drainage from Roman to Stuart times. Dotted lines show how county boundaries follow waterways now extinct

Map 2. The main rivers of the southern fens after drainage
(Maps based, by kind permission, on A.K. Astbury, *The Black Fens.*)

corn up to the troops in the north. Now that their farming is shown to have been mainly pastoral, it does not seem impossible that the Car Dyke also helped transport horses, cattle, sheep and their products to the north until it was geared to similar production. By Hadrian's time they were operating a well-planned water-control system. The Flaggrass site at March is one of the most interesting, and there is new evidence that their organizing centre was at Stonea Camp, Wimblington.

The Romans (with experience of the Po delta) operated by cutting rather than embanking: the earliest embankments including the so-called 'Roman Bank' (see Leverington) are Anglo-Saxon and Norman. The Romans concentrated, in making the Littleport-Brandon cut and similar improvements, on diverting the eastern fen rivers northward towards Lynn and so relieving pressure on the Well Stream (Upwell-Outwell) in time of flood. Their work was continued sporadically throughout the Middle Ages and in Elizabethan times, but carried through finally only by Vermuyden and Lord Bedford in the days of Charles I.

The main Roman developments are

roughly datable to *c.* AD 100–200. Then a decline may represent political confusion from 235 to 284 or 296: no funding for projects which did not bring a quick return! Thereafter, all went reasonably well till the British evicted the 'Raj' administrators, diocesan and civil, *c.* 407–10. By 599, the time the great king Raedwald arrived, the drains were blocked and the sedge had taken over.

Thereafter, the story of anchorites (see Thorney) and monasteries (Ely) is better known, and if the hard work of the medieval drainage commissions is not known, that is largely because the story is wearisome and confusing. One longs for a glimmer of light as when, in the 1420s, the abbess and nuns of Denny (Waterbeach) pressed the saintly Margery Kempe of Norwich to come to speak with them. Her first thought was to put them off for a year, and she was loth to go for it was pestilence time. 'But our Lord commanded her to go and comfort the ladies.' Meanwhile a Norwich friend begged her to stay to comfort her dying husband. Finally she came to the water's side at Norwich, and found that 'all the boats were forth to Cambridge-ward before she arrived.' And then something inside her told her not to be depressed, for the mission was good, and she should go safe and come safe again: 'and it fell so indeed' (*Book of Margery Kempe*, Early English Text Society, 1940).

Describing Ely in the gazetteer, I distinguish between the physical island on which Ely stands and 'The Isle', a much larger administrative district sometimes called 'The Liberty of St Etheldreda', which probably goes back to AD 970—when King Edgar granted to the Ely monks 'the two hundreds of the fen' (see Wisbech and Witchford), possibly even earlier.

The Great Drainage has changed life in the Fens more radically than any change of political boundaries. The stilts and the malarial agues have gone for ever, but so has the gliding in a punt through the reeds after duck, so hauntingly described by Wentworth Day (*A History of the Fens*, 1970). No more against the western sky the silhouettes of old John Butcher, of dark Bert Bailey, plodding homeward along the Lode bank, 'their donkeys straining at the barge tow-lines, the barges deep-laden with turf and reeds, the eel glaives and fish-darts poised in the bows against the sunset'. Now there are the black expanses of productive peat, and memories. My own earliest is of a train journey at Christmas, about 1931, from Suffolk through March to my mother's old home in Lincolnshire. It was a hard winter and the blackness had turned white for miles and there were skaters everywhere. It was not like any old Dutch winter-landscape, for there seemed to be no houses. I often think of that scene when I read of the skating in Edward Storey's early recollections (a few years later) or W.H. Barrett's *Tales from the Fens* (1963) and *More Tales from the Fens* (1964). Storey records the new breed of skaters with heated cars and flasks of hot coffee, himself among them. But how it seems to roll back the years, to come upon a notice of

> FENLAND ICE-SKATING CHAMPIONSHIPS
> BANTON FEN, LINCS
> FOR SKATERS LIVING WITHIN
> FORTY MILES OF MARCH,
> CAMBRIDGESHIRE

The local building materials

Admittedly, the local quarries and supplies of building materials are not exciting. Furthermore the relative ease with which the well-endowed colleges of Cambridge University could bring stone from the quarries of Northamptonshire, Rutland and Yorkshire to the

very banks of the Cam meant that the taste for the best imported materials developed early and well. Indeed, by adoption these grand stones have become almost denizens, locals, themselves. The same was true before the colleges got going in the later Middle Ages: it was easy for the well-endowed monasteries, notably Ely, to go to the best quarries; meanwhile those that closed at the Dissolution themselves became quarries. As well as monasteries and colleges, several parish churches obtained Northamptonshire stone. They often used it in modest but beautiful spires. It is curious that only one of these 'Midland' spires (in Cambridge itself) rises east of the Cam: but cross the river to St Peter's, Cambridge, or to Chesterton, or Coton, and you know that—in this building tradition at least—you have crossed a frontier from E Anglia to the Midlands.

Whether we are at great Ely or little Coton or wherever there is good Norman masonry, we can be reasonably sure we are looking at stone from the 'hills and holes' of Barnack: Ely's W front shows the most inspired use of the stone. But unless we are expert geologists, and carry a good hand lens, it is difficult always to be sure. The volumes of the Royal Commission of Historical Monuments (RCHM) are the most reliable sources to which those readers most interested will turn. In their Preface to *North-East Cambridgeshire* they say: 'In the 12th century and probably earlier [see Horningsea] the predominant material for church walls was rubble, with dressings of limestone. In order to preserve a traditional and generic term without inferring a precise provenance, this Jurassic limestone has been described in the inventory as "Barnack"', i.e. Barnack in inverted commas. I have sometimes been reduced to the phrase Jurassic limestone, off-putting and inadequate as it is. There is a good introduction to the grander limestones by Donovan Purcell,

called *Cambridge Stone* (1967, with illustrations). But the detailed treatment of all materials by the RCHM is superb. Alas, they seem unlikely to resume their work on Cambridgeshire.

What seems to me especially valuable is their unusually enlightened approach to ancient ways with the less grand materials. Writers from limestone country and places W of Wiltshire have a way of sniffing about flint or flint combined with, of all things, brick! Not so the RCHM men: they carefully and rightly record the very early appearance of knapped and flush black flint at Swaffham Bulbeck and Bottisham (*c.* 1300 and *c.* 1315). The medium caught on generally only in the 15th century. Even more discriminating, they note that at St Cyr's, Swaffham Prior, at the end of the 15th century, 'the plinth of the tower is enriched with chequerwork of red brick and limestone, and the parapet with flint flushwork.' So it is, and now beset by topiary, and unforgettable. Such flint chequer patterns are natural in all chalk counties , and across in Normandy (in Bec-Hellouin's gatehouse for instance).

Chalk is the mother of flint, the softest of building stones giving birth to the hardest. Known as 'clunch', 'Burwell rock', etc., chalk serves best indoors or as 'core' wall-filling. Indoors, it is 'all too easy to carve', as Alec Clifton-Taylor puts it (in Pevsner's Cambridgeshire volume), thinking of the excesses of Bishop Alcock's chantry in Ely cathedral. But there are masterpieces of clunch-carving in Cambridgeshire and most notably the interior of the nave at Burwell where, as the RCHM notes, the bases and lower courses are in limestone to avoid damage. Great St Mary's interior in Cambridge is another display of clunch superbly used. Then one thinks of Harlton's beautiful, tall 14th-century nave piers, and Grantchester's chancel, and Trumpington's smooth chancel going back to the 13th century. Isleham is one of my favourite Cambridge villages on account of its innocent, sound indulgence in the use of all available local materials, with a notable clunch wall in Pound Lane. But Anglesey Abbey was not too proud to incorporate it: nor Sawston Hall in one of Cambridgeshire's most delightful house fronts. The outdoor sample I delight in most is at Fen Ditton, in the front of No 6, High Street: the clunch laced spontaneously with courses of red brick.

From clunch we come to what most guide books refer to as 'rubble' or 'ragstone', rather pejorative words. Sometimes, as at Oakington church, it is difficult to eye these stones with enthusiasm, but often they lend some quality of colour or surface texture that enhances the building or links it to its surroundings.

One of the most appealing of these anonymous limestones I first noticed in the clerestory and S aisle of Cottenham church: it is a honey-coloured, shelly limestone in which is set, not at all to its disadvantage, a random patchwork of chocolate-coloured puddingstone from the neighbouring Lower Greensand beds. (If that reads like a confectioner's recipe it is unintentional.) Here again, rather against the rules, the strong bonding by a light-coloured mortar helps to make an impressive and beautiful wall. Other comparably attractive yellowish Jurassic ragstones clothe the distinguished tower at Orwell and much of St Wendred's at March and St Giles' church at Tydd. Equally pleasant, though browner, is the Jurassic stone, possibly cornbrash, of which St Mary's, Fen Drayton, is carefully composed ('pebble rubble' is Pevsner's reaction). One would give much to find a record of the source of just one of these pleasurable buildings.

Before leaving these poor relations of the 'quality' of Barnack and Weldon, Clipsham and Ketton, one must notice among the Jurassics, Elsworth Rock, taking its name from an agreeable village on the plateau W of Cambridge. It is sometimes visible in the village stream at Elsworth. Dr Forbes (Director of the Sedgwick Geological Museum of Cambridge) has identified some in Knapwell church tower. He found only one piece at Elsworth church itself; Boxworth church contains other pieces, all rather poor stuff, weathered back from the surface of surrounding stones.

Finally there is Lower Greensand. A belt of it crosses Cambridgeshire, appearing at Gamlingay, Lolworth, Cottenham, Wilburton and Ely. It very probably provided the distinctive brown stone of which Gamlingay's church is built. It is a green sandstone underground, but turns to a rich gingerbread colour. Another name for this cretaceous sandstone is carstone. Benwick church is a distinguished example of its use—improbably by the Victorian architect Teulon.

The characteristic brickwork of the Cambridge colleges varies from purple to yellow—not very beautiful—and is based on the Gault clay that runs close to the Lower Greensand from SW to NE. Queens' College opted for it in the 1440s, over a core of clunch, probably not wanting the expense of importing freestone. Jesus College and St John's also make handsome use of it.* But perhaps the best things of all are out in the country—much of Wisbech, especially Peckover House, Little Wilbraham's old rectory (with glazed pantiles) and the Bedford estate cottages at Thorney. Swaffham Bulbeck's old maltings also has beautiful gault-brick walling and roof tiles. Dullingham House's brickwork is lovely and red. Little Shelford's manor house was built c. 1750 by 'an opulent ironmonger of Cambridge' who chose bricks that were yellow. In Chesterton the terrace at Nos 13 and 14

---

* Already the brick surfaces were patterned ('diapered') in a way that suggests links with the Low Countries—Esquelbecque in French Flanders has distinguished examples.

Wisbech: North Brink: No. 7, in the middle, may owe the refinement of its *c*. 1750s stone front to the Cambridge am.

Church Street handsomely shows gault brick and tile, the brick dressings dark brown. Some of the most characteristic Cambridgeshire roof tiles are of the gault kind, best seen along Orchard Street in Cambridge (Walk 3).

I have not considered timber-building very earnestly, since Cambridgeshire is not outstanding in its repertoire. There are, of course, innumerable good old timber-framed houses; one thinks of Burgh Hall at Swaffham Bulbeck, a fine 'Wealden' house. A three-roomed, single-storey, 17th-century house at Swaffham Prior has been found to have swallowed up about seventy-nine stout oaks. Small wonder that the local supply dried up! Clapboard cladding is not very common: at Great Shelford, King's Mill and the thatched cottages opposite; at Soham the steelyard; at Christchurch, Upwell, a single-storey cottage opposite the church; a few dovehouses.

With the Fens at hand, it is surprising that reed-thatch is no longer a common sight: but

...chitect, Sir James Burrough

as reeds have given way to arable, so reed-thatch was replaced by wheatstraw. There are still two good thatched churches, at Long-stanton (St Michael's) and Rampton. At Newton, near Cambridge, a memorable clunch cottage is called Deep Thatch. Box-worth and Comberton, Lode, Whittlesey and Whittlesford show good specimens. The most

pleasant to record is James Wentworth Day's old house at Wicken. It is to be found in the detailed Gazetteer, which runs from Abington to Wratting. Cambridge is kept to its alphabetical place, since a principle of these county guides is to present county towns firmly within the visual and historical setting of their counties.

Swaffham Bulbeck ▷

Abington Pigotts: Down Hall gatehouse

Gazetteer

Usual abbreviations for main styles of medieval architecture: E.E., Early English, for most of the 13th century; Dec., c. 1290–1350; and Perp. going on into Tudor. Witchford and Over show need for caution in dating by style.
Places with linked histories, like Great and Little Abington, are described together here under their substantive names, not separated under Great and Little.
The numbers in brackets refer to the square where the place-name may be found on the map at the back of this Guide. The 1-inch Ordnance Survey sheets and their successors the 1:50,000 sheets are practically indispensable to the pleasures of sightseeing in this or any other county.

Abington, Great and **Little** [15] Two clusters of neat, thatched, timber-framed cottages lie with their churches in meadows on opposite banks of the stream. Stone causeway over meadow to *Great Abington*'s small church. Brown pebbly outer skin: inner walls whitewashed, misguidedly stripped of its smooth plaster in 1890s. 13th-century S arcade and lancet windows. Life-sized knight on his elbow in Caroline marble with iron sword, 1639. De Veres had manor here 1060s to 1570s; their mullet-badges (stars) carved in clunch on front of cottage No 109. Congenial signs of Cambridge Cottage Improvement Society; characteristic 'cottage Gothic' windows preserved. 'Jeremiah's Cottage' recalls Jeremiah Lagden, legendary highwayman of the Newmarket road; lived at Old House, Little Abington. Hall, remodelled late 18th century; now occupied by British Welding Research. *Little Abington*'s church, at edge of park, restored 1885, but pleasant Norman and E.E. remains, especially the narrow Norman S doorway. Criss-cross stone pattern on Norman doorway demonstrates source of dog-tooth moulding that (very notably in Cambridgeshire) went on into early Gothic design. Kempe window, 1901, depicts Adoration of Magi in medieval way.

Abington Pigotts [14] Old moats and unusually sequestered, tree-hidden, close-knit village: church a little apart beside Manor Farm, which is 17th-century, romantically gabled, ungated, with new brick cottages. Hawthorn trees line church path. Church unspoilt, like village. Norman fragments. Broad, aisleless nave. Chancel arch (and graffito) of 14th century. Nave darkened by stained benches and ceiling. Pre-Tractarian arrangement in NE corner; clerk's desk and iron candlestick, pulpit backed by Jacobean panels and topped by crucifix and by door opening out on to former rood-loft. Blissful small saints, angels, archangels in top gold-and-silver Perp. window-lights. Pigott memorials. Pigotts first presented to living in 1440, last killed in Flanders campaign 1794, but Fosters carried name to 1899. Medallion of a Foster Pigott with book and chalice, 1827, by Peter Rouw; his copy of the Prayer Book, 1796, still used. NW, above church, Bellus Hill occupied in Iron Age. To S, at Down Hall, a 15th-century timber-framed gatehouse stands behind the moat; smooth stuccoed and over-sailing.

Aldreth *see* Haddenham and Willingham

Anglesey Abbey *see* Lode

Arrington [14] was originally Earnington, the farm of the Earningas, Saxons named in Ermine Street, which cuts straight through their territory here: *Earningastraete*. Small church set up high to W of street. Fine E.E. work in chancel. Hardwicke Arms, Georgian. Visitors approach Wimpole now from E.

Ashley-cum-Silverley [12] *Ashley* village grouped about a duck-pond. Pleasant flint buildings. Uninteresting neo-Norman church but, a mile to S, the tower of *Silverley*'s ruined church stands hidden, with its yews, in shady picturesque copse at road junction.

Babraham [15] pronounced Baybr'm. Bounded like adjacent Abington by two Roman roads (this stretch of one of them, Wool Street, scheduled as site of special scientific interest). Copley Hill, 'great tumulus', crowned by beeches. Hall rebuilt 1829–32 for Adeane family by Philip Hardwick: 'Elizabethan', replacing a real Elizabethan house (long gallery and noble two-storey round bow windows), demolished 1767; home of Sir Horatio Palavicino, collector of papal dues in Mary's reign, alleged to have pocketed them at Elizabeth's accession. He died here, 'an extreme miser', in 1600. He used to be credited, improbably, with land drainage done in 1650s by Thomas Benet. St Peter's church looks Perp. but the fabric is earlier, pleasantly mixed clunch, flint and mortar, sand coloured in the sun. Cream-washed interior; old oak benches, oak clerk's desk and pulpit. Nave roof (1774) tied by massive beams, the ceiling blue between rafters. Aisle ceilings decorated with Adeane hatchments. Extraordinary scene at E end of S aisle: in white marble and the most lifelike theatrical attitudes, Richard and Thomas Benet, 'two Brothers, and both of them Baronetts'. They

married two sisters and died in 1658 and 1667. One of them addresses, with upturned hands, the congregation; the other awaits his turn. Unsigned: ?John Bushnell. Gilded reredos, 1700, with Creed and Commandments. Rustic oak altar rails, 1665, mark the return of settled churchmanship. Beautiful black marble, 1631, for Thomas Feltham's 'soldiership'. Organ gallery with royal arms at W end. E window suitably darkened and then set alight by glowing colours playing on St Peter's emblems: by Reyntiens and Piper. Mellow redbrick almshouse range, 1723–32.

Balsham [15] Parish bounded on three sides by Fleam Dyke, Icknield Way and Wool Street, one of the strip-shaped parishes of Radfield Hundred. Left to Ely by the Lady Leofflaed, whose father, Byrhtnoth, was the hero of the epic battle of Maldon (991) and whose husband and son died in the disastrous battle of Ringmere (18 May 1010), when only the men of Cambridgeshire stood firm against the Vikings. For three months after Ringmere the Vikings harried the region. A century and a half later, Henry of Huntingdon wrote the story of their massacring all the people of Balsham except one man, who defended himself in the church tower. In the very large church is a late Anglo-Saxon carved stone grave cover found in the churchyard, itself unusually large. Present W tower, massively buttressed 1589, reinforced 1973, may date from time of Hugh de Balsham, the bishop of Ely (1257–86) who founded the first Cambridge college. Edward I stayed with him here. Perp. nave clerestory reclad in yellow brick 1818. Dec. chancel of beautiful grey unknapped flint (? from Butterfield's 1875 restoration). Old wooden S door with Georgian injunction to keep sabbaths. Interior at first disappointing. Great nave with hefty aisle arcades seems bare. Tudor aisle roof timbers retain colour but have lost

Babraham east window

plaster ceilings. Font cover (F.E. Howard's design) still needs paint and gilt. Rood-loft and screen have been so obviously repainted and gilded that amateurs pass through it into chancel before grasping that it is furnished with some of the most striking 14th-century wooden stallwork in England. (Loft accommodated church band till 1840: see clarinet etc. at W end.) The twenty-four stalls, designed c. 1390, reflect the wealth of Ely's rectors here: they have armrests at two levels, so useful whether misericords were raised or lowered. Given by John de Sleaford, rector, they now frame two superb brasses. That on S side, Sleaford's own (d. 1401), records that he built the nave—'eclesia'. Window tracery denotes earlier 14th-century chancel. Stallwork just conceivably from workshop of Hugh Herland's glorious

Balsham churchyard

team of the King's carpenters, who roofed Westminster Hall in 1390s, for Sleaford was Master of Edward III's Wardrobe and Chaplain to Philippa of Hainault. The Latin phrase on this brass 'Loved by the King to the slow, sad end' points back to 1377, after the Queen's death, when Alice Perrers snared him and, as he died, pulled the rings off his fingers. The other brass commemorates John Blodwell (d. 1462), a Welshman trained in law at Bologna, practising it in Rome.

Barham *see* Linton

Barnwell *see* Cambridge

Barrington [14] lies in the plain below Chapel Hill (worth climbing for views) and the Mare Way, and be-

side the Ashwell Cam. Village mostly grouped about a large green. Old clunch workings, that gave white stone for the Gate of Honour at Caius in 1570s, now great quarries of Rugby Portland Cement Co. whose (former Hall) gates face the church and whose vesuvial smoke from two tall chimneys hangs over all. *Church* mostly clunch, including tower, white from cleaning, 1975. 13th-century doorway, defaced but fine, contains traceried 14th-century door. Clerestory lights heavily timbered roof. Four sets of five late-medieval pews are the church's chief pride. Stuart pulpit and tester well carved. Polished floors and astounding Victorian glass.

Bartlow [15] The 'mounds in the birch-trees' that gave the place its

English name are splendid Romano-British burial mounds (on Essex side of river). Sturdy Norman round tower of church retains abutment of SW corner of Norman nave, showing lowness of Norman roof. Fragmentary medieval wall-paintings. Cross-eyed lions in upper lights of 14th-century chancel windows, also a contemporary shield of royal arms. In NW corner of churchyard, *art-nouveau* metalwork gravehead, 1908. Hall rebuilt, 1960s, neo-Georgian, by Hon. C. Phillimore.

Barton [11] Radio Telescope deployed here: mechanical saucer-'ears', mobile, create landscape of robots. Barton's story of change since 1945 told in Robin Page's *Decline of an English Village*, 1974. Church and red-and-white brick

Carved stalls, **Balsham** ▷

Bottisham west porch

Victorian school secluded up Church Lane. W parts of chancel walls seem to be those of small chancel of *c.* 1100, extended. Inside, 'although narrow, extraordinarily decent and comelie', as John Layer found it before Civil War. 14th-century windows lit by plain glass; extensive remains of contemporary wall-paintings, mostly red; good screen tracery (dated 1374–88 by shields of arms painted on cusps) with two carved birds intact in central opening, and traces of red and green. From Layer's time, handsome pulpit and tester, 1635, initialled IR. Birds Farmhouse in fork of Arrington/Haslingfield roads bears name of owner *c.* 1440 and remains of hall of that time. New village housing well laid out and tree'd. Pevsner admired No 39, New Road (1965), flagrantly at odds with setting.

Barway *see* Soham

Bassingbourn-cum-Kneesworth [14] John Layer made clear the 17th-century use of the north-flowing bourn at Bassingbourn: 'It is a good corne ground, the town well watered, running by every doore every daie and never too much nor too little.' Air station, used by military, prominent. Sparse little township. Adjoining Royston, its prehistoric boundaries are impressive. Church tower rebuilt 1870s with recessed arcade like Orwell's. Small lead spire. Roomy traceried wooden porch. Nave and chancel of unusual width and design, all of a piece, just pre-Black Death, with slight ogival shaping of all arches, base of nave piers notably moulded. Traceried 1370s screen now garish colours. Chancel roof, light blue, deep blue and gold: boss carvings include Edward III's head. On floor, marble effigy of Henry Butler (d. 1647), given by his sister; he lies on his side in shroud. Parish library, 800 books, in tower till 1969, then sold to Cambridge and Essex universities.

Beach *see* Landbeach, Waterbeach

Benwick [15] is the one ancient Fen village not on an 'island' but sited carefully on a roddon, the parallel silt banks of the already extinct West Water, the original river Ouse, which once flowed here from Huntingdon and Earith to join an old course of the Nene: High Street occupies main stream. Chapel here mid-17th century: parish *church* replaced it, 1850: attractive 'Dec.' building by Teulon, using the brown carstone of NW Norfolk, but sited just off the silt bed, and subsidence has caused removal of tower and spire. Inside like being at sea. Roddons N of road to Doddington, also W of road to Whittlesey.

Bottisham [12] First syllables of name originally meant 'by ditches', a good description of the fen-drained N part of the parish that formed the new parish Lode (q.v.) in 1894. Barrows. Village now lines small open wedge of green and High Street. *Church*'s broad, lofty interior—one of the glories of Cambridgeshire. The eye delights in the window tracery, in the delicate limestone-and-clunch chancel screen, and especially in the arrangement of Dec. wooden screens at E end of each aisle, each enclosing a particularly affecting memorial. Earlier memorials include inscription for Elias de Beckingham, Edward I's upright judge. This nave may be his legacy. W chapels (Sir A. Richardson) in memory of Lady Fairhaven. Outside, the black knapped-flint panelling of aisle walls, *c.* 1315, is

Bottisham south aisle and porch

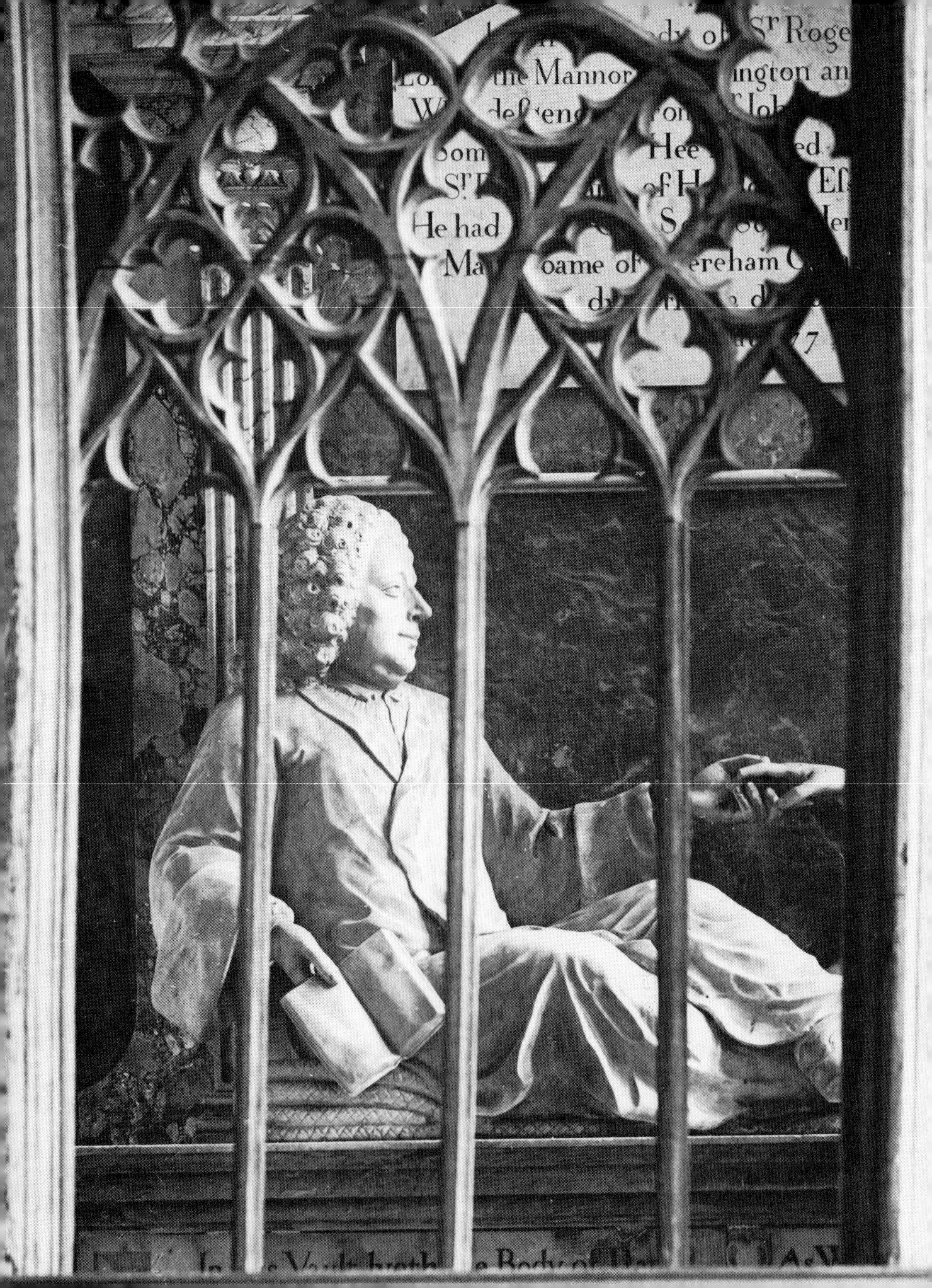

one of the earliest examples of such work. W porch a rare feature. *Hall*, white brick, pleasant in large beechy park, built 1797 on new site for Revd G.L. Jenyns.

Bourn [11] Picot, William the Conqueror's sheriff, built a castle here overlooking Ermine Street. The main enclosure is now occupied by Bourn Hall, a delightful-looking late-Elizabethan house, made progressively more 'Elizabethan' by J.A. Repton, *c.* 1817. He and his father Humphry Repton landscaped the park for the Sackville-Wests. It is now a famous clinic specializing in test-tube babies. Beside the park, and above the little village whose lanes were so much more frequented in the 13th century, the *church* of SS Helen and Mary: triple arcading of some elegance round three sides of belfry. Within, one sees the tower as a development from unusually graceful 12th-century colonnades, surmounted by roundel clerestories. From nave, fine view W: tall slender shafts of tower arcade. Late-medieval rood-screen, also tall and slender. 1934 reredos by Comper, centred on crucifix with children playing the parts. Comper windows. Dark weather-boarded post-mill, *c.* 1620 or earlier, oldest of its kind. Beside Longstowe road, Wysing Grange Farm has jettied Tudor front, with brick-nogging.

Boxworth [11] A secluded, wooded parish. Opposite the Golden Ball, Long Row is a terrace of thatched Georgian cottages. Church Farm, Georgian brick with gault pantiles, handsomely restored since 1972. *Church* behind, set in broad lawn-like churchyard for once acceptable, was all crenellated (1868) like a toy castle and has irresistible texture of multicoloured field-stones from the boulder clay, black-jointed and mingled with carved stonework from 12th century. Norman church

Bottisham conversation piece: Sir Roger and Dame Elizabeth Jenyns, 1728. Unsigned

given Dec. S aisle, all largely re-modelled after storm, 1636. All the old windows (except, alas, the E one) contain good late-Victorian glass by Kempe (twenty-one lights of it). Floor slab of Nicholas Saunderson, 'blind from his infancy, yet the miracle of his age for his Knowledge in Mathematics', 1739.

Brinkley [15] was carved late out of the mother parish, Burrough (Green). Market 13th–18th centuries. Follow the long boundary belt from Brinkley Wood (350ft contour) down into Six Mile Bottom (100ft) to see how many centuries the countrymen between Newmarket and Cambridge have been creating a rational landscape with green boundary hedgelines as straight as the formal plantations of the classical Enlightenment. *Church* late medieval with Essex and Suffolk

features and very flush black flints in 1874 chancel. A jettied house, rudely roofed and extended, frames SW side of churchyard. Dark stained box pews. Tablets to early Georgian infants. *Hall* adjoins, in pleasant green park with noble chestnut avenue. Sir Geoffrey Keynes lived at Lammas House.

Burrough Green [12] *c.* 1045 spelt *Burg* (Anglo-Saxon for 'fort'). The Green, Burrough's most obvious feature now, joined its name only in 16th century. On N edge of Park Wood, moated enclosure of unusual strength presumably defended lodge of park Count Alan had here in 1086; possibly the eponymous *burh*? Another hint of Burrough's antiquity is the church's dedication to *St Augustine*. The present fabric has several attractions but no features earlier than 14th century. By the

15th, nave and chancel had wide aisles, and before the Civil War John Layer noted here 'a merveillous faire and large quier for a parish church'. But the choir aisles were removed and only three bays of the nave aisles kept, each roofed by 17th-century cross-gables, which give the church a homely look: brick floors, flat ceiling. Rails round three sides of altar; unusual raised sanctuary. Elaborate late 14th-century royal arms in E window. Haphazard rearrangement of medieval effigies of De Burghs and Ingoldsthorpes. Adjacent pleasant (reduced) Elizabethan brick house with pedimented windows. Pilasters rise to eaves; roofs unfortunately slate. On E side, walls and earthworks of large gardens. Charming school building of 1714, the central block stone-faced (and slated); lively stone figures of rustic boy and girl.

◁ **Bourn** mill

Burwell: Old Maltings ▽

Burwell: Parsonage Farm

Burwell [12] A long village, skirts the fen. Its early Anglo-Saxon name, 'spring by the fort', showed that King Stephen's abortive castle here occupied a much earlier earthwork: under it, sure enough, remains of a large Roman building were found in 1935. The troublemaker Geoffrey Mandeville besieged it (1144) and was slain by an arrow. The castle was later used as a manor house by Ramsey abbots. The overgrown site makes a delightful walk. Below W end of churchyard, among roots of an ash-tree, the spring bubbles out, the original *bur-well*. You can follow its path N where it runs beside the *Low Road*, the former waterfront, past the *Hythe*, where it widens into *Burwell Lode*, for so long the main artery of the place. The path leads round to the N end of *North Street*, the old fenside commercial end of Burwell. The cottages and houses stand close together, end-gables to the street, which now has more importance than the Weirs to which they all run back. Nos. 91–7 are good examples. We return from the fen edge to High Town. Between the castle and St Mary's lie clunch quarries dug from Roman times to 1962: in Cambridgeshire, 'Burwell Rock'. Its use is beautifully demonstrated inside St

Mary's. *St Mary's* is one of the best examples of English Perp., the box-shaped temple of glass. But look first from NW corner of churchyard. From here you see (lower half of tower's N face) outlines of blocked tall round-headed lights and narrow ashlar buttresses, hints of former grand Romanesque building. Upper part of tower, octagonal, with smaller octagonal stair-turret in one corner: the natural influence of Ely's great W tower. Lead spirelet, 1799. The architect Reginald Ely worked on both Queens' College Gatehouse and King's College Chapel while St Mary's was building. Arthur Oswald noticed that the complex tracery in E window of S aisle, e.g., is identical with that in a S side-chapel at King's. Such fine connections become clearer inside: lofty nave clerestories superbly panelled in clunch, and the carved stone is roofed in by impressive carpentry. The stone walls are tied by huge cambered beams, delicately braced. Wood cornices display allegoric emblems: Annunciation, Assumption, elephants and castles, hare and hounds, tigers caught with mirrors (as in Pliny); meticulously listed and well illustrated in RCHM. Original inscription over chancel arch records that E wall and nave

roof carpentry were *completed in 1464* for John, Joan and Alice Benet. In chancel, canopied niches, sumptuously carved in clunch, are heavily restored. Corbels carved as angels, one with *shield* of John Higham who was vicar *1439–67*; evidently chancel and nave rebuilt together. Ramsey abbey responsible for chancel. Remains of convincing brass portrait of last abbot of Ramsey (d. 1542). In churchyard, one carved headstone displays large flaming heart, winged, symbol of seventy-eight people who died in barn fire while they watched puppets, 1727.

RCHM lists 115 secular buildings here, including Old Manor House, clunch-built, early 14th century, facing S entrance to old High Town; ground floor and first floor apartments, each with garderobe. Dr Eric Ennion's book, *Adventurers' Fen*, 1949, describes fen-edge Burwell with feeling. So does J. Wentworth Day's *A History of the Fens*, 1970.

Caldecote [11] began as a 'cold' hamlet of Bourn; was apparently a parish by the 12th century. Road in steep gully and church on bank where footpath crosses. Worth a glance for arboreal setting.

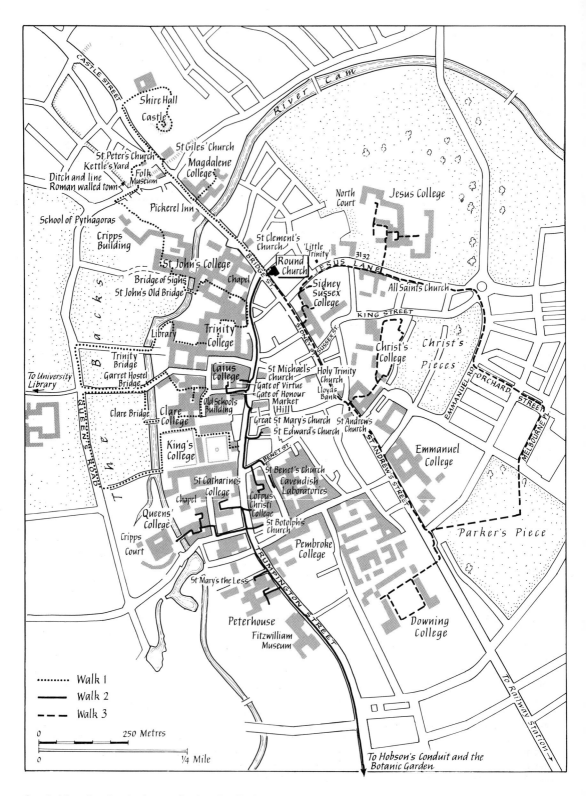

Cambridge showing the three walks described in the text

Walk 1 ··········
Walk 2 ─────
Walk 3 ─ ─ ─ ─

0   250 Metres

0   ¼ Mile

Cambridge [11] Whenever you come, it is best to walk round at your own pace. This is not another full-length guide to Cambridge; it is rather a pointer to ways of seeing the town in relation to its river and its belt of green commons, and the university and colleges in relation to the streets and parishes of the town. I have therefore devised three walks. Between them they take in all the major sights and many of the others. Each walk may be spread over a day, or taken more briskly in a half-day. Visitors with only a few hours for everything should start at Trinity College's library and Great Court, looking if possible into the Senate House, plunging into King's College Chapel, and dashing for the Fitzwilliam Museum. Provided they are lucky over opening hours, never safely predictable, these visitors-in-a-hurry will find their breath taken in other ways. Some of the main sights are in CAPITALS, so as to aid degrees of skipping. All three walks start at the Round Church at the main road junction of the old town.

WALK 1 *The Colleges by the Cam* (The Round Church—Magdalene Bridge—Magdalene College—the Castle—St John's College—the Backs—Trinity College—Trinity Hall—Clare—King's College)

We start at the ROUND CHURCH, which is not all it seems. Modelled *c.* 1130, midway between the first two Crusades, on the plan of the Holy Sepulchre in Jerusalem and replacing a still earlier church of St George, its atmosphere is that of Salvin, its Victorian rebuilder in 1842. The stubby columns and circular ground plan are of course original, but the round clerestory and cone replace a central sixteen-sided belltower: engravings show it carried—as well as late Gothic windows such as Salvin's friends despised—a wavy corbel-table, a very Norman feature (like Salvin's), and so it may have been an original Norman polygon such as the remarkable one on St Mary's, Swaffham Prior

(q.v.). It is now crowned with slates from Oxfordshire!

From the Round Church, one confronts *the chapel of St John's College*, impressive in its way, its architecture enhanced by two soaring fastigiate beech-trees, yet its scale and style offend because its designer, Scott, in the 1860s, was aiming at 'the highest perfection of pointed architecture'. His E end therefore echoes the polygonal apse of the Sainte Chapelle in Paris and his tower is an expanded copy in Ancaster stone of Pershore's, which he had just been restoring. The *genius loci* was thrown to the E Anglian winds. The part of the college facing Bridge Street (where we stand) is similarly inappropriate—the old town-dwellings were removed in 1939 and the town streets blandly ignored by the architect Maufe (who had won the competition to design Guildford cathedral in 1932): and he chose pink brick from Holland.

St Clement's church, usually shut: mural by F.R. Leach on E wall of sanctuary. Like nearly all the medieval graveyards of Cambridge, this admirably maintains sense of immemorial burial-ground and quiet garden; its ash-trees and the 'Old Vicarage' make amends for the undignified tower, 1821, an unfortunate memorial to the antiquary William Cole. Walking from it to the bridge, look mainly at the left side of the street beyond. It is the last real stretch of Tudor and Jacobean town street in Cambridge: plastered timber-framing, oversailing, with speckled gault-tiled roofs mansarded for headroom in the attics, and dormer windows.

Crossing *the Bridge*, replace the images of summer punts, sauntering under, by those of the black trading barges loading and unloading here all through the Middle Ages, gradually squeezed out by the colleges and the Backs and finally extinguished by the railway.

Just over Magdalene Bridge, glance in at the alley between 31 and the Pickerel Inn. Next on the left, Cross Keys Yard leads to Ben-

son Court and Mallory Court, where MAGDALENE has turned such 'vernacular' buildings to collegiate use: much of what we took for a town street is in fact a Magdalene annexe. It was bought for the college by A.C. Benson (who was Master, and wrote the words of 'Land of Hope and Glory') with money largely from a female American admirer of his books. To celebrate its fifth centenary in 1928, the college demolished Fisher Court, an enchanting row of cottages along the river, to make way for a ponderous purple range by Lutyens. Two more were planned, involving the demolition of Magdalene Street. Mercifully the money ran out. In the 1950s, David Roberts was commissioned to create what you see: an informal grouping of old and new.

Across the street, the Elizabethan brick front of Magdalene has lately been repointed all wrong: the flush joints make it look like a 1930s building by Maufe! Inside, First Court was rightly stripped of stucco in the 1950s: brick of various reds (over clunch). In 1428, the Abbot of Crowland built here a hostel, perhaps near present entrance, to shelter his students from secular snares. On right, separate staircases probably provided by several nearby monasteries. Staircase E (not open to public) actually retains original arrangement of tutor's room with three student cubicles leading off. Library, opposite, contains beautiful plasterwork from chapel, by William Collins, 1755. Superb hall, domestic in scale and candle-lit, remodelled in Queen Anne's reign, her arms dominating dais end. Theatrical double staircase at other end ascends to Combination (Cambridge for Common) Room. After that brick court, the pale tawny Ketton stone of the façade (only) of the PEPYS LIBRARY in next court comes as a nice surprise (and a stylistic puzzle—perhaps Elizabethan with Caroline colonnade and George II embellishments). Then the calm green Fellows' Garden flanked by brimming river. Pepys's

St John's College Old Bridge: Bridge of Sighs beyond

library was installed in 1724 behind those ornate first-floor windows, the 3,000 volumes kept as he arranged them in his twelve glazed cases in 1690s interior: housed now in SE wing.

As you return to the street, note the impressive oversailing structure opposite, with curved Jacobean brackets: similarly at corner of Northampton Street. Across Northampton Street, Nos 2 and 3 Castle Street, *Cambridge and County Folk Museum* in former White Horse Inn. Apart from the original bar, the series of small rooms on all levels is devoted to bygones of every kind. Essentially a 16th-century building, its timbers, surprisingly, are elm and (mostly) pine. Across Castle Street,

St Giles's church, tall, forbidding, occupies the probable site of the main Roman gate into Duroliponte from Colchester and replaces a late Saxon minster whose clergy resettled at Barnwell (q.v. below). The present church, 1875, retains the primitive, chunky, Norman chancel arch in its S aisle. E window one of Kempe's best: three others by him. Monument to Nicholas Carre (1524–68), Professor of Greek, by Jacobean daughter.

Those interested in earthworks and prospects will climb Castle Street to *Shire Hall*, its flag rather presumptuously bearing the three crowns of E Anglia; others will skip it and recross to St Peter's. Shire Hall stands beside its predecessor,

the great mound of the motte-and-bailey *Norman castle*, built upon the Roman foundation beneath. In 1068, twenty-seven houses made way for this castle. Paths wind to top of mound in S tip of former bailey, last remodelled to protect E Anglia against Charles I's troops; remains of Vaubanesque bastion immediately behind Shire Hall. On clear days, views from mound: Ely, Gogmagog, and Chapel Hill, Haslingfield.

Now back down the other side of Castle Street to *St Peter's* shady churchyard, padlocked: a misfortune, but the tower is held up by corner props. The small 14th-century stone spire signals that this is the Midland side of the river. The inter-

St John's Old Bridge. Panel with Neptune and young tritons. Notice, on another panel, Father Cam admiring the college

ior has one showpiece, a magnificent 12th-century font, a triton carved on each corner. On corner of street and Kettle's Yard, a stone marks the end of the Godmanchester turnpike. *Kettle's Yard* is the art collector H.S. Ede's delectable gift to the university and houses his collection, notably, of Gaudier-Brzeska's work. Filter through, and cross Northampton Street. The public lavatory at the junction of Honey Hill and Northampton Streets marks the S corner of the 4th-century walled town; its wall ran straight along Honey Hill and Mount Pleasant with a main gate at Albion Row. Walk along Northampton Street 50 yds past the Rose and Crown, then turn left into a yard, to face a Dutch gable.

This back entrance is the best approach to ST JOHN'S COLLEGE: a luxuriant greenhouse (built in 1979) flanks an irresistible series of gardens and lawns. But first keep left

of the Dutch gable and walk round MERTON HALL, one of only half a dozen substantial survivors in England from *c*.1200—the very time (1209) of the migration of scholars from Oxford here. The Elizabethans, carried away by its antiquity, gave it a name still used: the *School of Pythagoras*. Built of characteristic local mix of dark brown and pale sand-coloured ragstone for a family called Dunning, it was conveyed to Merton College, Oxford, in 1271, and only lately to St John's. Usual first-floor hall of the time. S corner, a 1374 extension, tallies exactly with building contract. Half-timbered Tudor and Stuart range, a little spoilt by recent removal of old plaster coat.

Now approach main courts of John's via the *Cripps Building* (1960s, by Powell and Moya), much acclaimed, especially for its extremely successful layout. Its massing is properly continuous with that of

New Court (to which we are coming) but is at once rendered more delightful by the open ground floor (with some protection from the winds) and by the shape and arrangement of the window-glazing with its reflections of the colour and mood of the green gardens and water-walks. The concrete structure is attractively faced with white Portland stone, full of fossil, and with a not unwelcome hint of travertine. Unfortunately the unfaced concrete of all the window lintels has already gone the way of all exposed concrete in our climate, smudging what Pevsner rightly designated 'a masterpiece'. Walk straight on to Staircase D, turn right, past the Boys Smith Room and on into a corridor of *New Court* (1825–31), a large three-sided block of late Georgian 'Picturesque' Tudor-Gothic, facing S and closed by a highly romantic 'Gothic' cloister screen. The designs (by the Birmingham medievalist

54

△ Merton Hall (School of
  Pythagoras), St John's College

◁ St Peter's church font

Rickman and his pupil Hutch-
inson) are sometimes disparaged,
and the octagonal lantern on the
main tower is called 'the wedding
cake', but the cloister and its carefully offset Bridge of Sighs spanning
the river to the older courts, are
deeply appealing in the terms of the
picturesque—the reason most visitors come, after all. These designs are
in part a response to such romantic
poetry as Wordsworth's, who came
up to John's in 1785, and Byron's,
next door at Trinity in 1805. Tennyson at Trinity saw this New Court
being built. As we reach the middle
of the tall cloister, a great pedimented arch with interior fan vault

St John's College: New Court and the Cripps Building

and pendant gives on to the sensational green turf of *The Backs*.

Big herbaceous borders flank the cloister and, to the right, lead to a secluded yew-hedged garden framing a venerable quince (*Cydonia*). Follow the border to the left and cross the *Old Bridge*, Wren's idea, realized in Weldon stone in 1712 by Robert Grumbold, about whom more later. From this bridge there is a good view of the *Bridge of Sighs* and St John's Library-end, prominently dated 1624 with the initials of its donor, and with its late use of 'the old fashion of church window'; deliberately chosen, so perhaps notably early Gothic revival and a proper neighbour for the Bridge of Sighs.

From the Old Bridge we can see the curved 'Dutch' gable-ends (1671) of the two other ranges of *Third Court* into which we now progress. The old gault brickwork was lately well scrubbed, making the entire court look uncannily as it first did. What Pevsner calls the 'playful' battlements, carried all round from the 1624 library, provide a truly enchanting unifier, and, especially over those library windows, recalling faintly but insistently that marvellous 'playful' battlement-cresting round the Doge's Palace.

Go through the large turreted gatehouse into Second Court, Elizabethan, dated 1599, and once again as clean as in that year. The gatehouse contains a lively statue (1671, by Thomas Burman) of Mary Shrewsbury, Bess of Hardwick's daughter (and daughter-in-law!), the principal donor of this Court. The next arch leads between the great hall and the kitchens, and is called a 'screens passage'—as in large medieval and Tudor houses and most old Oxbridge colleges. Furthermore the hall (to the left) has a bold hammerbeam roof, constructed perhaps by Thomas Loveday of Sudbury, on the lines of some famous church roofs. The First

St John's College: entrance gateway

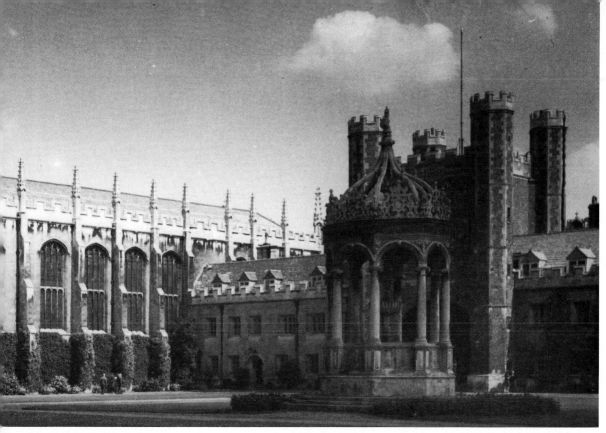

Trinity College Great Court

Court, blown open by Scott's chapel, nevertheless has his fine ironwork screen across the E side, presumably made by Skidmore Art Manufactory, Coventry. The S range, stonefaced, contains in the kitchen corner, Staircase F where Wordsworth occupied the 'nook obscure' he described in *The Prelude*. He was conscious, as the most unpoetic undergraduate and visitor must be, 'of generations of illustrious men' and could not always lightly 'sleep where they had slept' in 'that garden of great intellects'. Leaving by the great front *Gatehouse*, look carefully at the splendidly decorated frontispiece (1511–16), repainted and restored in 1981. Like that at Christ's, it pays tribute to the foundress, Henry VII's mother, the Lady Margaret, but here the statue above her arms is a work of 1662 by George Woodroff. It represents not the foundress but the patron, the evangelist John.

We are now in Trinity Street and turning right we proceed to the college of that name. The GREAT GATE OF TRINITY COLLEGE is a suitably grand entrance to the GREAT COURT within. In front of it, busy coming-and-going on the broad cobbled approach: beyond, less movement, individuals dwarfed by the expanses of the quiet academic piazza. Set in the front of the gate a 1615 statue of old Henry VIII, weathered into unintended burlesque, but confirming the majesty of the foundation as do the shields of Edward III's sons beneath. In the lower part of the gate, the pedestrian portal has stone carving identical with Wastell's on Bell Harry at Canterbury; done in Henry VII's time. One earlier college on the site, King's Hall, was founded by Edward III. Another, Michaelhouse, associated with St Michael's church across Trinity Street, was founded by a judge Her-

vey de Stanton in 1324. Acquiring Michaelhouse at the Dissolution, Henry VIII decided on a grandiose refoundation. In expanse what we step into is on the scale of a palace. Indeed Queen Mary, Henry's daughter, took a surprising interest and contributed the chapel; its series of eight Perp. windows within the court display a plain and rigid monotony. But it was at the end of Elizabeth I's reign, from 1593, that one of Trinity's great Masters, Thomas Nevile, completed the remodelling of the Great Court. Entering, we get our bearings.

The ranges that flank the Great Gate were part of King's Hall. The chapel itself runs W to another gatehouse, the earliest at Cambridge (*c*. 1430), called *King Edward's Tower*, moved here *c*.1600 (the date of its engaging statue of him) from its original position 30 yds to the south where it was part of the southern edge of the King's Hall Court.

◁ Trinity College Chapel

59

Trinity College Library

Nevile opened all this up, enlarging the court so that you now look diagonally across to his grand new hall beyond his fountain; to the left of the hall, the kitchens replaced the hall of Michaelhouse. To the right is the Master's Lodge. Behind King Edward's Tower, a further range of King's Hall survives and can be seen from the river. To the left, the fourth side of Great Court also contains a gatehouse: Queen's Gate, with

seated statue of Elizabeth I brought here by its London carver in 1597. Even from the Great Gate one sees that the stone for the facing of Nevile's fourth side was less elegantly reused. Trinity had acquired the building material of the dissolved Grey Friars (on the site of Sidney Sussex). They also acquired the water brought to that friary by aqueduct from the conduit head out beyond the Observatory and made

it play in their crowned fountain.

More even than the buildings of Trinity we think in the Great Court of the 'generations of illustrious men' who have heard that Franciscan fountain water splashing, day and night, through the centuries. On a single staircase between Great Gate and Chapel, Thackeray and Macaulay had rooms on the ground floor, Newton, Bishop Lightfoot, Jebb the brilliant Greek scholar

(Gwen Raverat's 'Uncle Dick'), and Frazer of *The Golden Bough* had rooms upstairs. Wherever their rooms were, in these courts we think of the early years of poets, of George Herbert, Cowley, Marvell, Dryden, Byron, Tennyson, FitzGerald, Housman; of formidable scholars, of course, like Bentley, Porson and again, Housman. Perhaps most important, for the modern understanding of our nuclear heredity in time, we think of Trinity's extraordinary natural philosophy tradition, from Barrow and Newton to Clerk Maxwell, Lord Rayleigh, J.J. Thomson and Rutherford (Cavendish Laboratory, Walk 2).

First, head right for the *Antechapel and Chapel*. In the antechapel one of the most famous statues in the world, Roubiliac's Newton (1755), standing, certainly shows 'his prism', but his stance suggests that 'his silent face' may at any moment address his thoughts to his companions: Whewell, seated, attentive, and Macaulay rather theatrically ready to listen. Tennyson is already entranced, Bacon slumped back deceptively. Among the smaller wall-monuments notice Hooper, by Roubiliac's admirable pupil N. Read, and Jones by Nollekens. Macaulay and Whewell are by Woolner. Fine Queen Anne reredos and early Georgian screen and stalls.

Continuing, pass in front of the Master's Lodge to flight of steps leading to *the hall*, and screens passage. Nevile's hall, begun in 1604, is conceived like the Great Court on an imposing scale: that of the hall of the Middle Temple. Francis Carter was master carpenter for the spectacular hammerbeam roof, in the Gothic tradition, but Classical in embellishment. Andrew Chapman was responsible for the wainscot, particularly impressive at the dais end as backcloth to Hans Eworth's dominant portrait of Henry VIII. Neither the portrait nor the royal arms stayed in place during Civil War and Interregnum; the headquarters of the Roundhead

Army was established here under Manchester and later Fairfax and Cromwell, and in this hall the Committee of the seven counties of the Eastern Association sat, under the chairmanship of a Bacon, one of Francis's nephews. We then move through into *Nevile's Court*, named after the remarkable Master who lived to see it finished in 1612.

Since Nevile paid out of his own pocket the college kept no detailed accounts, but John Symes may have continued as master builder with a craftsman named Pearce. Nevile's Court is now completed by Wren's Library. Nevile's N and S ranges were originally shorter, and closed on the W by a mere wall, with gate. Furthermore, they lost some Jacobean detail in 1755, when James

Essex renewed and to some extent rebuilt them. Nevertheless, Essex retained the arcades and the essentials of the design of these ranges and they are nearer to the spirit and feel of a cloister in Renaissance Italy than anything else in Jacobean Cambridge.

In 1672, sixty years after Nevile's work, his successor Isaac Barrow proposed a new LIBRARY, yielding 'much ornament to the University, and some honour to the Nation': not too high a claim for his friend Wren's designs, the gift of Wren to Trinity. From the hall end of the court, notice how the great architect has maintained the flow of the round-arched cloister with his necessarily sturdier columns, and laid the floor of his library at the

▽ Trinity College: library interior

Ketton stone mask at Trinity Hall ▷

Clare College

level of the springing of his arches, to continue the floor-level of the existing court. To mask this, he filled the arches with carved stone reliefs 'of which I have seen the effect abroad in good buildings . . . By this contrivance, the windows of the library rise high and give place for the desks against the walls, and being high may be afforded to be large. I have given no other frontispiece to the middle than statues, according to ancient example, because in this case I find anything else imperti-nent.' Gabriel Cibber's four statues personify (left to right) Divinity, Law, Physics and Mathematics; the last two proved especially propitious (though it was perhaps indecent of Cibber to show Mathematics count-ing on her fingers).

In summer, the cool colonnade beneath the library again recalls the classical Mediterranean: 'I have chosen middle pillars and lights outward, rather than a middle wall, as being the same expense, more graceful, and according to the man-ner of the ancients who made double walks about the forum.' Fine iron gates (from London) give on to the river bank. We first climb the stair-case to see the library itself, rightly acclaimed 'one of the noblest works in England and bears comparison with the Library of St Mark's at Venice'. Wren's design included Cornelius Austin's carved oak book-cases, also their decorations and the busts above done by Grinling Gib-bons and C. Austin. Only two of the original busts survive (Anacreon

Clare Bridge ▷

and Ben Jonson, in wood), but exquisite details in rosewood remain from these glorious early 1690s (the building was begun in 1677). Since that day another set of busts has been placed at the bookcase ends, those by Roubiliac especially brilliant. Again one observes the extraordinary sequence of Trinity men who have contributed to our life and thought. At the end of the room sits Thorwaldsen's fine statue of Byron (1829)—rejected by Westminster Abbey on grounds of Byron's immorality! Here he sits beneath a delightful Georgian window based on a design by Cipriani, a founder-member of the R. Academy: Fame is introducing Newton to George III while Bacon writes. Newton's own books and papers are in a nearby alcove.

Leaving by that river-gate, follow the bank. Good view of the Rickman Gothic of St John's New Court and of the river façade of Wren's library; the Ketton stonework's natural patterns of pink and saffron have full play in the monumental base storey, the library's floor-level then masked within three massive Doric doorways.

Cross *Trinity Bridge* (1765, James Essex) and walk along The Avenue (of limes) through the fine iron gate from Horseheath (q.v.) and left, under chestnuts, to Garret Hostel Lane. Over to the right, the University Library (1930s, awful, by G.G. Scott), its storage tower a portentous landmark: some good interiors: open only to MAs and ticket-holders. Garret Hostel Lane, leading back to the river, is a causeway between watery ditches; in summer moorhens are less evident than discarded drink-cans. Now cross *Garret Hostel Bridge*: its sure high concrete curve (granite-finished and its bronze rail polished) was trajected in 1960 by Timothy Morgan, an undergraduate in the School of Architecture, who died that year. It supplies a bold, even a superior, platform for viewing its fine Palladian neighbours, the bridges of Clare and Trinity, through the overhanging willows.

We are now approaching, through its 14th-century gate, the college confusingly called *Trinity Hall*. Step gables denote the unpretending Elizabethan brick library (it contains its five original bookcases). Pass through hall passage into the Principal Court, 14th-century but behind a Georgian mask of Ketton stone, 1740s, by Sir James Burrough, who became Master of Caius College (pronounced Kees), adjacent, and did much, as we shall see, to transform Cambridge over the years 1728–63. Chapel contains unusual plaster ceiling, 1730, and retains its medieval buttresses (*c.*1360) in South Court where the brick façade of H Staircase is, deplorably, painted over. Emerge through main front of college (by Salvin, in Ancaster stone), turn right and experience the unmistakable and glorious scale of King's College Chapel.

On the left, a large stone gatehouse of 1441, much restored and lately cleaned, is now part of the 'Old Schools' (Walk 2) but was the original court of King's College, built in 1441. The King (Henry VI) soon realized he wanted something on a much grander scale and so (1443–6) he closed thoroughfares, bought up houses and demolished the ancient church of St John Zachary near the W front of the great chapel; the chapel's foundation stone he laid in person on 25 July 1446. The clearance was on a scale recalling the Conqueror's building of the Castle, but here the dispossessed had sold willingly. And in what a splendid cause we best see by an indirect approach-route through CLARE COLLEGE.

So turn right between Clare's stone gateposts, urn-finialled by Edward Pearce, 1675, and supporting superb gates of 1714. A lavender-lined path leads to a fan-vaulted entrance, a very old fashion, for this court was begun a year or two before the interruptions of the Civil War and resumed soon after. Clare's great quadrangular building displays much that is most memorable about Cambridge's college architecture. It is characteristic of several buildings put up in the century between 1567, the date of Dr Caius's Gate of Virtue, and 1665, the year Wren's Pembroke College chapel was consecrated (both in Walk 2): a combination of traditional Gothic with classical forms. The E front's oriel windows go back to Kirtling (q.v.), etc. The inner, court side of this entrance displays the ingredients better, with Gothic niches surmounted by voluted scrolls and reclining angels of the northern Renaissance. Much interest derives from Clare's full records of the building, beginning with this E range and the Bridge (1638–40) and the S range (1640–2). John Westley was master mason and the masons included Thomas Grumbold, one of generations of that family who originated in the Northamptonshire stone-quarrying village of Weldon; the first worked on Great St Mary's tower in the 1590s. Robert's name appeared, you remember, as builder of the Old Bridge at St John's. Thomas, of the previous generation, did the drawing for and built Clare Bridge and we naturally find close similarities. Before leaving the court, look into the chapel, Sir James Burrough's last work (finished by James Essex, 1763–9): octagonal antechapel with dome, chapel with barrel-vault and apse, all delicately decorated like two stately rooms by Adam. Also look into the hall, remodelled with rich ceiling in 1870. In the panelling behind high table, comic portrait of principal foundress (Elizabeth de Clare, '1346') recalls three centuries of the college before its present buildings: other portraits include Hugh Latimer's and our own contemporary Lord Ashby. Now through to *Clare Bridge*, with richly bordered lawns beside, and further elaborate iron gates ahead.

The bridge's parapet bears a series of beautiful stone balls and the central arch seems to sag proudly under their weight. The bridge is usually assumed to have been

The Backs at King's College

undertaken early in Clare's rebuilding programme to enable materials to be carted direct to the site, but we may suppose that all those tons of Weldon and Ketton stone and Collyweston slates arrived at this bank by barge. Notice the carved dies on the outside of the main pedestals above the cutwaters. A bard failing to keep his seat on a lobster (SE pedestal) is a kinsman of Father Cam on St John's Old Bridge by the younger Grumbold (Robert).

Pause now, for this is the best standpoint for taking in *Clare's river front*, and its remarkably natural relationship to its grand neighbours at King's. Robert Grumbold's palatial composition, seventeen bays in Ketton stone, 1669–76, is divided by a central, rusticated gateway and then each bay flanked by Tuscan column-pilasters surmounted by great Ionic ones.

Turn right, just over Clare Bridge, cross Clare College garden, then gaining the Backs, turn left and enter the grounds of King's College through monumental gates (Wilkins, 1819, whose front screen we see later). Suddenly, walking back towards the river, we are at Wilkins's bridge. There it is: the most unforgettable broad lawn in the world separates the Cam, and us, from the Gibbs' Building (1724–31) and CHAPEL OF KING'S COLLEGE.

This slow approach round the lawn from the river imprints on us the essential proportions of the famous chapel. Its narrowness and

King's College Chapel and Gibbs Building △

◁ King's College Chapel (*left and below*)

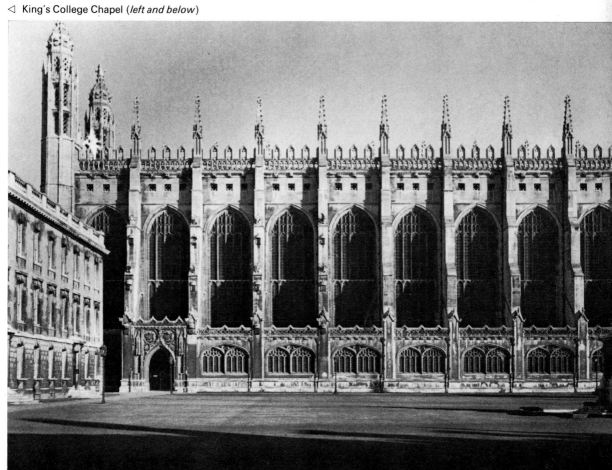

its height (conveniently contrasted with Gibbs's Building) are somehow balanced by the gentle arch of the roof-line and matching width of the W window. The proportions, exactly as given in Henry VI's memorandum of 1448, combine an internal height of 80 ft with a breadth of no less than 40 ft; the overall length runs very nearly to 300 ft. Before entering, take a look at the length from the S side, for it helps prepare one for the extraordinary unity of the conception within. Construction went ahead in three separate bouts of activity spread over about seventy years. The first came to an end with Henry VI's débâcle in 1461 and its progress is marked by the line of white Yorkshire stone used till 1460. After 1460, the stone came from King's Cliff and Weldon (and closely matches that from Yorkshire). By 1485, at the end of a second advance, the five E bays were timber-roofed but not vaulted. The chapel's greatest benefactor was Henry VII. In his last year, 1508–9, his grants totalled £6,400, enabling the main masonry to be finished. Under his will, a further grant of £5,000 in 1512 paid for the vault, some of the glass and much woodwork. In 1515 the fabric was finished and the glazing begun. More money was found, this time probably by Henry VIII. The screen was set up bearing Henry VIII's and Anne Boleyn's initials, in 1533–6. The glazing was not finished till 1547. After a whole century in construction all we can now see was ready.

That persistent phrase 'King of Kings' in Handel's most famous chorus takes on a fuller meaning as one experiences this glorious interior. Might, majesty and the utmost grace are stated in stone and wood and glass. On a dull day the lithe intricacies of the stonework preside; on a brilliant day the lights and colours of the glass prevail. The soaring shafts are hung about with crowns, in themselves more than substantial enough to orbit the skull of Henry VIII, and each serving as a kind of crocketed canopy to the roses and grim portcullises of the Tudors, but each crown crowned by crosses. Again, the splendid heraldic beasts on the screen, though they insist first on Henry VIII's supremacy as Head of the Church, do not omit the crosses over all.

The Crucifixion itself occupies the terminal position in the E window, the enormously tall cross totally eclipsing Pilate on his princely throne, washing his hands in vain. And if the details of decoration were contributed by the Tudors, so was the bulk of the cash. They transgressed the Founder's 'will' (1448) which instructed them to avoid 'superfluity of too great curious works . . . and busy moulding'; only 'large form' remains as Henry VI ordained, antechapel and chapel, divided by the screen, but united by a fantastic triumph of height and breadth, weightlessness and weight, in an inevitability of proportion that marks it among the finest buildings of the world.

The records are fortunately full for the last phase of construction, from 1508. The heroes of this superb phase, the conclusion of the whole enterprise, are John Wastell (see Trinity Great Gate), the master mason who (perhaps from an earlier design by John Wolrich) created the great vault, the pinnacles on the buttresses, the exquisitely finished angle-turrets, and the vaults of all but two of the eighteen side-chapels; and Thomas Stockton, the master carver, whose intricate crowns seem almost independent of the wall. Another hero is the Provost of King's, Robert Hacomblen, a gifted musician as well as a considerable humanist scholar, commemorated in the middle side-chapel NE of the screen; he signed the contracts with Wastell as he did fourteen years later with Galyon Hone and a number of his remarkable fellow glaziers. It is strange that a humanist should have agreed to the scheme of the subjects depicted in the glass—the highly legendary life of the Virgin Mary (one of the college's two patron saints), including the life, passion and resurrection of her son, together with all 'the prophesies and prefigurings' of all this in the Old Testament. Colet had rejected much of the 'prefiguring' in lectures Erasmus had attended at Oxford over a quarter of a century earlier. In fact this was a last fling of the old medieval theology, given a sort of immortality under the auspices of a Renaissance prince.

Clearly, a detailed list and commentary are needed if each of these subjects is to be identified and understood. Such booklets are available at the sales counter. The name of Dirck Vellert has lately been emphasized as perhaps the chief designer. For most visitors it will be enough to wonder at the realism of the drawing, the brilliance of the pictures and the lights they throw into the chapel. It is perhaps best seen in the morning sunlight when the golds melt into the gilding on the great organ, its trumpeting 17th-century angels facing the congregation like the Winged Victories they represented.

Two more heroes deserve commemoration. Dr Samuel Collins, Provost from 1615–45, so nourished the intellectual eminence of the college that when Manchester supplanted him by Benjamin Whichcote, that 'noblest of the Cambridge Platonists' (Walk 3) cared for old Collins and did his best to stand between the Fellows and the Puritan dictatorship. Collins's integrity may have helped to preserve all those priceless windows; when Dowsing, the official iconoclast, visited chapel on Boxing Day, 1643, all he could scribble in his Journal was '1 thousand superstitious pictures'. Some influence, unrecorded, restrained the smasher's hand.

In 1962, Rubens's great picture of the Adoration of the Magi was given to the college and was finally installed behind a lowered altar.

As we reel away from this bombardment of images, we look across at the more humdrum staircases on the far side of the court and start thinking what Kingsmen have done. Until 1873 virtually all were from Eton, under Henry VI's terms. A century later they have come to include Kingswomen. It has to be admitted that economists like Maynard Keynes come to mind, rather than statesmen. Many will remember, even before they give the chapel a thought, the first-floor room of E.M. Forster. Auden's sonnet from America to him, on the brink of World War II, conjures him up compactly: 'Though Italy and Kings are far away,/ And Truth a

subject only bombs discuss,/ Our ears unfriendly, still you speak to us,/ Insisting that the inner life can pay . . .'

Finally, come to the Porter's Lodge and see how cleverly it forms part of a Ketton stone screen that carries across the front of the court the screen design of those eighteen side-chapels we vow to inspect on another visit. This external screen is the creation (1824–8) of William Wilkins, not for nothing the son of a theatrical manager. We shall see more of his work on Walks 2 and 3.

Porter's Lodge, King's College

WALK 2 *To the Botanic Garden* (Trinity Street, King's Parade, Trumpington Street: St Michael's church—Gonville and Caius—Senate House—Old Schools—Great St Mary's, St Edward's and St Benet's churches—Cavendish Laboratory—Corpus Christi—St Catharine's—St Botolph's church—Queens'—Pembroke—Little St Mary's church—Peterhouse—Fitzwilliam Museum—Botanic Garden)

Starting again at the Round Church, along Trinity Street past the gates of St John's, and Trinity and the Victorian bulk of Caius. Opposite the Great Gate, Trinity has two interesting extensions: Whewell's Court, Victorian, by Salvin, really a sequence of three (lately refaced) small courts, and, beside the second, the Wolfson Building, 1969–71 (by Architects Co-partnership) makes ingenious use of the enclosure to provide comfortable rooms for about eighty students—entrance of shuttered concrete painted to suggest striped tent! Heffers' great Bookshop adjoins. Opposite Caius *St Michael's church* was given to Michaelhouse (Trinity College, Walk 1) by Hervey de Stanton who rebuilt the church, and was buried in it in 1327 just before it was finished: his (S) chapel is light, with exuberant niches and remains of 15th-century glass. In 1966 the church was sensibly partitioned, the nave becoming a community hall (for use e.g. by overseas children's groups in the summer); the chancel, large and clearly designed for collegiate use, now serving as a chapel: its glory is the roof.

Recross the street and, before being exposed to a very famous view, do not fail to enter the quiet front court of *Gonville and Caius* (normally abbreviated to 'Kees', which indeed is how its second founder's name was spelt when he became a scholar here at Gonville Hall in 1532). Beyond the court, called, since 1658, Tree Court, the walk has been replanted with an attractive young alley of Swedish Whitebeam

(*Sorbus intermedia*): it leads straight to the *Gate of Virtue*. Looking at and through this gateway is another of those rare experiences, as in Nevile's Court at Trinity (Walk 1): the brief illusion of being in Renaissance Italy. But this one is half a century earlier than Nevile's Court. On the far side the gate is inscribed 'Io. Caius Posuit Sapientiae 1567'. John 'Caius' had gone to Padua in 1539, worked and lived with Vesalius, taken his MD there, and returned home to become physician to Edward VI and Mary and President of the Royal College of Physicians. About 1556 he decided to re-endow his old college. He was not the only Cambridge man to experience the Italian Renaissance, but he was the first to bring back its architectural ideas. His original entrance to the college, labelled 'Humilitas', a mere gateway in a wall, was removed to the Master's Garden in 1868 when Waterhouse erected his hideous and unhumble French gate-tower. Caius's idea (nobody has produced a better) was for a student to enter with humility, walk the straight path to virtue and leave, across the next court, through the Gate of Honour (which opens directly on to the 'Old Schools' where the University's lectures and examinations were held).

The Gate of Virtue is highly interesting for its (appropriately) correct use of Classical detail. In its spandrels, for the Victories he saw on Padua's town hall, Caius substituted those engaging females Fame and Fortune (or Wealth). Although the GATE OF HONOUR was built in the two years following Caius's death, 1573–5, 'it was wrought according to the very form and figure which Dr Caius in his lifetime had himself traced out for the architect'. It raises a charming signal of greeting to the more ornate terminal turrets of King's Chapel. Awareness of neighbours is not a virtue much cultivated these days by architects or their historians.

Back in Trinity Street, rejoice in the view opening up on the right:

the E front of King's College Chapel is attended by a noble chestnut, its gently cascading outlines soft against the adjacent geometry. They are flanked, further right, by the two chief contributions of the University (as distinct from its colleges) to Cambridge architecture—beside Chapel and chestnut tree, Stephen Wright's Palladian E range of the medieval 'Old Schools' quadrangle, a prettier version of the middle block of the Horse Guards; and, at right angles, facing S down King's Parade, Gibbs's SENATE HOUSE, both in very (newly cleaned) white Portland stone. Both sprang from the need to find room for George I's magnificent gift of the late Bishop of Ely's books and manuscripts to the University. (The University's own library and rooms for lectures and committees were known as 'the Schools'.) With the library overflowing, a new three-sided court was planned, open towards St Mary's. In 1721 James Gibbs came in to advise.

Gibbs might well have brought into being, here at the University's heart, something of the monumental *forum academicum* he so triumphantly crowned at Oxford when he added the Radcliffe Camera to Schools Quad, Clarendon Building, Old Ashmolean, and Wren's Sheldonian Theatre. But it would have been at the expense of the view of King's Chapel. The threat to this view was one of the reasons given for curtailing Gibbs's three-sided scheme. Other reasons, familiar to us, were shortage of funds and change of political control. Gibbs's patrons were Tories. When the new S front of the Old Schools came to be rebuilt (1754), its beautiful medieval gateway went up to Madingley; meanwhile the great Whig manipulator, the Duke of Newcastle, was Chancellor of the University and his Palladian man, Stephen Wright, did a fine enough job on the Schools. On the immaculate green turf between the two fronts sits a bronze

Gonville and Caius, Gate of Honour: sundials flank the hexagonal crown above a one-man triumphal arch ▷

(Birmingham) copy of the Warwick Vase, given in 1842, inscription by Eric Gill, 1936.

Entering Gibbs's Senate House by the door between the fluted three-quarter columns of the S front (these exquisite forms of Corinthian capitals Gibbs had noted in Rome in the ruined temple of Jupiter Stator), one's eyes are at once distracted by two superb marbles—life-size standing figures of the Duke of Somerset (Newcastle's predecessor as Chancellor, 1689–1748) and the younger Pitt, Pembroke College's great man. Both are masterpieces, carved 'to the life', though both posthumously: Somerset, relaxed, by Rysbrack, 1756; Pitt by Nollekens, 1812, drawn up, as always in public, to face Destiny. Returning to the Senate House we let our eyes wander to the riches of woodcarving and plasterwork. To his two regular plasterers Gibbs himself paid proper tribute, writing of this building simply: 'It is of the Corinthian order, having all its Members Enrich'd: the Ceiling and Inside-Walls are beautify'd by Signor Artari and Bagutti.'

Outside, a few steps W to the one range that was erected of C.R. Cockerell's masterly remodelling (1837) of the N wing of the Old Schools, now containing the Law Library and, in 'the Regent House', the *University Combination Room* (common-room for senior members of the University, not necessarily College Fellows). Beside the entrance, notice medieval walls and windows on left, again the snuff-coloured ragstone that gives such a pleasant character to medieval buildings in much of Cambridgeshire. With permission, or discretion, at top of stairs on first floor, one may peep into the Combination Room. Its alarmingly broad medieval roof is masked delightfully by an Elizabethan plaster ceiling, the plasterwork faithfully enfolding some of the long horizontal timbers, wrapping them in patterns of vines. Underfoot, the carpet is a famous

Senate House with Old Schools beyond

Corpus Christi College: chapel and Cambridge-Venetian lamp

one by William Morris, *c.* 1890. At the W end of the Law Library, two more exceptionally fine sculptures, again posthumous, the kings clad comically as Romans: George I by Rysbrack, George II by Joseph Wilton.

Now back across King's Parade to GREAT ST MARY'S, the medieval University church and, like St Mary's at Oxford, a part not only of the main street but also of the *forum academicum*; it was used for examinations and degree ceremonies before the Schools were built in the 14th century. Then there were all those University sermons, from Martin Bucer and Latimer, not to mention, as Rose Macaulay did in her poem 'Trinity Sunday', the Master of Caius. Outside, the endearing features are the octagonal corner pinnacles of the tower, echoing not only Haslingfield, but the W front of Ely. The tower was begun in 1491 but stuck just above the W window. It was completed, 1593–1608, by two of those Northamptonshire Grumbolds (see Clare, Walk 1). Inside is a church of surprising nobility. The beautiful traceried spandrels above the slender nave arcade are best seen in the quiet glow of the winter afternoon sun. The similarity with Saffron Walden's church is unmistakable, where the work was contracted with Simon Clark and John Wastell, freemasons (see Trinity Great Gate, Walk 1). Here the spandrels of the chancel arch, most unusually, are traceried, very delicately, as high as the springing of the broad and splendid roof, which is curiously chocolate-coloured. The timber for this roof was given by Henry VII in 1506—a hundred oaks in Chesterford Park. A general rebuilding of this church had been going on since 1478 as the result of an appeal by the University. The stone of the chancel walls was re-used from the previous church, going back at the very least to 1205, refaced 1857 by Salvin with Ketton stone. The galleries, 1735, running the length of each aisle, detract only a little from the delight of the arcade. Aisle roofs fine. Good late-Victorian glass (by Powell's) in clerestory windows, two to a bay, each separated by wall-post of tie-beam.

Beyond St Mary's, just along the pavement, is No. 19 King's Parade, built c. 1700, with steep original staircase. Turn up St Edward's Passage into a charming small square formed round *St Edward's* gardened churchyard. (Unluckily all the surrounding buildings have been marred by having their brickwork painted.) The church's dedication suggests a pre-Conquest origin. The little building is famous as one of the potent dynamos of the English Reformation. Here on Christmas Eve 1525, Robert Barnes denounced bishops, and four years later Latimer preached his famous English Reformation sermons on the metaphor of cards, making hearts and works of mercy triumph over ceremonies and pilgrimages. In this small nave, only four bays long, the panelled early-Tudor pulpit stands on spindly legs that scarcely look strong enough to support such impassioned preaching. The arcades are appropriately spiky and narrow and a main impression is, naturally, of the empty matrixes in the floorstones from which 'superstitious' memorial-brasses were later ripped by a second generation of Reformists, the Puritans. (Dowsing celebrated New Year, 1644, by breaking forty picture-windows.) The font seems to be supported by secular figures. Near it is a memorial by E. and M. Gillick to F.D. Maurice, 1835–72, founder of the Working-Men's College and Queen's College for Women in London. His bust stands in the Old Schools. A white marble on the S wall recalls John Mortlock (1755–1816), woollen draper, who controlled Cambridge in the younger Pitt's interest from 1787. Nowadays, the bookshops and the Arts Theatre's restaurant are the main centres of life in this little square.

Continuing along King's Parade, notice a distinguished modern architect's junction between King's and Cat's (St Catherine's): lines, mass, height of oriel window, all seem wrong, including the use of Portland stone, its texture usually pleasant but here an obtrusion instead of a link.

Just round the corner, in Benet Street, stands one of Cambridge's most delightful surprises—*St Benet's church* (short for Benedict's), with a magnificent Saxon tower, framed in a well-gardened churchyard as usual in this town. In the churchyard a handsome gadrooned casket-tomb (Sarah Newton, 1725) and the shaped headstone of Thomas Grumbold, 1657, with the emblems of mortality: the author of Clare's bridge and, probably, the cresting on St John's library and balusters on Christ's Fellows' building. Not only the tower, but the four corners of the nave and much of the S wall of the chancel are 'Anglo-Saxon', from perhaps c. 1030, so really Anglo-Danish. The quoins of the tower display the 'long and short' laying of the limestone, the manner that characterizes pre-Norman masonry: the rest of the walling is of the traditional honey-coloured rag-stone. Walk S from the tower and observe the original main entrance to Corpus Christi (formerly St Benet's College) to which we return. Inside the church, the pre-Conquest tower-arch is of splendid proportions, though the capitals are comically 'unclassical' and the arch springs from two endearing lions, twitching their moustaches and swishing their tails above their backs. Six bells: Fabian Steadman, inventor of change ringing, was parish clerk in mid-17th century. So here emerged that 'sweet uproar'.

Across Benet Street, the Bath Hotel has Georgian features, and the Eagle, once the Post House, goes back to c. 1600; in this courtyard the upper rooms are entered from an open gallery. (Benet Street leads into Wheeler Street, where the Tourist Information office is situated.)

At the E end of Benet's churchyard, turn into the pleasant Free School Lane for another of Cambridge's great surprises, *The Cavendish Laboratory*. Built on the site of the University's 18th-century Botanic Garden, it looks just like any other Victorian academic building, stone faced, with Gothic windows and a gateway, a small ogival arch echoing Christ's and John's, surmounted by a statue of the Duke of Devonshire, Chancellor of the University, who provided the necessary £6,500. An equally unobtrusive plaque marks the centenary of the building, 1874–1974, and says 'it housed the Department of Physics from the time of the first Cavendish Professor, Clerk Maxwell, until its move to new laboratories in West Cambridge.' It is hard to imagine a more classic understatement. Here, under Clerk Maxwell, the foundations of electrical science were laid in the 1870s. Inside, a brass plate on a ground-floor pillar records the place where the uncertainty of the ohm was reduced to very small dimensions. Nearby, J.J. Thomson established the identity of the

electron and, later, Rutherford accomplished the artificial disintegration of the atom; the neutron was announced in 1932. Next year, just through the entrance arch, the Royal Society's Mond Laboratory was opened with, engraved in the brickwork, Eric Gill's crocodile: a creature that never turns its back, and hence symbolized Rutherford's career. When its first occupant, P. Kapitza, was detained in Russia he was sent all the apparatus he needed to pursue his researches. Rutherford believed scientific discovery was for all nations, everyone. Perhaps he

College buildings of the '60s:
left: Queens' Erasmus building
below: Caius' Harvey Court by Leslie Martin and Colin St J. Wilson
opposite: Corpus' Leckhampton House

President's Lodge, Queens' College

was lucky to die in 1937. Anyway, here, overlooking this Anglo-Saxon churchyard, between the 1870s and the 1930s, discoveries were made that seem to surpass even Newton's in their significance for mankind in relation to the universe. The crocodile building now houses the admirable Aerial Photography department, another of Cambridge's pioneer undertakings. But it is the recollection of those physicists that causes us to approach Gill's crocodile with such awe.

Back round St Benet's churchyard, we enter *Corpus Christi College* through a small Gibbsian postern. It leads into Old Court, one of the best-preserved medieval college quadrangles, and the oldest, dating from 1352–77; three sides containing sets of rooms, and the S side contained former Hall, common-room, Master's Lodge and library over. An awkward remodelling of windows commemorates two former Corpus Christi men: Marlowe, the most brilliant and challenging of Shakespeare's contemporaries, a student here in the 1580s when that Anglo-Saxon tower was being refurbished, and John Fletcher, the delightful playwright, Beaumont's friend and collaborator, a student in the 1590s. To the S, a complete new court was built by Wilkins in 1823–7 in rigid, theatrical rather than medieval, Gothic; since its repair and wash in 1952, the Ketton stone has kept very clean. His chapel, opposite the main gate, contains six pairs of elegant candelabra, and four windows of Rhenish glass, *c.* 1510, apparently imported by him. The Hall also has four fine candelabra and much distressing Victorian decoration. The library contains a superb collection of manuscripts given by Archbishop Matthew Parker, many of them 'rescued' from monastic libraries at the Dissolution.

St Catharine's College, opposite, is a rebuilding by Robert Grumbold in 1674, less genial than his work at Clare, in a dark blue-red brick. It is relieved by a stone centre-piece gateway austerely classical in deference to Wren's work. To the right, half the N wing had its windows absurdly Tudorized by the Victorians. The other half contains the chapel, deeply impressive in the simplicity of its interior: a plain wainscot throws into relief the tall wooden reredos, its baroque round arch supported on two pairs of Corinthian columns, and all is lit by very tall, thin candles.

Across the street, *St Botolph's church* has a delectable garden on its S side, with wooden seats among the headstones, geraniums and flowering shrubs, and on the S wall of the chancel the monument to Robert Grumbold, master mason, 1721 (see Clare College, Walk 1, particularly). On the top corners of the tower (*c.* 1400), tall stone emblems of the Evangelists look slightly sheepish without their weather-vanes. The (mainly) early 14th-century interior has fragments of 12th-century carving reused in bases of two of the arcade-piers. The font has a Jacobean case like an old well-head. William IV's royal arms on canvas are painted like a good inn sign. Victorian stencilled ceiling in nave, chancel by Bodley, 1872, oak and gilt, with Georgian copy of Van

Queens' main gate from Front Court

Dyck *Crucifixion* in reredos, another *Crucifixion* by Kempe in E window of N aisle.

Cross over to Silver Street, turn up Queens' Lane into *Queens' College* through the Old Main Gate—yet another of these late medieval East Anglian country-house entrances. In the head of the arch, the male figure with scroll represents Andrew Docket, the first President and virtual founder in 1448: the two queens involved in the launching were Margaret of Anjou and Elizabeth Woodville. Docket was rector of St Botolph's. The front court, brick over clunch, is more or less as designed in 1448–9, the master

mason probably Reginald Ely, the carpenters from Elsenham, Essex. Bear right, through Walnut Court to Bodley's lofty chapel, 1890, one of the best Victorian contributions to Cambridge. Inside, the E wall, in fading purple, sage green and gold, is very impressive, the reredos and E window within one high recess— the window (and five more on N side) by Kempe, facing four (slighter designs) by Hardman. Reredos contains late 15th-century S German Triptych, dramatizing Christ's Betrayal, Resurrection, Appearance to the Apostles. Brasses in antechapel include Martin Dunstan, servant to Mr Andrew Dokett;

also an Elizabethan Fellow is shown in ruff saying 'Lord Jesu Receive my sperit', 1591. Back into Old Court to Old Hall: roof carpentry by Thomas Sturgeon of Elsenham, 1449, restored 1845, rich and exciting redecoration by Morris and Bodley, 1862 and 1875. On into Cloister Court: walk to the middle of this mellow gault-brick court with its picturesque covered way round three sides—built c. 1495 and new when Erasmus lived here 1510–14. His rooms (according to tradition) were in the narrow tower, brick with stone quoins, to the S of the Old Hall range. To the N, the remarkable timber-framed Elizabethan President's Lodge with its long gallery. As the College's own guide leaflet admits of this major example of timber-framing in Cambridge, the studs (vertical posts) were not meant to be exposed and were plastered over, like the rest of the wall, until 1912, since when their diseased-looking, nail-pocked stripes have set a wretched example to other owners of such fine old buildings.

Through the W arch, the river is spanned by a 1902 facsimile of James Essex's *Mathematical Bridge* of 1749, constructed solely of timbers pegged together without resort to any nail. Here one sometimes gets the nostalgic watery whiff of the Venice canals. This is where the Backs end, and they end with a bang architecturally. Across the silvery stone of Silver Street bridge, Scudamore's boatyards find themselves in the strange company of the least congenial of all modern Cambridge buildings—the so-called *University Centre*, its aggressive fenestration connected by small squares and oblongs of bolted-on stone cladding; these façades are further disrupted vertically by what look like Gothic stair-turrets, concrete of a different dinginess, and weathering to something worse. Reverting, gratefully, to *Queens'*: it has leapt the river with its buildings, like St John's at the other end of the Backs, but with nothing like the élan. The curved 1930s red-brick range, named after

Erasmus's friend Fisher, we used to laugh at for its unfashionableness: beside its new neighbours, the University Centre and the latest Queens' building, it looks positively agreeable. The newcomer bares its backside, bicycle stores, etc., under the very windows of the Fisher rooms. It includes a new hall, with 'high table' but of course no dais. The students' rooms look comfortable to the point of luxury. One thinks of Erasmus finishing the first stage of his great work on the Greek New Testament here at Queens' in 1513 and 'when he had been sore at his boke, for lacke of better exercise he wolde take his horse and ryde about the Markette Hill and come agayne.' If the design of Cripps' Court seems hardly to justify its intrusion into the priceless green of the Backs, the beech-shaded bank alongside provides a good platform for viewing Basil Spence's Erasmus Building, 1961, a model of trim, unshowy design, the right scale, sensitive use of materials and colour in positive harmony with all its neighbours. *O si sic omnes!*

Back to St Botolph's and the corner of St Botolph's Lane (a pleasant street marred by having the brickwork of all its old cottages and houses, with one notable exception, painted over), and along to the corner of Pembroke Street, flanked by Pembroke College's 14th-century wall. At this point we meet *the water-runnels of Trumpington Street*, their ripples and splashes a reminder of the town water supply brought here in 1614 from Shelford by the benefaction of Hobson the Carrier (see later in this walk). One of its functions was to flush out the King's Ditch, a possibly late Anglo-Danish defence-work, perhaps contemporary with St Botolph's church, improved by an 8-ft walk alongside when Henry III was here trying to cope with the barons based at Ely. The King's Ditch ran from the river up the N side of Mill Lane and Pembroke Street, turning to pass Christ's College and down Hobson Street and Park Street, to rejoin the river.

It was a town moat, Cambridge's natural form of town wall. The need to flush it through had been discussed since 1574: Hobson provided the means.

Now enter *Pembroke College*'s delightful late 14th-century gateway (refaced in Ketton stone, 1717, but otherwise unaltered), the oriel windows overhead reminding one of old Northamptonshire houses. Inside, on left, Old Library; converted c.1690 (from previous chapel) with astonishing plaster ceiling by Henry Doogood—swans flying about and a cupid trying to arrange a ride on one. The new CHAPEL was given by Matthew Wren, Bishop of Ely, released from over eighteen years' imprisonment in 1660. On that account, and from its remarkable quality, we assume the design was by his nephew Christopher Wren, a brilliant mathematician and scientist, and Professor at Oxford. It was built in 1663–5, one of Wren's first two buildings in Cambridge, and certainly the university's first sight of something so very like a classical temple. It appears to have been inspired by a reconstruction, published in 1611, of 'the temple by the river at Tivoli'. The sanctuary is an addition of 1880, sympathetic. In the reredos, the painting of the Deposition was in Sir Joshua Reynolds's collection. The remarkable decorations and fittings of this chapel are worth long appraisal.

The unaccountable Victorians let Waterhouse loose on this college. His (Louis XII) range S of the chapel, on Trumpington Street, has lately been cleaned: its bright red brickwork looks as if laid in 1972 instead of a century earlier. His library, 1875, to the W, with egregious clock tower, might be thought 'a gem of its kind'. His hall range, W of Old Court, bears downpipes dated 1926 from a remodelling by Maurice Webb. Murray Easton had another go in 1949—all very depressing. The poet Gray would have been appalled by it all. To get to 'the New Building', a sort of Arts and Crafts 'Grumbold' design,

◁ *p.84*: Pembroke College Chapel
p.85: Peterhouse Chapel from Trumpington Street and from Old Court

1907, by the younger G. Scott, you pass what Waterhouse built as Master's Lodge, a truly sinister thing, hung now with ivy and Virginia creepers, guarded by gargoyle dragons and fronted by a dreadful garden. Let us quickly think of Bishop Ridley's farewell: he recalled the orchard at Pembroke where he had learnt all the Epistles by heart.

Retreating through the main gate, notice the University Press building opposite, a colossal Tudor-Gothic tower, rising from a wholly classical plan, 1831, and usually known as 'the Pitt Press' since it was built with funds oversubscribed from a statue for Pitt in London in 1802. Take no notice of the aggressive Emmanuel Free Church tower, 1875, and make for Little St Mary's Lane alongside. In yet another enticing garden, the church of *St Mary the Less* offers a light, spacious interior, N, S and E windows as broad as Perp. ones but full of Dec. tracery and dating from 1352: the N windows retraceried 1857; glowing E and W windows and NE window by Kempe, S window by F.C. Eden (the altar by Comper). Dowsing smashed '60 superstitious pictures, some Popes and Crucifyxes and God and Father sitting in a chayer and holding a Glasse in his hand'! Beautiful pulpit, 1741. Before 1352 this was the church of St Peter outside the Trumpington Gate (King's Ditch): Peterhouse took its name from it, indeed used it as college chapel till 1632, much as Corpus did Benet's. Details of the Norman building survive at W end, so do a few fragments of Anglo-Danish carved interlace, reset in S wall outside. Some 14th-century brickwork in bone-hole under vestry; early for brick here.

Next along Trumpington Street, *Peterhouse*'s Master's Lodge, dated 1702, was built for himself by one of the Fellows, who then left it to house succeeding Masters; dignified 'builder's domestic' at the beginning of the best period. It faces the Front Court of the college, the Perne Library range, 1633, in brick on the left; on the right James Burrough's Building, Ketton-faced, 1742, and PETERHOUSE CHAPEL, with its raking shaped gable like a breaking wave, an idiosyncratic silhouette that will remain in the memory almost as persistently as Trinity Great Gate or Clare from the bridge. Here the motive is High Anglican and the begetters were two Laudian Masters: Matthew Wren, who gave Pembroke its chapel after his release in 1660, but who had begun this chapel and much else at Peterhouse 1625–35; and his successor, a Norwich man, John Cosin, Master 1635–44 and 1660, under whom the chapel was completed. Cosin gave the walls their stone face, with a final gift of this E face in 1665. By then he was Bishop of Durham, and Hendrik de Keyser III was collaborating in his building programme there. The de Keysers were a family of Amsterdam master masons and it seems reasonable to link the original and very 'Dutch' frontispieces of Peterhouse chapel with their name, also, perhaps, to see Pembroke's as a response to Peterhouse's challenge. The Cromwellian Puritans accepted the challenge of Peterhouse chapel by sending Dowsing to wreck it: 'pulled down 2 mighty great Angells with wings and divers other Angells, and the 4 Evangelists and Peter with his Keies over the Chapell Dore and about 100 Chirubims and Angells, and divers superstitious Letters in gold'. The E window, *c*.1630, a harrowing Crucifixion scene, probably by Bernard van Linge, had been removed to safety: now the curious gloom of the interior enhances the horror of the subject. The eight scenes in the remaining windows, vivid like early magic-lantern slides, were by Professor Ainmüller of Munich, inserted *c*. 1855. In the reredos, a fine late 15th-century French wood Pietà was given in memory of Eileen Power (Postan). The arcades, with galleries over, linking chapel with buildings N and S and closing Front Court, were done 1709–11 'according to a paper delivered by Mr Grumbold'.

Constructing the Front Court in the 17th-century meant destroying the two hostels of 1284, the earliest 'college buildings' in Cambridge—established by Hugh de Balsham, Bishop of Ely, 'according to the rule of the scholars of Oxford called Merton'. In 1286 a Hall was built for them—to the left across Old Court. It was largely rebuilt by G.G. Scott junr., 1868–70, and redecorated with tiles, stencilled murals and stained glass by William Morris's firm, most of the glass designed by Ford Madox Brown and perhaps hard to live with. The redecoration includes older portrait-panels of, e.g., Edward, Lord North (*see Kirtling*) and Bishop Cosin. Going on through the screens passage, you emerge through a 13th-century doorway between two buttresses and see what survives of the buff-coloured limestone walls, the original walls of the earliest college hall built in Cambridge. Here one also pauses to regret the destruction of the old Garden House Hotel. Admirers of Morris and Co. will wish to experience the 'romantic atmosphere' of the Peterhouse Combination Room with windows designed mainly by Burne-Jones.

Beyond Peterhouse, Trumpington Street takes the character of a pleasant old suburb, with a Tudor timber-framed pub, The Little Rose, and No. 32, now Fitzwilliam House, built for John Halsted in 1727, his front door flanked by simple Corinthian pilasters and the grey and red brickwork vertically patterned. Meanwhile, THE FITZWILLIAM MUSEUM has suddenly appeared, a properly monumental building to house and display one of the greatest and most varied art collections in this country. We approach the first of the glittering prizes for the undaunted who have come so far:

Peterhouse Front Court through arcade

the second, the treasure garden of the botanists, is at hand with more relaxing delights. Both are liable to compel repeated visits at leisure.

Paintings by Rembrandt, Titian, Veronese and Palma Vecchio, prints, illuminated manuscripts, a library and £100,000—when Lord Fitzwilliam left all this to his old university in 1816, the very recent pure Grecian architecture of Wilkins's Downing College (Walk 3) was understandably admired. But by the time the University organized its competition (1834) for a building fit to receive the collection, fashion had changed and George Basevi won. His orders 'are not Gre-

cian but Roman and the spirit is more Roman still, but Roman of the later Empire in the East, as at Baalbek and Palmyra' (H.-R. Hitchcock). This suits some of the collections particularly well: the initial bequest was generous enough to ensure a splendid succession. A valuable extension by David Roberts to the building was recently completed.

Mounting the steps to the portico, you are aware of the extraordinary richness of the frieze and coffering of the portico ceiling; it really is a bit like icing on a gigantic Parnassian cake. The sculpture is the work of W.G. Nicholl (the design for the

pediment—nine muses, Pegasus and the Hippocrene fountain—by Eastlake). Nicholl went on to carve for the Taylorian at Oxford, the pediment and lions for St George's Hall, Liverpool, and the reredos at Waltham Abbey. Basevi was killed by a fall in Ely cathedral in 1845 before the Fitzwilliam was finished. C.R. Cockerell succeeded him and designed the dome above the staircase hall, which is otherwise Basevi's: the feeling in this hall is depressingly that of a portentous London club. But there the resemblance ceases. Downstairs, the Gayer-Anderson Egyptian room is superbly arranged: vivid mummy portraits of

87

the Roman period, the noble granite sarcophagus of Rameses III (c.1198–1166 BC) deified as Osiris, and so on. Greek, Etruscan and Roman rooms lead to Porcelain galleries; there is a Glory made by Giovanni Baratta in Florence, 1715, for Marlborough.

At the head of the main staircase, a very fine array of sculpture includes a Milan Venus, 1829, very classical, Chantrey's bust of a Professor of Mineralogy, 1824, and his Horne Tooke, John Bushnell's terracotta of Charles II and Roubiliac's 9th Earl of Pembroke. Ahead, a noble room lures one on to see Eworth's *Unknown lady, formerly called Mary I*, Reynolds's unfinished *Rockingham and Burke*, and Carlo Dolci's *Finch and Baines*, painted in Florence when Finch was minister to the Grand Duke of Tuscany, their skull-like heads draped in dark wigs and lit by living eyes, their sculptured monument at Christ's (Walk 3) one of the finest of its kind. Such local connections at the heart of the building create an illusion that we are visiting some Cambridge nobleman's house, which in a sense we are. Here is Joseph Wright's charming portrait of him, Richard, 7th Viscount Fitzwilliam as a young man, near two busts by Wilton and two by Nollekens, Stubbs's *Gimcrack on Newmarket Heath* and Gainsborough's early Suffolk portraits of the old Kirbys and the young Heneage Lloyds and one of his small delicious landscapes.

There is no need to list the Corots, Courbets, beautiful Pissarros, a ravishing Renoir; but, confirming the sense of local connection, we soon come to Constable's portraits of his closest friend Archdeacon John Fisher, and of Fisher's wife, and more Constables including a Dorset watermill looking just like the one in Dedham Vale. Then, among the Braques and two small Rouaults, an early Wilson Steer of girls paddling on Southwold beach in Suffolk, not many walls away from Sickert's *Hugh Walpole* with background of paddling boys.

Only a door divides all this from the world of the Italians. Whatever else you walk past, stand before two wonderful small Venezianos from humanist Florence; an *Annunciation*, and the *Miracle of St Zenobius*, restoring to life a child run over by an ox-cart. You are unlikely to miss the glorious collection of Venetian paintings, their size and richness of colour dominate and mesmerize. There is an enchanting Bellotto and a pair of Canalettos grouped with a painting of an allegorical monument. It is by G.B. Pittoni with D. and G. Valeriani, and the monument is to Sir Isaac Newton: once more we are back in Cambridge.

Here one can only hint at the variety, without space to do more than mention the W Asiatic antiquities, the ceramics, glass, armour, enamels, textiles, all the forms of Oriental art, then the coins, the illuminated manuscripts, the music, and so on. The displays and special exhibitions are admirable. There is now a good refreshment room and bookshop.

Opposite the main entrance, the domestic 1720s scale of Fitzwilliam House is agreeably continued in the gently bent terraced houses of Fitzwilliam Street, an unchanged street of the 1820s. As we pass the Museum's bookshop on the right, the curious range of the old Addenbrooke's Hospital appears, mostly 1863 by M.D. Wyatt, but preserving a 1740 core behind. Here the street curves slowly right, maintaining its pleasant width and water margins. St Peter's Terrace, 1850, with Tuscan porches, 'Roman and contemporary styles combined with virtuosity', is conveniently set back behind a fence of iron spears, yew, plane and chestnut. Scroope Terrace follows (including the Royal Cambridge Hotel), 1839 and 1864, and brings us to the Leys School on the edge of Coe Fen.

The edge of the town is signalled by *Hobson's Conduit*, a large, delightful ornamented stone pepperpot surmounted by a gilded fir-cone: the town's answer to the Trinity Great Court fountain. It stood on Market Hill 1614–1856, when the Cambridge Water Company's piped water supply seemed to make it redundant. It was brought here, where Hobson's Brook, an artificial stream from Shelford, runs into culverts. One we have seen, reappearing in Trumpington Street; another goes under Tennis Court Road on its way to Market Hill; a third by Lensfield Road to St Andrew's Street, feeding by the way the gardens of Emmanuel and Christ's (Walk 3). Thomas Hobson, 1544–1630, was the highly successful Cambridge carrier, a chief benefactor of the conduit. He is more widely known through his horse-hiring activities: you took the horse he offered, or none, so that 'Hobson's choice' has become synonymous with 'no option'. Milton wrote uncharacteristically 'undergraduate' verses on him.

Walk on beside his brook as far as Bateman Street. Near the corner is the entrance to the UNIVERSITY BOTANIC GARDEN. At the office and bookstall it is worth picking up a leaflet showing the layout of the 40 acres, with grid-references to all the principal trees and plants. Entrance is free to the public, though the garden was established here, in 1846, chiefly for the teaching and research in the University's Department of Botany. Members of the Director's staff welcome serious enquiries. Most members of the public will appreciate the chance to roam in such beautifully arranged and kept and *labelled* gardens, where indeed the bird life is nearly as absorbing as that of the plants. The excitement begins with a black walnut and a prodigious growth of Caucasian wing-nut, the suckers grown from one that blew down in 1886. As at the Fitzwilliam, here is more than the completers of Walk 2 will even glimpse. But they will be readier to appreciate the fine *Catalpa erubescens* at Christ's, and the noble *Platanus orientalis* at Emmanuel, on Walk 3.

Trumpington Street from Fitzwilliam Museum (*top*); Fitzwilliam Museum portico ceiling (*bottom*) ▷

(*above and opposite*): Lloyds Bank

From the Round Church, walk left, past Joshua Taylor's, Georgian street-fronts preserved on the right until you reach *Sidney Sussex*, founded in the 1590s by Frances Sidney, Countess of Sussex. Much recent stone renewal has replaced the unattractive cement rendering of Wyatville's 1821–31 'remodelling': a central porter's lodge separating two apparently '1820s Elizabethan' courts. What he remodelled in Hall Court (to the left) was Elizabethan, the real thing. In 1831, Wyatville moved a beautiful rusticated Doric former main gateway (of 1749) from Hall Court to the wall in Jesus Lane as part of his overall neo-Elizabethan scheme, embracing Chapel Court as well. In 1891, J.L. Pearson went even farther, extending the Hall range with memorably awful bulbous bay-windowed and cloistered buildings, reproducing the opulence but not the lightness of the originals: they stand frowning over the beautifully tree'd (and sensibly labelled) old garden, which contains an enormous spreading chestnut. The cloister contains a 1966 plaque to Duns Scotus, the 13th-century 'Dr Subtilis', presumably on the score that this was the site of the Franciscans, some of whom claim him; in Erasmus's time he came to be thought of as the original 'Dunce'. The chapel (with what echoes of Biblical exposition) was rebuilt in 1776, and again in 1910 from a dignified design by T.H. Lyon that makes one want to go to look for his church of St George in Chesterton. The enchanting *Nativity* by G.B. Pittoni was brought from Venice in 1783. Oliver Cromwell

was a Sidney Sussex man. In the antechapel an oval plaque marks the grave, nearby, of his head, brought here in 1960 after long residence with an Anglican canon in Suffolk.

On through (slightly curving) Georgian brick ravine, past Galloway and Porter's bookshop to Sussex Street, the creation of E.R. Barrow, 1938, 'the best piece of pre-war urban planning in Cambridge' (Pevsner), certainly a most attractive contrast to what we see of Petty Cury a little farther on. At the corner of Market Street, *Holy Trinity* church became an engine of Jacobean Puritanism, 1610–34, then one of Evangelicalism under Charles Simeon, 1759–1836, Senior Fellow of King's and 54 years vicar here. A gallery in the S transept remains from his day, also various relics in

the vestry, including his 'preaching Bible' and his green umbrella. He is commemorated in the chancel alongside several oriental scholar/ missionaries in India. Another wall monument recalls Sir Robert Tabor, 1681, whose expertise with quinine saved the lives of Charles II, the Dauphin and the Queen of Spain. The spire, the only medieval stone spire standing E of the Cam, was rebuilt in 1901. Churchyard-garden redesigned 1974. Stonework cleaned in 1981, not to its advantage: ragstone of a suspiciously uniform colour, resembling chunks of creamy cheese, it would look better well 'rendered'.

Boots' store adjacent bears insignificant notice of Darwin's residence on the site in 1828 (he was at Christ's). Next, Petty Cury's offensively uniform roof-line along its far

side betrays this piece of 'comprehensive redevelopment' of 1975. The great red lion from the yard of the wonderfully atmospheric medieval Red Lion Inn destroyed in this cause looks understandably savage. An ugly cylinder bearing the names of those chiefly responsible is already cracking within six years of its erection. What is worth looking at, and now beautifully cleaned and renewed, is *Lloyds Bank* formerly Fosters, with a clock tower related to Pembroke Library's; the bank is by A. and P. Waterhouse, 1891, with a pale neo-Tudor extension of 1935; the remarkable glazed-tiled interior is intact, a perfect period piece.

The NW wall of *St Andrew's* churchyard, opposite, marks the line of the former Tibbs Row and the King's Ditch (Walk 2) which crossed here, its line continued by Hobson Street. Barnwell Gate stood beside the Ditch, and the church was 'St Andrew without Barnwell Gate'. A famous scene of Elizabethan and Jacobean pulpit Puritanism, it was largely rebuilt in 1660, then again in 1842, with cast-iron piers and wooden galleries, to hold 1,000 of the swelling population. Several interesting wall monuments were kept, some marking the early deaths of undergraduates at Christ's, the main gate of which we now face.

CHRIST'S COLLEGE began as God's House here in 1446, expressly to train teachers. At the turn of that century, John Fisher, the leading reviver of learning in Cambridge, became confessor to the Lady Margaret, Henry VII's mother, and began to interest her in his projects. With his help, she re-endowed God's House as Christ's College in 1505 (they also went on to found St John's, Walk 1).

In 1714, the clunch-and-brick front was refaced (by Robert Grumbold) in Ketton stone, and in 1760 the whole inner court was given its comfortable, domestic-classical, sash-windowed appearance, in Ketton stone, by James Essex. This most welcoming little court probably goes back, in the core of the two ranges to left of entrance, to God's House; the Lady Margaret and Fisher enlarged the chapel in the far left corner, then that too was refitted, chiefly in 1702.

First, walk over to the far right corner and through the screens passage out into the second court, where you confront the Fellows' Building and the Fellows' Garden beyond. They bring the 17th century vividly to mind. Milton, just 16, came to Christ's in 1625; he was here seven years, his first-floor rooms in N range, Front Court. Already spurred 'to scorn delights, and live laborious days', he drew from these years at Christ's much of the beauty and strength of his later sublime utterance. His last year here, 1632, he celebrated with the

Christ's College: Fellows' Garden: the Bath and Mead's urn

Allegro and *Penseroso*, two of the most magic of immortal poems, ending with a famous tribute to the college chapel: 'storied windows richly dight,/ Casting a dim religious light./ There let the pealing organ blow,/ To the full-voiced choir below . . ./ Dissolve me into ecstasies,/ And bring all Heaven before mine eyes.' Nothing very puritanical, but Paradise had been seen in Christ's chapel, and perhaps in the garden.

In 1608, the year of Milton's nativity, the college planted 300 mulberry trees to gratify James I, keen to produce English silk. Naturally the venerable mulberry in this garden has become associated with the poet. Unluckily his two tutors seem to have exposed him to a dreary scholasticism, 'studies fruitless as they are joyless', almost as though Fisher and Erasmus had had no impact on teaching. Things might have gone very differently had Joseph Mead been his tutor. We come to Mead's urn in this garden, and need to know what he stood for. An open-minded Biblical scholar from his schooldays, and a remark-

able tutor, Mead expressed such disarming ideas as: 'I cannot believe that truth can be prejudiced by the discovery of truth.' In that way lay the future. The 'Cambridge Platonists', or 'Latitude-Men', shaped the divinity thinking of the Georgian Age: Christianity to be tested by reasonableness rather than revelation. Mead was succeeded as Fellow (1639–87) by Henry More, a leader of the Platonists (his daunting belief was 'God reserves his closest secrets for the purest minds'). These two were men of impressive simplicity, declining all preferment. It was More who introduced John Finch to Thomas Baines in 1648, and in 1682 composed their epitaph on the most remarkable monument in the chapel.

The Fellows' Building, 'the boldest building of these years, 1630–70, and one of the most original of its date in England', was erected in 1640–2. The name of its designer is unrecorded. What is unmistakable in the Fellows' Building is its Cambridgeness—a family likeness with so much of the best building here in

Christ's College: Fellows' Garden

that creative century between the Gate of Virtue and Pembroke Chapel. We walk through it and on round the *Fellows' Garden*, a crescent of beehives representing sweetness and work, and the Bath (an early 18th-century oblong bathing-pool supplied from Hobson's Conduit) with adjoining pretty summerhouse, representing leisure. Beside the Bath, three Georgian busts preside on pedestals: Milton, Cudworth (another of the Platonists) and Saunderson (a mathematician), with two urns, one of them Georgian for Joseph Mead ('Mede'), the other for Charles Percy (Lord) Snow. C.P. Snow's own writing, not least his novel *The Masters*, about Christ's, is a fitter memorial. Monumental plane-trees and beautifully flowering catalpa must be resolutely forsaken if the chapel is to be seen.

The main story of *the chapel* is clear in the antechapel: the timber-panelled ceiling of Lady Margaret's time is supported on piers encased as Corinthian columns by John Austin, 1702. The light is moderately dim and religious still, two small 15th-century windows showing Edward the Confessor and Edward IV, three rather more interesting ones of *c*.1505 seem to show Henry VII, Elizabeth of York and Henry VI all at prayer. An upper window from the Master's Lodge, where the Lady Margaret used to hear mass, was reopened in 1899 (when the oriel was made). The brass eagle lectern dates from her time. The lunatic Dowsing clawed an inscription from it. The organ is a renewal of 1705.

The most beautiful object in the chapel is a monument to Sir John Finch and Sir Thomas Baines, sculpted with virtuosity by Joseph Catterns, 1684, in white and black marble and undisguised wood. Catterns was a member of the Joiners' Company and this is his only identified work. There must be much more. He clearly based his carving of the heads on the portraits by Carlo Dolci, much at home now in the Fitzwilliam (Walk 2). Christ's also has portraits of them, by Mary Beale. Brass nearby shows John Sycling, 1506, last head of God's House, first Master of Christ's, as D.D. In ante-chapel, notice brass of Thomas Fowler, gentleman usher 'with the famous King Edward IV, and his wife, gentlewoman to the Lady Margaret'; and floor slab of John Covel, 1722, Master, chaplain with Finch and Baines in Constantinople, who wrote travel journals, and left Christ's the cupola and clock above Grumbold's chapel turret.

We leave Christ's, easily omitting Sir Denys Lasdun's terraced building, offensive to King Street. Grimly we head along St Andrew's Street, passing the recent plate-glass shopping arcade that replaced a medieval yard of timber-framed buildings, towards Emmanuel and Downing.

If God's House had been founded to train teachers, *Emmanuel College* was founded by Sir Walter Mildmay in 1584, to prepare 'pastors' with sacred theology for 'preaching the Word'. Mildmay's Essex neighbour, Lady Sussex, modelled Sidney Sussex on it. What is more, of the 130 University men who migrated

Emmanuel College, North Court

across the North Atlantic before 1646, 100 were from Cambridge and no fewer than 35 from Emmanuel, easily the biggest, most influential contingent at work on the mind of New England. They included John Cotton, the leading divine of Massachusetts, and John Harvard: a tablet here in the chapel records his emigration to Massachusetts Bay, 'and there dying in 1638 he bequeathed to a college newly established . . . his library and one half of his estate.' Mildmay's college disseminated 'the Word' more effectively than he can have dreamed. Then, like Christ's, it mellowed into 'Platonism'.

Theological activity evidently proved popular, for Emmanuel increased rapidly to become fourth largest college. As interest in Puritanism collapsed with Cromwell's Protectorate, the college then turned to William Sancroft, later Archbishop. He became Master in 1662, and was instrumental in getting the new chapel built by Wren. As you enter the college through James Essex's front screen-range (1775) your eyes rest on Wren's EMMANUEL CHAPEL (1668–77) straight ahead. In its lateral 'cloister' arcade, with galleries over, it resembles the Peterhouse arrangement (q.v.) but in fact that was modelled on this. Here Wren combined the wings intrinsically with his noble main front of the chapel; a giant order, as at Pembroke Chapel, but the cupola here supported on a square (clock-faced) pedestal by the two inner columns. The feel is Palladian, not all that far from Inigo Jones and Covent Garden: indeed he may have had in mind a design in an early edition of Vitruvius. Furthermore, as you look at this façade, you see the making, in Wren's mind, of his London church towers. The masons, Simon Wise and Nicholas Ashby, came from Deene (Northants) and Ketton (Rutland) as did the stone. Robert Grumbold had a hand, widening the central arch in 1677.

As you advance towards the chapel, register the point that in the range on your left the Hall, modestly refitted by James Essex (1760s),

Downing College

apparently occupies the ancient (13th-century) fabric of the church of the Blackfriars of St Dominic: it is one of those rare continuities from medieval to modern we celebrate when we reach Jesus College. On the right the range was Elizabethan, rebuilt 1719 by gift of the earl of Westmorland, badly burnt in 1811, but retaining the George I stair-cases. The Chapel's interior is won-derfully light. The superb plaster-work of the ceiling, by John Grove, who worked for Wren at Trinity, has a central oval wreath of fruit and flowers in very high relief, the four Gospels lying open in the four cor-ners of an outer frame. The wood-work, London-designed but made by Cornelius Austin, was the gift of

Sancroft. The organ case is *c.* 1730, the cut-glass chandelier, just right in this small temple of light, was given in 1732, and Jacopo Amigoni's beautiful painting of the Prodigal Son was given in 1734, then framed as reredos. It remains to note the marble, on the W wall, to Richard Farmer, Master 1775–97, with epi-taph by Dr Parr; in 1765 Dr John-son had a 'joyous meeting' with him here. Two years later, Farmer's *Essay on the Learning of Shakespeare* showed effectively that the Bard's knowledge of the classics was der-ived from English translations. Thereafter, he freely indulged his three loves, 'old port, old clothes, and old books', Georgian Emman-uel's answer to all those Puritans.

In the garden a pleasant lake is fed by Hobson's Brook, and so, over the wall in the Fellows' Garden, is a swimming pool among five copper beeches and a marvellous oriental plane-tree. Looking the other way, running S away from the chapel, is the Brick Building of 1633, with curved 'Dutch' gable-end, and at right angles the new Library, begun in 1909 by Leonard Stokes: next year he also did the excellent North Court, across Emmanuel Street. South Court, near the Library, is well designed by Tom Hancock, who also did the Master's Lodge in 1963.

Leaving 'Emma', we press on through the poor street-scenery of St Andrew's Street, crossing the road a few yards from the University Arms Hotel. Here it becomes Regent Street, with respectable white-brick Regency houses (No 41 was the first home, 1871–5, of Newnham College), but we turn right through an unremarkable black-ironwork gateway into the campus of an architecturally most distinguished Regency college, Downing—its distinction wronged by egotism and insensibility in our own century.

DOWNING COLLEGE was begun in 1807 with the endowment of the 3rd Sir George Downing, who had built himself a large house at Gamlingay, at the end of Queen Anne's reign. In his will he devised the estate to cousins but, if the line failed, a college was to be founded. The widow of the last childless cousin did all she could to obstruct the foundation and destroy the value of the endowment, reducing the Gamlingay house to the present melancholy earthworks. Litigation ceased only in 1807, when the first stones were laid of a beautifully conceived group of authentically Greek-style buildings. They were designed by William Wilkins, aged 24 and just back from four years in Asia Minor, Greece and Italy: his details and grouping as impressive as the timing of his return.

This was the first foundation in Cambridge since Sidney Sussex. The shift of emphasis from theology to law and medicine is reflected in the design, a large verdant open square closed on two opposite sides, E and W, by classical ranges, graceful Ionic porticoes emphasizing the residences of the two professors in the middle of each range, the Master's Lodge and the Hall facing each other at the S extremities of each wing. The scholars occupy the intervening ranges.

The entrance to Downing was to have been from the N through the columns of a magnificent gateway leading between the two residential flanks to a colonnaded chapel and library. Downing's money ran out in 1821 before the E and W sides were quite complete, but enough was done to give Wilkins a gratifying view from the house he built himself to the S, just across Lensfield Road (pulled down in 1955 in favour of immense chemistry laboratories). These two flanking ranges were completed approximately to Wilkins's design by E.M. Barry, 1874–6, one good architect showing proper regard for the work of another. Unhappily in 1931 and 1951, when the planned formal N approach became impracticable, Wilkins's scheme was inverted and a sprawling chapel block with L-shaped corners was erected across the N side by Sir Herbert Baker and A.T. Scott. More recently a surprising addition to the Hall end has been made by a Cambridge Professor of Architecture: it is in the Japanese, or perhaps Tibetan, manner. Its designer's intention may not have been to demonstrate the superiority of Greek architecture, but his very interesting building instantly does!

None of the 20th-century degrading of young Wilkins's fine conception need surprise us. His invention of 'the college campus' is a measure of his originality: it was followed a decade later by Jefferson in his University of Virginia at Charlottesville, where the two flanking ranges were designed to lead the eye out into the distance from the Roman Pantheon placed centrally as university library. Even sooner than at Downing, Jefferson's masterpiece was undone by leading architects who, as H.-R. Hitchcock remarks, 'professed the greatest admiration for the work of such predecessors as Jefferson and proceeded to destroy its essence whenever the opportunity arose!'

Wilkins's noble edifice at Downing also has to contend with gross intrusions from outside the campus, notably the massive tower and 220-ft spire of the 1890s Roman Catholic church of Our Lady and the English Martyrs where Regent Street reaches 'Hyde Park Corner' and becomes the Hills Road. This church contains an oak carving, half life size, of Virgin and suckling child, mid 16th-century and alleged to be from Emmanuel, where the Dominicans had a statue of 'Our Lady of Grace' in 1515; also an impressive woodcarving by Pugin, 1843, of St Andrew on his cross. 'The most conspicuous place of worship in all Cambridge' might be a more acceptable claim if the building were in a style at all identifiable with the place, but, as with Scott's chapel of St John's College, its very prominence in this beautiful setting emphasizes its alien character.

Those not impelled to visit the church should recross the road to the University Arms and walk out to where the paths cross in the middle of *Parker's Piece*. Parker's Piece is the very extensive open space acquired in 1613 by the town from Trinity College (the college cook, Edward Parker, had the lease and is thus immortalized) in exchange for a section of 'the Backs' on both banks of the Cam; it is framed by small houses and lime-trees. Now turn left, cross the road at Parkside, continue along Melbourne Place to ORCHARD STREET.

Orchard Street crosses Clarendon Street, and flanking its right side is a strikingly picturesque terrace of humble single-storey cottages, of *c.* 1825—easily the most attractive row of dwellings of its kind in the county: local grey-brick and tile, a great unbroken stretch of Mansard roof following the curve of the street (the attics lit by dormer windows at the rear), brief gardens before simple pedimented front doors, a sash window either side, and a series of massive chimney-stacks above.

Orchard Street emerges opposite *Christ's Pieces*, another of Cambridge's generous endowments of public green spaces—formerly 'pieces' in the open fields—and adjoining Christ's Fellows' Garden; it provides shade and seats for weary walkers. We turn right and pass New Square, its terraces built 1825–38, part of Cambridge's great expansion this way in those years. The population of this (Barnwell) parish rose from 250 to 9,500 in the

first forty years of the 19th century—more than the entire population of Cambridge in 1800. The delightful physical evidence of it throughout this neighbourhood is an object lesson all too apparently ignored in our time. New Square itself was long disfigured as a car park. Short Street leads to a traffic roundabout, where we turn left along Jesus Lane.

Along Jesus Lane, the spire of Bodley's famous church of All Saints still attracts the eye, though the church has been redundant since 1973. We shall appreciate its interior the more after visiting JESUS COLLEGE, through the gateway immediately opposite. The gateway to Jesus is R. Grumbold's work, 1703, with ball finials on gadrooned pedestals, the wrought-iron gates a little later. They lead into 'the Chimney', the narrow paved approach, walled in the 17th century, between the Master's Garden (right) and that of the Fellows (left). Suddenly it is like being out in the Isle of Ely again, with Bishop Alcock, the founder, greeting us over the arch of his beautiful gate-tower, his canopied statue surmounted by the familiar cock (unexpectedly black) on its gold orb. The red brick came from his claypits. After his death, in 1500, the top of the tower was completed with a rather sketchy diaper pattern in yellow gault bricks, perhaps the earliest example of their use?

This gate-tower is assumed to stand on the site of the gatehouse of St Radegund's priory of Benedictine nuns, founded in the 1130s. In 1496, Alcock, the diocesan bishop, established in its place a college, known almost from the start as Jesus College. What is more extraordinary is the extent to which the college continues the life of a cloistered community begun some eight and a half centuries ago. When we bemoan the Tudor circumstances that cut off, as by axe, the life and purpose of a

Jesus College Chapel:
(*left*): the chancel
(*right*): ceiling coving by William Morris

Fountains, or a Tintern Abbey, we usually forget this remarkable exception beside the Cam.

The range to left of gatehouse was a grammar school from *c.* 1505 till absorbed in college in 1570: top storey 1718. Past the porter, straight ahead is a dull 1638 copy of the grammar-school range but we head half right, for a doorway signed with another painted cock-rebus. It leads into the cloister, that of the nuns, the timber roofs Alcock's, the brickwork redone in 1760s. Immediately to left, upon an undercroft, the Hall sits within the very walls of the nuns' refectory, heightened and bricked by Alcock; its best feature a vaulted oriel beside high table. Going clockwise round the cloister, notice that the fine early 13th-century portal of the nuns' chapter house was found in 1840 by young Osmond Fisher, son of Constable's great friend, while still an undergraduate. In the later 1840s, as a Fellow, he helped Pugin in his great work of transforming the chancel of the superb Benedictine priory church that serves as College chapel. Straight ahead, the S range of the cloister gives modest access to it.

Alcock removed N and S aisles of nave and chancel and took the W two-thirds of the nave for the Master's Lodge, but the remaining third continued as parish church till 1555; with the N and S transepts it forms something like one of the grand Oxford college ante-chapels. The N transept retains solemn Romanesque features from the time of the first building. We cannot appreciate what we see without knowing what Pugin, Bodley and Morris and Co. did. The dim religious light helps, both in showing up the Pre-Raphaelite windows to their advantage and in enabling us to think ourselves back into the time before Alcock turned nunnery into college. (An electric light-switch just inside the entrance beautifully reveals the painted ceiling of the 'nave'.)

This was an ambitious late-Romanesque cruciform church, the ambition continuing into the middle of the 13th century when the chancel was gloriously rebuilt, lancet windows especially fine on N side and notable sedilia and piscina to S. Thereafter, accidents and mismanagement. Alcock reduced the size and put in a Perp. E window, but enough evidence of the previous linked lancet-windows survived to enable Pugin to reconstruct the originals convincingly. When Pugin was called in, in 1846, the chapel was in a poor way. He resurrected the chancel, largely rebuilding the E wall and, with the help of Osmond Fisher and James Rattee, a Cambridge carver, created the altar, the ceiling, stalls (including a few notable originals) and the great screen. He also designed window glass and brass lectern both for Hardman to make—the lectern modelled on the famous one in St Mark's, Venice (English work, but that fact was not known to Pugin), the glass based on a special visit he made to Chartres. Pugin died in 1852, and ten years later the tower, transepts and nave all needed strengthening.

G.F. Bodley, making designs for a new All Saints', opposite, did the necessary work for Jesus Chapel, with new ceilings in nave, crossing-tower and chancel. William Morris supervised the painting of the nave ceiling by F R. Leach, the Cambridge craftsman (see St Clement's church) and himself did the angels with scrolls round the coving: the remaining ceiling designs were Philip Webb's, the execution by Leach. Bodley designed the floors, undertaken in stone and tiles by Minton. Bodley then pressed the college to commission the remaining windows from Morris and Co. He finally succeeded in 1872, the designs mostly by Burne-Jones, but a few by Ford Madox Brown and Morris himself. One may be content simply to admire the medieval and Victorian qualities of this remarkable chapel.

The W wall is hung with a well-carved monument to Tobias Rustat, 1693, Yeoman of the Robes to Charles II: very possibly one of those lost carvings of the excellent Joseph Catterns. In the N transept floor a brass plate recalls Constable's promising eldest boy, a friend of Osmond Fisher: too fearless in his medical research into scarlet fever, he died of it at 24. Osmond left to the Fitzwilliam Constable's 'Gillingham Mill'. One of the Fitzwilliam's most surprising treasures is a large medieval wax candle found in this chapel by Pugin: painted with vine tendrils in red and gold.

Pugin's chancel is wonderfully convincing '13th-century' from the outside, especially since the 'rendering' was replaced by beautiful stone facing in the 1930s. Returning towards the (first) Outer Court, we see David Roberts's large new North Court building, 1963–6, in a sandy-coloured brick, a pleasant contrast to Waterhouse's plum-red brick barracks of a building in prolongation. Admirably thought out, North Court is one of the best three or four major college extensions in Cambridge since 1945 and must be one of the most agreeable to live in. The gardens of Jesus, too, are among the best in the University; there is a particularly well-considered flower-bed on the W side of Outer Court, with *Datura suaveolens knightii* flowering happily among the Michaelmas daisies.

Back down 'the Chimney', we cross the road to Bodley's *parish church of All Saints*; first to see where to collect the key, then to enter, preferably from the very modest NW porch. The medieval All Saints', immediately opposite St John's College, could hold only 400 of the 1,400 parishioners it found itself with in 1854. Jesus College, patron of the living, offered the new site, and a former Fellow proposed Bodley as architect. His first (very French) design proved too expensive; the second, in 1862, was adopted and was in many ways remarkable. First, it 'stands out in the history of English architecture, marking the point at which the Gothic Revival demonstrated the ability to learn from past styles and to build from their principles rather

Bodley's All Saints

than to plunder them for individual features and precedents'. This breakthrough was recognized by Bodley's contemporaries. As we just saw in Jesus Chapel and, earlier in Queens' (Walk 2), Bodley went on to envisage the complete scheme of decoration as an integral part of the architectural design: late Gothic ideas of 'darker painting on the walls, while the glass was made delicate and silvery in tone'. As at Jesus, the main collaboration was with Morris; F.R. Leach, of Cambridge, carried out the major part of the actual painting of roofs and walls—the nave roof at his own cost. C.E. Kempe supervised the work.

The interior is majestic, a tall, broad nave, with fine arcade to a S aisle; the chancel, also lofty, is seen through a tower raised above the chancel in 1869. The 'darker painting' of the walls seems sombre now that the church so urgently needs cleaning and restoring, but the glass is much as Bodley hoped. The famous E window's five lights each contain four single figures of saints, the central light rising to a charming Christ in Majesty (Burne-Jones). Morris and Ford Madox Brown contributed a few of the figures (some of them identifiable members of the Pre-Raphaelite group). Kempe, Kempe's cousin Walter Tower, and Ward and Hughes later contributed good windows. Christ in Glory is painted in tempera over the chancel arch, and the pulpit has St John Chrysostom, St Peter and John the Baptist painted on gesso: both works apparently by 'Mr Hughes' under Kempe's direction, 1878 (?Arthur Hughes). To the relief of its Friends, All Saints was in 1981 vested in the Redundant Churches Fund. Next door, Westcott House, a Church of England establishment founded in 1881, has a most attractive brick court and garden.

We complete the length of Jesus Lane, starting with two admirable Georgian brick houses beyond Jesus Fellows' Garden: No 32, red brick with mansard roof, c.1740, and No 31, white brick and almost a century later. Wesley House, by contrast, displays the depressingly rigid refusal of modern urban designers to incorporate existing street lines. But it is quickly forgotten as No 16, 'Little Trinity', comes into view, set well back beyond gatepiers bearing urns; truly urbane, early Georgian, three storeys of unusual grey-brick 'header-bond' (only the small side of each brick showing), trimmed with rubbed red brick and ashlar: 'perhaps the most handsome private house in Cambridge' (Pevsner): no longer private. Finally, the University Pitt Club, with that famous profile—abundant nose, scarce chin—in a roundel in a smart Ionic little temple built as late as 1865, and turned to Conservative politics after use as a Turkish bath.

Suburbs *Newnham* and *Barnwell* (Darwin, Arts Faculty, Museum of Classical Archaeology, Newnham, Leckhampton House, Robinson, Churchill, Observatory, Barnwell, Stourbridge)

Visitors curious about the contribution of modern architecture to Cambridge have seen some of the most considerable examples at Magdalene and John's (Walk 1), and Queens' (Walk 2), Emmanuel and Jesus (Walk 3). The incurably curious will want more for it is widely known that a great outcrop of new buildings was reared here in the 1960s. Sir Nikolaus Pevsner was taken aback by the extent to which new fashions in architecture were adopted between 1958 and 1968, when the 1st and 2nd editions appeared of his *Cambridgeshire* volume in 'The Buildings of England' series: he described it as 'astounding'. The 'Postscript to the Introduction' in his 2nd edition is very instructive. He is naturally appreciative of the response by so many Cambridge academic committees to the 'International Modern' style he personally did so much to promote. But he is careful to distinguish between what he calls the 'crisp logical' architecture of the 1930s–1950s and the tendencies to the 'over-dramatic, aggressive and highly individual' of the 1960s. He uses mild phrases such as 'individualist' where many of us think of 'pigheaded'. At all events, the pity is that the ideas swept Cambridge precisely then, in the 1960s, so that many laymen are left bitterly regretting the over-saturation of the architectural schools in the dogma of 'International Modern', apparently irreversible.

To see more of this, a short excursion may be made into that neighbourhood W of the river known since the Middle Ages as *Newnham*. Across Silver Street bridge, past Queens' new buildings, on the left before the traffic lights is *Darwin College*, commemorating a Cambridge dynasty as well as the author of *The Origin of Species*. It is a small college of graduates founded in 1964. It incorporates the riverside house, Newnham Grange, bought in 1885 by Charles's son George, Plumian Professor of Astronomy, and immortalized by George's daughter, Gwen Raverat, in *Period Piece* (1952). The architects Howell, Killick, Partridge and Amis managed to insert an octagonal dining-hall on stilts in a way that does the firm much more credit than their University Centre just over the river. Gwen Raverat's father himself planned the wooden bridges over to the islands. Writing of his other modifications to Newnham Grange, she already observed: 'What very odd minds architects do have.'

At the traffic lights, go straight forward to Sidgwick Avenue (named after another of the Cambridge intellectual dynasties). Not far, on the right—the recent *Arts Faculty* buildings, of the University (as distinct from Colleges). In the first, through an upper corner window, the lively cheeks of the Vatican's *Quoit-player of Naucydes* beckon the visitor upstairs to *the Museum of Classical Archaeology*. This invaluable collection of plaster-casts of antique figures is very comprehensive and crowded. As in its previous setting beside Peterhouse, the grouping together, cheek by jowl, of such widely separate creatures is at first disconcerting: the Apollo Belvedere paired off with the Versailles Artemis, the Farnese Hermes quelled by the very superior Hermes of Praxiteles, and—in the most arresting group—confronted by the just plight of Niobe, all the men are stood with eyes averted: the Ludovisi Ares, Agias from Delphi, Apoxyomenos from the Vatican, the Lansdowne sandal-binder and the Lansdowne Heracles, old Aeschines from Herculaneum, and the Hermes from Andros. In this Cambridge gallery we step from Delphi to Athens, to the Capitoline Hill and back to Olympus: the plaster is often like the real marble, and sometimes retains details now lost in the originals.

Outside, we confront the 'crisp' lines (1952) of Sir Hugh Casson and Neville Conder's Philosophy Library, English Faculty Library, etc. The chalk-pale cladding is pleasing in this clunch country, and the concrete impressively dressed up as granite. Unluckily, by the time construction started (1958), the site was restricted by the promoters and neighbours, and all hope of the original fine landscape design abandoned. Alongside, the gigantic descending Wurlitzer organ, of glittering glass and tomato ketchup red hanging tiles, serves as History Faculty library. Or is it a segment of a huge polygonal greenhouse built into a right-angle of sheer glass cliffs? A few tomato plants in pots were ailing on an exposed upper landing ledge of the 'cliff' when I last looked, in 1981. More seriously, Tanner and Hall's scaffolding was deployed in rehanging tiles that had ceased to hang, and there were disgusting details of metal corrosion: so soon! The books are stacked forlornly around the base of the glass cascade. Clearly, a prize-winning masterpiece. 'Visitors allowed in only from midday till 2 p.m.' Queues do not form.

On the other side of Sidgwick Avenue, Lyster and Grillet's lighthearted extension, 1961, of Newnham College's library. It would be a pity for visitors who do not know Newnham College to miss the chance of going round to see the S front, a whole range of buildings composed 1875–*c*.1900 by Basil Champneys in attractive variations on the red-brick and white-paint William-and-Mary Dutch made fashionable by Norman Shaw. Champneys's glorious bronze gates, 1893, in memory of the first principal, Anne Jemima Clough, the poet's sister, were made by Elsley's: a match for those models of the 1690s. At the end of Sidgwick Avenue, turn right into Grange Road and immediately left, opposite Selwyn College, to see Leckhampton House. Built in 1963 for graduates of Corpus Christi, and designed by

◁ Museum of Classical Archaeology (old setting 'The Ark': these famous characters have all been regrouped with equal success in their new setting)

History Faculty Library

Sir Philip Dowson of Arup Associates, it is one of the better designed and sited of Cambridge's post-war buildings. The pre-cast concrete frames are, for once, elegant shapes in themselves and stand well clear of, seeming almost free of, the glass-fronted rooms hanging from them. All well grouped with trees and an unusually human (as distinct from monumental) seated figure by Henry Moore.

Continue N along Grange Road. On the left, a fairly daunting red-brick fort, with mock portcullis over the entrance and windows that at first glance look barred, turns out to be ROBINSON COLLEGE,

opened in 1981 and the most interesting of the new creations. It is by Andrew MacMillan and Isi Metzstein of Gillespie Kidd and Coia, and bears the strong stamp of that Glasgow group. They are the first to appreciate the need to exclude the cold Fen winds. You feel the warm shelter of the red-brick walls as soon as you enter. The library (behind the big black grille to left of entrance) is carefully planned for quiet and study. The chapel has two windows by Piper; one is a little masterpiece, with Virgin and Child in the heavens separated from the Last Supper by monsters of the kind that lurk above Ely's S portals. This

design was prompted by a carving at Neuilly-en-Donjon (Allier), and extends the fortress image here. The other window gently distils the Light of the World. New garden beyond.

Farther on, turn left into Madingley Road to face Richard Sheppard's *Churchill College*, looking as remote and unfriendly as Girton, without Girton's tree shelter. The good Stamfordstone brickwork would please the great patriot commemorated. His reaction to the sculpture by Henry Moore and Barbara Hepworth, and to the exiling of the small chapel to the far corner of the grounds, is easy to imagine.

Seventy per cent of the members of Churchill are scientists. A more beautiful scientific institution stands a few hundred yards on towards Madingley. Built in 1821, and still in the Greek fashion of Downing, the *University Observatory* greets you, at the head of an evergreen drive, with the sunny golden stone of a convincing Doric portico now thought inappropriate to the study of astronomy. Two other new colleges, New Hall and Fitzwilliam, do little to draw Cambridge visitors any farther this way, on to the Huntingdon Road.

The Newmarket Road to *Barnwell*, however, disagreeable though it becomes beyond the pleasant white-brick terraces of Maid's Causeway, repays a brief visit, preferably by car, though the walk is scarcely more than a mile from the end of Jesus Lane. The first stop is less than half a mile out, just beyond the Elizabeth Way roundabout. On the left, as you pass the roundabout, notice the tall square Elizabethan brick chimney-shafts of *Abbey House*: it is a delightful, rambling house, the later half dating from 1678, as appears on a shaped 'Dutch' gable. Given to the Cambridge Folk Museum by Lord Fairhaven in 1946, it is not normally open to the public. Two stone arches in the garden are made up of 12th- and 13th-century fragments of the remarkable *Priory* of Augustinian canons, the subject of a *Book of Observance* written here in 1295–6, and which is one of our freshest descriptions of medieval monastic life.

Back on the Newmarket Road, take the fifth turning left, into Garlic Row, leading to the meadows of *Stourbridge Common*. At the bottom on the left, opposite a lorry park, *Oyster House*, with early 18th-century rooms, stood till recently at about the middle of the site of *Stourbridge Fair*. Oyster Row replaces it!

The fair had begun in John's reign as the modest endowment of a leper hospital of St Mary Magdalene, whose original chapel has survived (see below). By Elizabethan times, as in Defoe's, the fair was one

Newnham College

of the greatest in Europe, comparable with Nijny Novgorod. Defoe described it unforgettably in 1722, concluding: 'To attend this fair, and the prodigious conflux of people which come to it, there are sometimes no less than fifty hackney coaches which come from London, and ply night and morning to carry the people to and from Cambridge; for there the gross of the people lodge; nay which is still more strange, there are wherries brought from London on waggons to ply upon the little river Cam, and to row people up and down from the town

and from the fair as occasion presents ... The last day of the fair is the horse-fair, where the whole is closed with both horse and foot-races, to divert the meaner sort of people only. Thus ends the fair, and in less than a week more there is scarce any sign left, except for the heaps of dung and straw, as good as a summer's fallow for dunging to the land.'

Alas there is little to commemorate this now, though the river is still there, rowed mostly for pleasure, and immemorial cattle graze the common. We drive to the Romanesque

Churchill College

leper-hospital's chapel beside the railway bridge. The key is at the adjacent Barnwell (former) junction station-house. Much Barnack or Weldon stone in walls of chancel, which had its S doorway widened in the 19th century to house stall equipment for the fair. There is a blocked upper E window from a former 'caretaker's flat'. The chancel roof was originally stone-vaulted: the corner piers survive from which it sprang. The upper W window is a superfluous invention by G.G. Scott, 1867. The two round W windows are original. The graceful wooden roofs, with wall posts, are *c*.1400. After many vicissitudes, the chapel was bought in 1816 by the Rev Thomas Kerrich who conveyed it to the University. In 1954 it passed to the Cambridge Preservation Society, to whom it now belongs.

Driving back into Cambridge, you may notice after the Elizabeth Way roundabout, set back a little on the left between Wellington Street and Napier Street, a rather shabby-looking storehouse labelled 'Festival Theatre'. This is the *Theatre Royal,* or *Barnwell Theatre*, which in 1814 replaced an earlier Barnwell Theatre. Built for William Wilkins senr., the E Anglian theatrical manager, it is presumably the work, like that at Bury St Edmunds in 1819, of his remarkable architect son. Its 'season' coincided, of course, with the fair, and the demise of the fair somehow killed the need for a theatre in this suburb. It managed to open as a theatre between the wars. Like Bury's Theatre Royal, it retains the original auditorium with lower, middle and upper circles.

Camps, Castle [15] Like Canfield, Hedingham and Earls Colne in Essex, this woodland manor of one of Edward the Confessor's thegns was given by the Conqueror to the De Veres, who chose Hedingham for their headquarters. By the 13th century, Camps was one of their hunting-lodges, with great park, four leagues round, running up to and along the E boundary of the parish. No sign of any castle-mound here within the great inner moat, only a 'keep-and bailey' earthwork. Name 'Castle' added in 14th century: 'camps' merely implies early enclosures. Layout intelligible if you walk through wooden gate in NW corner of churchyard and stand SW of tower; inner court lay S of church, and Great Park beyond. Head and shoulders of Berghane Lodge (former rectory) rise above fields to SW, rebuilt by rector who died in 1724. Church tower rebuilt 1851, then all coarsely restored, 1882. Mural marble to James Reynolds, 1747, whose villa on nearby Olmstead Green was demolished, 1969.

Camps, Shudy [15] *Shudy* added in the 13th century, apparently implying disdainful 'shed-like' or 'shanty', but charming approach from E, with Georgian park on right, and blacksmith's cottage, thatched, behind willows on left. At Bramleys, there are remains of the very primitive 'cruck' timber structure common in the Midlands and abroad but virtually non-existent in E Anglia. Church imparts small sense of God's glory, nor that of the Dayrells, whose monuments, by Thomas Carter, ungainly, are beginning to lose cherubs, wreaths, etc. Industrial expansion planned 1980: 200 acres, for 2,000 new jobs.

Carlton-cum-Willingham [15] parishes united in 15th century. At W end of green, Willingham's church vanishing in Tudor times. At E end of green, picturesque low plastered cottage with tall thatched roof. Carlton's tree-shaded church retains simple plastered exterior and two late medieval bells in rebuilt bell-cote. Thick sloping walls probably 12th century, handsome Perp. chancel arch, single tie-beam and crown-post nave roof. Elegant 15th-century screen makes vestry at W end. Sir Thomas Elyot, More's friend, buried here 1546. Lophams Hall, Tudor, remote, dilapidated, being restored 1980.

Castle Camps *see Camps, Castle*

Caxton [11] A one-armed raddled wooden gibbet (replica) on its little mound near A45 crossing, and the grandeur of former coaching inns in the main village along Ermine Street, survive from days of the turnpike. The George now Caxton Manor, the Crown now Crown House, opposite site of market 13th–18th century. The county toll-gate here lasted only 1663–8, for the traffic learnt to slip past on W loop road by church and Hall. As usual, manorial centres were scattered; the parish is marked with their moats. Church coarsely restored 1860s.

Chatteris [8] The old Bedford Ouse made its way from Earith to Wisbech, not Lynn, and made it for $3\frac{1}{2}$ miles along the W boundary of Chatteris, providing the surprising last syllable of the place name—'ric', Old English for a stream. This ancient Ouse, or 'West Water', supplied the first 'modern' means of communication across the swamps with Chatteris, whose 22 square miles spread E over Langwood Fen (only a few scattered oaks remind one of the wood) and N to Honey Hill near the Wimblington boundary. One needs the OS map for these ancient sites and bounds. Honey Hill represents the ancient 'Huna's Island' and the Huna in question was a devoted chaplain of St Etheldreda who, when he had buried her in her monastery at Ely, retired here. Cures were experienced at his grave, whereupon his bones were removed to Thorney. D. and S. Lysons (1810) recorded presumed remains of his chapel under Hunny Farm. Three-quarters of medieval Chatteris was Thorney's endowment, the rest supported small abbey of nuns founded here by Abbot of Ramsey and his sister c.1006–16; later, it was given to Ely. Map of Fens in 1636 still showed no road between Chatteris and Ely. The A142 was built for security reasons in 1643 when Cromwell made Henry Ireton Deputy Governor of the Isle of Ely. Between Chatteris and Sutton the road is still called Ireton's Way. Before Ireton, traffic was either waterborne or confined to tops of winding canal banks. Gault-yellow Congregational chapel, 1838, pleasantly Gothic (in grounds of old nunnery). The Particular Baptists preferred round-headed windows for their Zion, 1839. Bits of abbey wall survive in E Park Street and S Park Street; rest of its line traced by W Park Street and Park Street, where Skeel's pleasant old plumber's workshop preserves the true feel of the place. Nos 4 and 6 Wenny Road (another medieval island name) provide examples of the merits of local brick when *cleaned* instead of painted. Elegant church tower probably survives from before devastating fire in 1310, and wears a little spire. Rest of church largely rebuilt by Blomfield, 1910.

Cherry Hinton [11] Now swallowed by Cambridge, its 'abundance of cherry-trees' only a memory in 1789. *War Ditches* is an unfinished Iron Age fort whose single rampart failed to save its inhabitants from massacre c.AD 50. N side of St Andrew's churchyard quick with cowparsley in May. Base of 14th-century cross S of S porch. Chancel, Barnack with clunch (and gault brick in the repairs)—a ravishing design. Pevsner describes it as early English 'at its best, that is of c.1230–1250'. From outside, the tall pairs of lancets give something of the effect of a glazed building seldom seen in England before the 15th century and Perp. Key well worth fetching: interior beautifully kept. Norman jambs in Perp. tower arch.

Cherry Hinton

In chancel, handsome, slender, screen-effect of E.E. shafts separating the eight lancet windows, four pairs each side. Flaxman's simple marble to Capt Walter Serocold, killed by a grape-shot while getting the last gun into place at the siege of Calvi, in Corsica, 1794.

Chesterton [11] Cambridge castle (Cambridge Walk 1) stands within the bounds of Chesterton and, till 1922, within shire as distinct from borough. The name, meaning 'ton [farm] near the fortified place', refers back to the Romano-British walled town. Old Chesterton's church lies some way E, downstream, but since the enclosure of the 'open fields' in 1840, New Chesterton has spread right across N side of Cambridge, out to and across Arbury Road. Arbury's name denotes another pre-Saxon earthwork, a circular bank and ditch now largely waste and flattened. Near junction of Akeman Street with the medieval (possibly prehistoric) trackway leading N to Belsar's Hill and Aldreth, it now occupies uneasy position on Chesterton-Impington boundary, N of Arbury Road, on brink of relentless suburban spread of Kings Hedges (another old name for Arbury), countryside till after World War II. SE Dykes Bower's church of the Good Shepherd (1957–64), pronounced 'reactionary to a degree almost unbelievable' by Pevsner, is carefully designed in red and purple brick of excellent workmanship. *Chesterton Tower* was built mid-14th century as residence for proctor of Canons Regular of Vercelli, near Turin, to whom Chesterton church (near by) was given in 13th century; an agreeable squarish house of brown ragstone with turrets. *St George's*, signalled by thin campanile, 1938 Italianate by T. H. Lyon. *Chesterton Hall*, a dark redbrick house, Jacobean, with shaped 'Dutch' gable-ends and dormers, now unluckily abuts 'Elizabeth Way', a hectic traffic roundabout dominated by office block. *St Andrew's church* in quiet churchyard with Ketton headstones, signals position on Mercian bank of river with its beautiful slender Midland spire, 14th century, ashlar, on tower of soft pale-gold ragstone. Clerestory and aisle parapet of local pebble, clunch and ragstone lower down. On N wall, Anna Maria Vassa's tablet, 'Daughter of Gustavus Vassa the

African', a rescued slave: 1797, aged 4 years: 'Know that there lies beside this humble stone/A child of colour haply not thine own . . ./To bury her, the village children came,/And dropp'd choice flowers, and lisp'd her early fame.' Bench ends include two young men in clothes of *c.*1430. 15th-century Doom painting over chancel arch. Large royal arms of James II in tower base. Outside again, headstone records ferryman, Ben Colley, 1790–1876, 'well known for almost half a century . . . as CHARON'; evokes images of towpath walks from Cambridge and the lost world of Edward FitzGerald's *Euphranor*. It sends one along Water Street past the Tudor pub, The Green Dragon, and the concrete footbridge, to the famous *Pike and Eel*, beside chestnuts and the river, and looking over to a great meadow.

Chettisham *see* Ely

Cheveley [12] A sleeve-shaped parish, designed to combine boulder clay at S end (Broad Green, Cheveley village and Park) with long chalk downland slopes that here include Warren Hill and Long Hill (two of the most famous scenes of racehorse exercises) and end at the Icknield Way in Newmarket itself. Cheveley was an Anglo-Saxon and Norman royal manor. However, the castle earthworks in the Park date no farther back than Edward III's reign when (1341) a City financier was licensed to crenellate his house here: 'built of flintstone and mortar, foursquare, at every corner a small tower', but only square ditch and fragments survive. Flintstone and brick predominate in this pleasant village. The church (St Mary and the Sacred Host of Heaven) is a distinguished building of the late 13th and early 14th centuries, cruciform, with central tower crowned by a small bell-cote. The tower itself is an octagon rising from a square in the admirable Cambridgeshire fashion: octagon partly masked by attached stair-turret, running up above the tower and

said to have served as look-out. In Charles II's day, Lord Dover's house here was a great centre of entertainment: partially wrecked about the time of the 1688 Revolution. Later the seat of the 5th Duke of Rutland, it was replaced in 1892 by Col. H. McCalmont's mansion. There are very fine iron gates (from the Alington house at Horseheath) at the handsome Georgian Glebe House, opposite church, also at the Banstead Manor Stud at Broad Green.

Childerley [11] Only 1069 acres, it supported two medieval parishes, Great and Little, reunited 1489. By the time Charles I spent a night at the Hall in captivity in 1647, its owner, Sir John Cutt, had created the classic 'Deserted Village' of today. Only the Victorianized Tudor Hall survives with its separate Jacobean brick chapel, draped forlornly in ivy, beside a vanished formal Tudor garden. The Jacobean wainscot of 'King Charles's Chamber' now seems sombre and depressing—painted with luxuriant vegetation, spaniels, serpents, owl and central monkey. Here he was interviewed by Fairfax, Cromwell and 'the chief men of the Army' one day in early June.

Chippenham [12] Ancient planned parish running from chalky heath, on Icknield Way, down to fen; indeed the best bit of surviving fen after Wicken. Village and parish subordinate to Hall and Park since Admiral Edward Russell, Lord Orford, swept the old community away in Queen Anne's time. In her careful anatomy of the previous Chippenham (*Contrasting Communities*, CUP, 1974), Margaret Spufford showed how populous medieval High Street continued SE from church (ignoring the elbow bend caused by park boundary) to village green (now swallowed in the park). In those days the manor house served the Infirmary of the Hospitallers in England. Presumably,

convalescent brethren 'once strolled in the three courtyards and the great garden within the moat, before returning to the heat of Rhodes'. Parts of Orford's house are embedded in building of 1886. Lodges by Wyatt. The cottages of the Estate Village are picturesque, and the school, 1714 with four tall round-headed windows either side of the front entrance, is agreeably Dutch in appearance, as might be expected of so active a supporter of the Prince of Orange. *Badingham Manor*, a pleasing timber-framed post-Reformation house, was a grange of Sibton Abbey (Suffolk). The church's S porch is guarded by two formidable gargoyles. Interior of tremendous character. One arch frames perfectly a great ochre-and-black St Christopher. Red colouring survives on piers, and colour on N wall E of St Christopher and behind the parclose monuments. Hatchments.

Chishill, Great and Little [14] transferred from Essex 1895. On chalk hills, at edge of boulder clay. Good views out (W) from *Great Chishill*'s churchyard and in from N and W. In 1798, fire wiped out four-fifths of the village, but missed St Swithun's church. Its lofty S porch had upper chamber. Dull interior, but rococo organ-case and graffiti (15th-century keys). Lynchets worth visiting for views. *Little Chishill* church set up alongside Rectory Farm (where peacocks cry). Flint and rubble walls outside, but rather grand clunch on S entrance to porch has been sealed: effect very waxy. The inside has been made the most of—cream walls, clear glass, plain seats—a model of what can be done with a relatively ordinary medieval church.

Chittering *see* Waterbeach

Christchurch [6] Built in wide Upwell parish 1864, where winding Norfolk boundary marks stream of former Wisbech Ouse (Old Croft river) from Littleport. 'Skirtland', where black peat meets more

Little Chishill (*above and below*) ▷

Croydon (*left and above*)

undulating tidal silts of Marshland. Redbrick cruciform church, calm and quiet. Simple waggon-roof structure in nave and decorated cellure in apse. Middle of three E windows looks as if from William Morris's workshop: 'It is finished.' Dorothy Sayers's father rector, which explains marshland setting of *The Nine Tailors*, 1934. Roman Fen Causeway crosses W to E and there was an important Roman farm here. Euximoor Fen was Yekeswellemoor 1431, 'marsh by cuckoo's spring or stream'.

Clayhithe *see* Horningsea

Clopton *see* Croydon

Coates *see* Whittlesey

Comberton [11] pronounced Cumberton, as originally spelt. *Cumbre* was a polite word for a Welshman or Briton. Site of Roman villa beside Bourn brook, S of church; it was built of Ketton stone and had lead pipes. At Green End, with duckpond beside main crossroads, ancient 50-ft maze given to care of village school, and disappeared. Some good old houses among much suburban. Down near church Old Vicarage contains medieval hall and cross-wing, timber-framed, beautifully plastered and reed-thatched. The church's clunch W tower (early 14th century) and W

Wood Ditton

pears to lean a little to the W. Rusticated W doorway almost conceals the medieval W window. Inside, pantheon effect created by elliptical-headed recesses (keystoned) alongside the windows, and overcast with gloom of the Victorian chancel. *Monuments*. Start with Alice Cotton's, 1657, carved for her for £20 by Edward or Joshua Marshall in her lifetime. Clearly the matriarch here, she was the second wife of the antiquary's only son, the 2nd baronet, and she had six children by him. Their second son's only son Robert died aged 14 in 1697; portrait bust *signed* by Grinling Gibbons. Next, Dingley Askham, creator of the family shrine in 1737, who died in 1781: two daughters died at 15 and 16, their unsigned memorial, with charming medallion profiles, speaks of a violent contagious fever. In churchyard, Tom Sawyear's headstone, 1728, is carved with instruments of the Passion. Hollow-way signs of former settlement just S and E of churchyard.

Coton [11] First called Cotes, meaning cottages, and rhymes with *verboten*. A most attractive small village, still free from Cambridge's sprawl. The church at once proclaims, with modest 'Midland' stone spire, that we are W of the Cam. Norman ashlared Jurassic-stone chancel with sturdy shafted and moulded windows. Moulding also shows the outside SE corner of the original aisle-less Norman nave. 14th-century aisles of brown pebble with reused limestone, perhaps Ancaster. Inside, Victorian tile floor gleaming and oak pews shining. Base of tower, clunch-walled, makes notable baptistry—limestone marble font carved with Romanesque arcading as crude as Bayeux Tapestry's. Long medieval chest alongside and painted Commandment Board. The mouldings of the tower arch seem to tie it to a datable group with four others in the neighbourhood, *c*.1377–1422, a graffito on S side suggests 1481, but may have been misread or 'improved'.

wall of S aisle had lost their stucco coat in 1973, looked miserable. Clerestory and other walls of attractive buff ragstone and field stones. Inside, pleasant broad nave with beautiful set of late medieval tracery-panelled benches. Traceried wooden screen in not very broad chancel arch. ('The young want it away, so that they can walk through arm-in-arm the only time we see them here.') Early Tudor N aisle roof very well carved; several pairs of angels' wings in wall plate.

Conington [11] Beside the old Huntingdonshire boundary but not to be confused with the Conington *in* Hunts., both notable for their links with the family of the great antiquary Sir Robert Cotton, both pronounced Cunningt'n and originally meaning King's manor. Present handsome Hall and church largely the creation of Dingley Askham after his marriage to a Cotton heiress in 1729. Hall echoes Peterhouse Master's Lodge (1702). Church powerfully attractive as you arrive at Church Farm and see it across a duck-pond and through a screen of fine trees, redbrick nave redesigned as a pantheon, 1737, and medieval tower with tall slender spire that ap-

Fen Ditton Hall

rebuilding, ?middle 15th century, using a lot of honey-coloured shelly limestone from ?Northants, with a random patchwork of chocolate (-coloured) puddingstone from the neighbouring Lower Greensand beds, as well as pieces of reused ashlar from the earlier Norman fabric; two pieces of chevron moulding, e.g., in the S chancel wall. Here, because the stone colours are fairly warm and the texture rough, one welcomes the strong bonding with a light-coloured mortar, holding the old pattern together as naturally as winding ivy stems. Interior disappointing apart from grand scale and symmetry. Just across the road from the church, behind the pleasant old rectory, a dense grove of trees marks the quay at the head of the Old Cottenham Lode, which originally joined the Ouse where the A10 crosses it. At this quay, in 1068, the Conqueror dumped timber and stones for fishing boats to transport upstream to Aldreth causeway, where the assault on Hereward was launched. If you fork left 500 yds N of church, then take the first turn right towards Setchel Fen, just past Willow Farm, on the right you will see some remarkable earthworks of a Roman village site: 'Bullocks Haste Common'.

Clunch wall-tablet, 1627, gorgeously repainted. SE of church, where Grantchester road crosses stream and (?still) elmy public footpath to Barton road, a 6-ft shaft of a medieval cross.

Cottenham [11] At the edge of the fen, famous for its rich green pastures. In 1810 there were 'never fewer than 1,200 milch cows kept in the parish', and dairies produced a celebrated cheese. The long history of the village is evoked in J.R. Ravensdale's book, *Liable to Floods*, 1974. He records the fires that almost wiped out the village in 1676 and again in 1850, and how the strange ancient layout persists. The village streets seem very long and well built, mainly of yellow-grey brick; well over a mile, from Green End in the S to Church End and the astonishing church tower, one of the landmarks of Cambridgeshire. Set among chestnuts and yews in Church Close, the church's great attractions lie in the colour and texture of its building materials and in the bold Jacobean design of its tower. The tower itself stands on a medieval base of silvery ashlar, then rises through white gault brick to a bright red brick and a stepped stone parapet with four endearing, slightly fantastic, stone corner pinnacles, bulbous like small Orthodox domes. Donors' names carved, 1617. The rest of the large aisled and clerestoried church is a delightful

Coveney [9] In the generation before 1066, Aethelswyth, Leofflaed's daughter (see Balsham) retired here with her maids to work at weaving and embroidery. The present 13th-century church (St Peter ad Vincula) is at the N end of a small village street lining the ridge of the island. Small graceful tower has passage through, looks down W over fen to its outlying hamlet, Wardy Hill. Pleasant 14th-century E window faces Ely over willows and three miles of fen. Interior, 'High Church', dominated by dark-stained and discreetly painted modern rood screen complete with rood high among rafters. Brass chandelier. Tudor benches. Painted pulpit, 1706, Danish. Modern canopy-of-honour over altar set against E wall with German carved reredos *c*.1500, painted in fairground colours and given by Athelstan Riley. *Coveney Mansion*, a delightful thatched house, timber-framed, jettied, plastered and brick gabled.

Croxton's [10] boundary with St Neots, the old county boundary with Huntingdonshire, climbs S from A45 over broad clay fields and to the N follows an oak-studded hedge towards a willowy brook. The 'village' has various thatched cottages, variously maintained, set in marvellous trees and grouped beside the park near Manor House and well. This settlement succeeded one marked by earthworks in the park nearer the church. The park is one of spectacular beauty. The church on a slight rise stands none-the-less down among meadows. Church a pleasant rust-colour—limestone in the solid-looking tower, which has

Doddington ▷

(*below and right*) : Headstones at **Doddington**

unusually delicate carved ornaments in lower string-course and round hood of W window: a basic version of Haslingfield's finer tower. The restored fabric of the chancel has that prominent jointing which one admires at Cottenham. Surprises in N porch: fragments of 12th-century respond and medieval coffin-lids; a 17th-century door itself contains reset carved fragments including (?French) Renaissance nativity. Inside, still more surprise and pleasure: rustic medieval traceried parclose-screens ranged all round one and a third of the three-bay N and S aisles, forming large aisle chapels immediately on left as you enter N door. Furthermore, whole nave and part of the N aisle retain their blocks of medieval pews. S parclose serves as family pew with modern sofas recovered, in commemoration of Elizabeth II's coronation, in embroidery worked by Muriel Lady Huntingfield (1887–1953). A small, chaste, no-longer-coloured stone tomb contains brass effigy of Edward Leeds in doctor's gown: he was chaplain to Archbishop Parker, became Master of Clare and then retired here. Other Leeds memorials. Leaning uneasily from the four corners of the nave roof, reconstructed 1659, four angels with gilded locks and gilded, feathered wings clutch the arms of Leeds. E window by Kempe, successful, 1900. In the Park, the house originally built by the Elizabethan Edward Leeds was rebuilt by his descendant and namesake in 1761 and is still in fine order.

Croydon with Clopton [14] Croydon occupies the top of a 250-ft spur and hangs down the S slopes to a stream of the Cam in the plain. Its original name, Croy*den*, proclaims it a valley village. Its western neighbour *Clopton*, where Picot, the Norman sheriff, had a garden in 1086 and which had a market in the 13th century, was enclosed and dispeopled 1495–1518. Croydon itself has five deserted medieval moated sites. Very rustic church stands just

below ridge on attractive approach lane. Chancel, and part of S transept, red-brick rebuilding by second Sir George Downing, 1685. Interior delightfully unspoilt, arcades and walls all leaning outwards. Norman font, box pews and bizarre harmonium. V.W.H. Gape, his family here in 18th century, killed at Sollum, Libya, 1941, at 23. The walk, about a mile SW, to the earthwork remains of *Clopton* is curiously moving. Just below the crest of the hill ahead, the ridged grass marks the slope of the medieval open field. Beneath it, even with RCHM map, the arrangement of streets and buildings almost impossible to make out.

Denny *see* Waterbeach

Ditton, Fen [11] '*Tun* on the *dic*', i.e. on Fleam Dyke. The prefix 'Fen' readily distinguishes it from Wood Ditton (q.v.). Christopher Taylor showed how this is probably the defended S edge of a Roman estate based on Horningsea and transmitted fairly intact to the English and the bishops of Ely, whose 14th-century house here, known as *Biggin Abbey*, is now covered with grey cement and grouped with disagreeable farm buildings. Main village street occupies line of the Dyke, some of the substantial 17th-century houses standing on the flattened bank. No 6 High Street provides a model for use of the local materials, alternate courses of squared clunch and pink gault brick. Part of the village lines river, and popular tea-garden also supplies scenes and sounds of oarsmanship. *The Hall*, S of the church, is a famous example of old red brickwork with shaped gables of *c*.1635; it was constructed on a grand scale round a late-medieval timbered house. Whole W half of long S front removed *c*.1821. Sudden rise in lawn of old walled garden asserts presence of Roman defensive *vallum*. Church, with walls of jumbled rubble and clunch, is redeemed by early 14th-century tracery of tall chancel, by the lofty early 15th-century porch, and the serene tower by Pearson,

1881, apparently following earlier design. Inside, pleasant cream-white walls, but the chancel's fine conception (1316–37) is marred by ruthless restoration. Good Victorian glass, especially Kempe, 1897. *Old Rectory* presents lovely red-brick front, *c*.1711–32, to churchyard.

Ditton, Wood [12] '*Tun* on the *dic*', this time on the Devil's Dyke, and distinguished from Fen Ditton by its position behind the Dyke where it entered the old clay woodland. Rolling, open, stud country; the church stands in green mown churchyard flanked by chestnuts: most headstones serried in interests of grass-cutting. William Simonds, 1673–1753, had his dripping pan fixed to his: 'Here lies my corpse who was the man that lov'd a sop in dripping pan.' Noble square tower with octagonal top in the good Cambridgeshire fashion. Carved wood bosses and hammer-beams in S porch and ?Tudor S door (locked). Interior less immediately impressive, but with interesting details. Brass effigies of Sir Henrie Englissh and wife Margaret, 1393.

Doddington [5] Originally about 38,000 acres of very rich fen, including Benwick, March and Wimblington, hived off in 1868. The village straggles along the Ely-Chatteris-Wisbech road. In the S churchyard, finely carved headstones 1730–1850, presumably Ketton stone. Base of 14th-century cross N of churchyard. Hooded N chancel porch gives 13th-century date to the chancel, of Jurassic ragstone, with 15th-century window design of great dignity. Interior dull, but beautifully feathery-winged angels survive in largely restored nave roof. Christopher Tye retired here early in Elizabeth's reign: he did much to see English church music through the Reformation. An apparently early William Morris window in N aisle, a powerful Crucifixion. Good Victorian *grisaille*. Brass commemorates Elliott Yorke, 1895, early victim of bicycle age.

Downham Tower Farm

Downham [9] Sometimes 'Little Downham', yet not very little, with 3,000 acres of 'upland' and 7,000 of fen. Here we are at the 'brink' of the Isle, the road W to Pyemore drops noticeably steeply, and at Tower Farm (the remains of a favourite palace of the bishops) Wisbech, 15 miles away, can be seen on a clear day, and to the S, Ely. Bishop Alcock, 1486–1500, built what is left here, in diapered brick, with prominent stone-dressings, and a small gateway for pedestrians. Bishop Wren was arrested here in 1642, the place fell into disrepair, and has been let ever since. There are late Norman features in the church (St Leonard's) at the time of Transition to Gothic: in the tower, and in the interesting S doorway beset with 26 carved heads of beasts, biting bishops, etc. The narrow aisles have, unusually, lancets in W walls. Victorian tapestry reredos, under E window of Kempe school. Just N of Pyemore and the point where the March-Ely railway crosses the Hundred Foot Drain, the Hundred Foot Pumping Station bears two plaques; one has the dates of the various improvements from 18th-century windmill-pump to present oil-fired engine, the other was erected proudly in 1830: 'These *Fens* have oft times been by *Water* drown'd./Science a remedy in *Water* found.'

Drayton, Dry [11] The name implies '*tun* on a stiff slope up which things were *dragged*', and the parish does occupy clay slopes above the Huntingdon road, which supplies its N boundary. 'Dry' merely distinguished it from the Drayton over by the Fen (see below). Medieval village layout in parallel lanes, Petits Lane, Butchers Lane, etc., ignoring 'High Street'. Site of Crow-land manor house (Park) just E of church: pulled down when manor bought by rector, Revd Dr Samuel Smith (d.1841), who rebuilt pleasant white-brick rectory, 1830, and is depicted at prayer in window by Willement, 1853, in impressively rebuilt chancel. At the Dissolution, the Huttons acquired the manor and are portrayed in fine brass effigies. Clay does not make a steady foundation, and the church's patched exterior is partly due to subsidence, partly to the random collection of stones. At *Bar Hill*, a 'new village' planned in the 1960s, with much discussion of suitable densities, 'vernacular' buildings and so forth. Yet here 2,000 'new villagers' live in houses that might be almost anywhere.

Drayton, Fen [11] Connected to Ouse by brief waterway fed by brook running slowly N beside the

High Street, and crossed by footbridges and by Horse-and-Gate Street. On brook side, The Homestead has curved brick gables and a round pediment of ?*c*.1720. Two timbered houses alongside include Home Farm, thatched. Opposite, a remarkable steeply step-gabled house, The Old Manor Farm, has been restored as three cottages by Cambs Cottage Improvement Society and given a Civic Trust award: gables red brick, body of house timber-framed, the first-floor studs (numbered I–XX) exposed. Round the corner in Cootes Lane, old Methodist church, tall, Gothic, with polychrome brickwork and tiles. The extremely 'Dutch' feel of this place is crystallized opposite the church in the reed-thatched cottage with pediment board over front porch, painted with the date 1713 and the Puritan maxim in Dutch: 'NIET ZONDER ARBYT'—nothing without work. Count Alan of Brittany was one of the chief holders of Drayton in 1086 (cf. Fulbourn, Isleham and Swavesey), and the *church* belonged early and improbably to the abbaye de Bon Repos now a stark ruin in deepest Brittany. It is built very pleasantly in horizontal ('stratified') courses of brown pebbles and ragstone from a local Jurassic bed, perhaps 'Cornbrash'. Freestone nave parapets and broached Midland spire. Nave roof on charming rustic corbels. Screen hacked about. Good 'country' Elizabethan holy table. Richly painted E window by E.R. Suffling.

Dry Drayton *see* Drayton, Dry

Dullingham [12] A 6-mile long sleeve-shaped parish stretching from Newmarket 'Round Course', in the chalk, to the old boulder-clay enclosures and Suffolk boundary at Bradley, where Widgham Woods are replanted with conifers by the Forestry Commission. In 1086, main manor belonged to abbot of St Wandrille near Caudebec. Main village along S edge of Reptonized (1801) grounds of Dullingham House (dignified early 18th-century red-brick) and contains highly picturesque heavily thatched and embowered stone 'estate' cottages. Thatched guildhall with jettied first floor and exposed studwork, painted chocolate. At crossroads, a small green was former Camping (medieval football) Close. *Church* stands modestly behind a great burgeoning

(*below and opposite*): St John's, **Duxford**

Old House, **Eltisley**

sycamore. Flint and field-stone church with E Anglian W tower. Striking 1903 pulpit of dappled green marble, as in an Italian church. Font retains colouring in armorial shields (painted with royal coats in 1603). Several Jeaffreson monuments include Mrs Elizabeth, 1778, by Westmacott, 'chastest Louis XVI style' (Pevsner).

Duxford [14] (formerly Duxworth), its open downland fields lying W of Essex Cam. There is a collection of prominent industrial buildings (producing aircraft adhesives such as Araldite) by celebrated architects, near the Ickleton boundary. *St Peter's church* has massive Norman W tower, with corner shafts rising the full height: on a low mound standing straight out of water-meadows on three sides. Interior very gloomy.⊦ Broad low Norman tower arch spans 11 ft. medieval S door. All restored by Ewan Christian, 1884–91. Along these river-meadows, sites of four moated medieval manor houses. *St John's* disused *church*, with small green, is highly picturesque with creeper hanging over half the central Norman (and *c*.1300) tower, surmounted by slender lead spire. Churchyard now a lawn. A hospital of St John was founded before 1230 beside the Icknield Way at Whittlesford Bridge. It stood on the S (Duxford) side of the road and probably served as a sort of wayfarers' hostel till the Reformation. Since then its functions have been maintained by the Red Lion Inn. One room has richly carved ceiling beams, early Tudor, with elusive shield of arms and rebus. Clapboarded pigeon-house and simple, well restored early medieval chapel adjacent. Duxford Airfield, beside the old Royston road (A505), established *c*.1917, unforgettable for its part in fighter defence of east coast, 1940, transferred to the Americans 1942, closed 1961. Since 1972, part of *Imperial War Museum*, displaying over 70 aircraft of 1910–82, US and German as well as British, also tanks, midget submar-

ines, artillery. Open daily to 31 October. Good special exhibitions and *Handbook*. Immensely popular in school holidays.

East Hatley *see* Hatley, East

Elm [5] spelt *eolum* in 973, so possibly a place for eels rather than elms. They would have teemed when all those Midland rivers rushed past Elm to get to the Wash at Wisbech. A profusion of Roman sites has been detected by aerial photography, mainly in the S parts of the parish about Coldham. It was, to some extent, in order to relieve the flooding of these settlements that Roman engineers deflected much of the great outflow to Lynn (*see* p. 25). Elm's magnificent 13th-century church may mark the first effective reclamation after Roman times. The W tower, with its broad storeys of lancet arcading, is like a trial run for West Walton (Norfolk). Top belfry stage, with clasping buttresses carried up to four octagonal corner turrets, and belltower, itself octagonal and battlemented (and capped with small leaded spire) are in the most splendid Cambridgeshire fashion, culminating in the spectacular crown of Ely's central W tower. A delightful finishing touch is the 'nail-head' stone frieze running right round the church, at first storey level in the tower, and under the eaves of aisles, clerestory and chancel. Inside, the fine broad 'E Anglian' nave roof has delicately carved spandrels that require *binoculars*. N aisle roof repaired in 1620: 'Franses Smith Franses Brustr churchwardens: William Gyles, vicar' (vicar 1599–1641). Nave roof crudely repaired 1760–2: recent repairs fine. The superb W end, W of the porches, is kept uncluttered and the architecture speaks (?sings) for itself. Alec Clifton-Taylor rightly complains that the overall lurid glazing 'serves no conceivable purpose'. There are finely carved (?Ketton) headstones and box graves. The Black Horse Inn is a piece of spectacular 'Norfolk' brickwork of 1665. Elm House and The

Limes are two good 18th-century brick houses, The Limes with local stone roof slates. At the approach to Wisbech, the village was divided by the Wisbech Canal (formerly the Well Stream, the cause of so many medieval commissions and litigations), becoming the new Churchill Road of the 1960s in Wisbech. Of the hamlets, *Begdale* has very good orchards. At *Friday Bridge*, Needham Hall (1804), replacing what sounds like a medieval aisled hall, is approached by a broad avenue. The Chequers Inn (Georgian), Wesleyan Chapel (1843) and modern water-tower (resembling some ambitious Georgian church tower) all exemplify both the hardness and the attractions of the local red/buff bricks. The great distinction of Friday Bridge is provided by the leaning yellowbrick E. E. tower and spire of its pleasant Victorian church. The weight of the tower has pulled the whole W end of the building down into the peat with it so that inside even the font is askew. W of Friday Bridge, between Lilypool House and Speedwell Farm, one of the few probable instances of Roman strip-cultivation in the Fen has been found. *Coldham's* church, isolated, with a very pleasant Victorian brick vicarage, is built of the same unpleasant stone as Wimblington's. Roman leather sandals have been found on Whitehouse Farm, S of Coldham Hall.

Elmeney *see* Waterbeach

Elsworth [11] A beautiful elmshaded (still, in 1982) village, lying in a broad saucer of shallow sloping fields. A Corallian limestone outcrop, exposed in the village stream, is sometimes called 'Elsworth rock'. It was used in some of the local church walls, low down in the W wall of the tower at Knapwell, for instance; subject to frostbite, and only one piece seems to have been used in the cladding of Elsworth's own church (W end of N aisle, 2½ ft from N corner). This village gains much of its character from several timber-framed, plastered, white-painted and thatched houses and cottages. The two most attractive are Dears Farmhouse, 1601, in Fardell's Lane (to N), and a cottage with roof ridges at two levels in Smith Street (to W). A grassy brook runs down from the S, giving its name to Brook Street, with footbridges over it. A steep causeway rises E from the Brook to the *church*. Unpleasant stucco on tower: pleasant texture of sandy limestone inside. Whole church rebuilt in first half of 14th century; only the chancel arch is 13th century and on a less lofty scale. Attractive 17th-century stencilled flower pattern painted on the rafters. W end of N aisle occupied by very fine reredos with pediment and Ionic columns, Lord's Prayer, Creed and Commandments, gift of Elizabeth Holworthy, 1745–9. (Holworthy Cottages stand in Brook Street.) In chancel, monument to her and husband. W half of chancel fitted with stalls, mostly Tudor; book cupboards under the desks with original doors, carved and hinged. John Watson, a friend of Erasmus, became rector in 1516, with 'a pretty parsonage' where he hoped Erasmus would visit him. The pulpit is the one he occupied.

Eltisley [11] A large boulder-clay parish straddling the A45 near St Neots and focused on church and green, now by-passed. Church with tall graceful Midland spire is well matched by nearby timber-framed 'Old House' built in 1612. Another well-preserved house stands beside the green: a late medieval hall house, hall now in two storeys. By 1086, the Conqueror had given Eltisley to the canons of Bayeux, which does nothing to explain the strange dedication of the *church* to St Pandonia (locally now Pandionia!). Leland gathered she was a King of Scots' daughter who fled for her honour to a kinswoman, prioress of a nunnery here. Dying here, *c*.904, she was buried by a well, and her body translated into the church in 1344. Leland said the well was 'in

the S aisle of the choir' presumably just outside the (now yellow-brick) S wall of the chancel, where unevenness suggests subsidence. In 1576 the vicar 'brake it down' as it was used for 'superstitious purposes'. (He also decapitated some 13th-century effigies.) The church is 13th century with an E.E. dog-toothed S doorway and sturdy 1200-ish piers of three-bay arcades to N and S aisles: handsome carved capitals. Brass inscription, 1640.

Ely [9] The cathedral rests majestically on the biggest of the Fen 'islands', one that rears up out of the black peat at Aldreth and Haddenham in the SW and stretches N to the Littleport causeway. This physical island is only part of what was virtually a county palatine called *The Isle of Ely*, reaching right across to Whittlesey (q.v.). Here, I am describing neither 'The Isle' nor the physical island as a whole, but just the cathedral (for which nothing quite prepares one) and the little city, with its quays down beside the Ouse and its two ancient parishes spread out E across the common fen to Stuntney and Prickwillow (q.v.). The two parishes are printed across 24 square miles on the Ordnance Survey map as 'Holy Trinity with St Mary'. Dedicated to Peter, Mary and Etheldreda in the Middle Ages, the cathedral transferred at the Reformation to the patronage of the *Trinity*. Trinity parish was based originally on the cathedral nave, moved out to a church built N of the nave in the 14th century, then occupied the cathedral's Lady Chapel from 1566—when the parish church came down—until 1938, its benefice united with St Mary's. Beside the Green, just W of the cathedral, *St Mary's* provides one of the reasons for looking, however briefly, at the town before walking in among all the wonders of the cathedral. St Mary's Barnack spire does nothing to indicate the qualities of the N doorway and the seven-arched nave arcades, curiously exciting examples of the Transition, in King John's

day (and Bishop Eustace's), from the weight of Norman to the upspring of E.E., a transition notably illustrated in Ely and at large in Cambridgeshire. The extraordinary elegance of the nave is enhanced by the flat panelled ceiling, painted in distemper from designs by the architect F. Franey of Lambeth during the careful 1876 restoration. Art nouveau candelabrum, 1890, in S chapel. Kempe E window, 1904. The poor fellows hanged nearby after the Littleport riot lie here in one grave, commemorated on a tower buttress. Leaving St Mary's, look towards the cathedral across Palace Green, and sense being in the angle of a much bigger ancient green: Fire Engine House opposite (which has long served very good food), and two beautiful early Georgian houses are encroachments on that older green, which was bounded on the N by St Mary's Street. Before succumbing to the cathedral, you may have time to walk a little way W passing *Cromwell House*, where Oliver lived as Steward of the Ely Tithes before 1640, when he went off to represent Cambridge in the Long Parliament. If not, skip straight to p. 128. If so, 300 yds farther, in West End, a spectacular Barnack-and-brick step-gabled house embodies 13th-century remains of *hospital of Mary Magdalen*, amalgamated in 1240 with a *hospital of St John*, 130 yds farther still, in St John's Road; this is now a farm building, displaying a badly weathered carved stone, once recorded as showing a man blowing a horn as he rode backwards on a cross-horned beast. Eroded, it resembles the Breedon (Leics.) sculptures, which would take it back to the pre-Danish abbey here. Three hospitals marked the edge of medieval Ely at its main entrance from Aldreth. The most attractive survivals of the Tudor town are in Silver Street, near the Porta. Glance now at the cathedral's setting N of the precinct wall, along the *High Street*. Built into this wall is the buttressed undercroft (*c*.1200) of the *Almoner*

Ely west front and detail

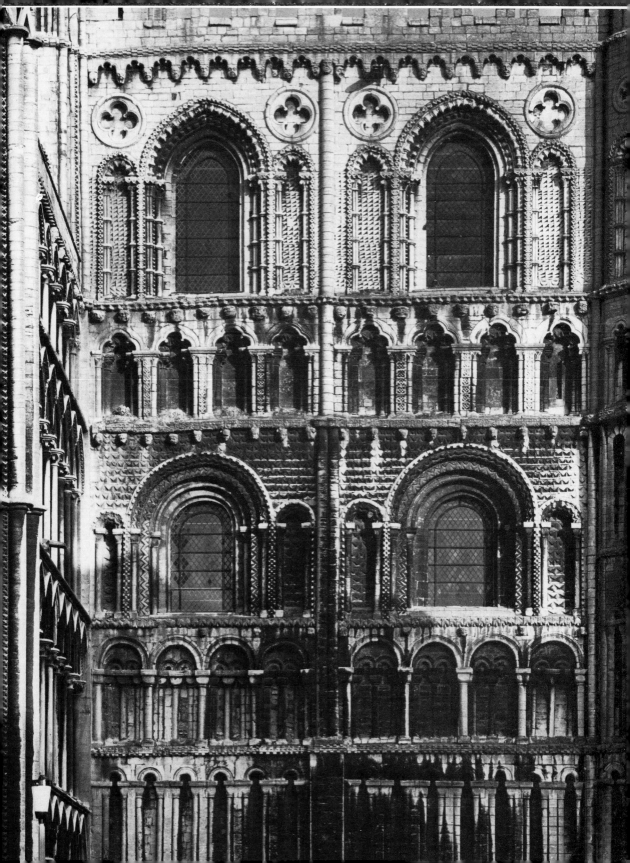

(opposite the E end of the cathedral); then W of that the 14th-century walls of the offices of the *Sacrist*, built by the greatest of them, Alan of Walsingham, who masterminded the cathedral's huge central lantern. The sacrist was responsible for collecting town rents and market tolls (as well as for the building and maintenance of the cathedral) and the almoner ran the school and helped the poor. So the market place was laid out here: these two officials occupied the physical junction between town and monastery. The *market place*, with contemptible modern buildings, originally stretched N to Market Street, where No 41 still bears the painted sign of the proprietors of the vans, fly and stage-waggons passing through from Lynn to Cambridge and Bishopsgate Street, 'EVERY DAY'—until the railways came. Round the *Lynn Road* corner, the Bishop's gaol (now muniment room) still has septaria (a rough medieval building stone) in its front wall and rings for securing the prisoners to the floor: a byword for severity before its abolition in 1837. A few yards along the Lynn Road, the Shire Hall has an attractive Doric portico, 1820. From the market place, Fore Hill descends steeply E to *Waterside*, a curved street with terraces and gabled houses of several periods, mostly brick, leading farther down to the Quay, a wide open space, as for a market. In *Broad Street*, following line of E wall of precinct, view of cathedral from car park, and, near the corner of Castle Hithe, *St Peter's church*, 1890. Noble Comper screen and rood. Mosaics. Kempe E window, 1891, with portrait of benefactor in gear of St Michael. Castle Hithe marks the proximity of the motte-and-bailey, established on the 50-ft contour, to hold Ely against attacks across the Stuntney causeway. The motte is known as *Cherry Hill*, though there are no cherries. It probably goes back to William I, certainly to Henry I; by 1229 it served as mill mount. Defended now by deplorable

barbed wire, it still bears a graceful Ionic column celebrating the 70th year (1779) of James Bentham, historian and benefactor of Ely. An inscription added in 1879 by Dean Merivale refers to Bentham's grove of oaks (see end of *Ely* entry): here the scruffy boscage does include *Quercus ilex*. Close by, the *Porta*, the impressive, broad three-storey gateway at this SW edge of the precinct, was begun in 1396/7. Even more than High Street (Steeple Row), this great gate preserves the sense of an embattled community, already secured by the surrounding fen. Now complete the outer circuit of the precinct, approaching the cathedral along a pleasant street called *The Gallery* (because a long bridge enabled the bishop to cross from palace to S front of W transept, and descend into the cathedral from the triforium). Built into the wall on the right, a remarkable range of monastic buildings is occupied mostly by the King's School (founded at the Reformation, but in a sense a continuation of the one run by the Almoner) and by the Bishop's House. On the left, beautiful great plane-trees are seen above the garden wall of the former *Palace*, now a Red Cross School for physically handicapped children (facing closure 1983; inadequate funds). Standing on the green and looking S at it, you see this curious structure: front court separating two four-storey brick towers, Bishop Alcock's (1486–1501) on the left a gate-tower, the main passage-way filled in, beneath three canopied niches. Tons of Cambridge's Tudor bricks came from Ely: Trinity's Great Gate's, for instance. Now we are ready to start looking at *the cathedral*.

The West Front. Some cathedral pundits say: 'Go straight in', but that is ill-advised here. You are looking at the most remarkable 12th-century *façade principale* in England and may not feel strong enough to eye it attentively after a first venture inside. Ignore for a moment the 13th-century Gothic porch, the late 14th-century top

storey of the tower (and the mysterious absence of the complete N wing of the W transept, which probably fell early in the 15th century), and see for yourself the proud elevation of this most elaborate Barnack masonry, at once intricate and monumental. The dark and light weathering of the stone seems to add to the effect. The windows lighting the triforium are framed within a triple arcade that always reminds one of Georgian 'Venetian' windows. This form is introduced here at clerestory level all the length of the nave. On the W front this tier is given a background of diaper-patterned stone and then, above the triforium, the style changes. Small trefoil arches support 'Venetian' clerestory windows. Suddenly the arches are pointed. We have reached the 'Transition' from Romanesque to Gothic: instead of a diapered Romanesque background, there are (Romanesque) roundels, each with a (Gothic) quatrefoil centre, beneath the fringe of a (Gothic) corbel-table. This tiered pattern on the W front may be followed, with variations, round the twin staircase turrets at the S corners of the transept (where the exact moment occurred of the transition to pointed arches) and, on a magnificent scale, round the great W tower (ignoring the 14th-century top). Where do you go to match these twin turrets? They begin twenty-sided, almost as round as Pisa, and end ten-sided; on the W front but not the S, strange shafting, like rainwater down-pipes, divides, instead of framing, each face. Their rounded unangular form is another of the means by which 'Ely' Gothic seems to have been modified—even civilized—by Romanesque, something to be considered when we look at the 14th century's contributions. First visitors should resist plunging in for just a little longer. If they can't, and find themselves inside the W door, they should stand to the left, look up into the tower and then S to see the reverse of the arcaded transept they appraised outside, and then E. This

E vista has been described as 'one of the finest architectural experiences in Europe'. I confess to a sense of disappointment, for there is a monotony in the design of the massive nave, and whereas at Norwich the Norman nave seems to soar up into its 15th-century fountains of rib-vaulting, and at Peterborough one sees right through to the majestically vaulted and windowed retro-choir, at Ely Bishop Hugh Northwold's excellent E lancets make a poor impression from the W—from which they were of course screened in the Middle Ages and down to 1770 by a wall (known as the pulpitum) on which, as at King's College, the great organ stood. But there are more positive reasons for entering the building from the S, through the Monks' Doorway from their cloister, and the first reason is that you feel less a visitor, more able to comprehend their ceaseless routine of devotion.

The East Front. So, now approach the middle of the great building from the S. The quickest way is back through the Porta (skipping this section). Those wishing to see the E front before entering may walk past the N side, noticing the timbered oversailing Steeple Gate entrance to the precinct from High Street: this was the main approach for pilgrims, who made for a doorway in the N transept. That doorway is now distinguished as Ketton stonework, 1702, by Wren's mason at Trinity Library. Wren's uncle had been bishop here 1638–67, imprisoned eighteen years in the Rebellion. The Lady Chapel projects NE from the cathedral. One of its greatest distinctions, the widest medieval vault in the country (46 ft, i.e. 6 ft wider than King's College chapel: only 18 ins higher in the middle than at the sides), makes its effect inside: outside, the chapel merely looks broad for its height and the battlements and niches too frilly. The loss of the medieval glass is lamentable wherever one is. We come to Northwold's E front. Extended to allow the pilgrims freer

perambulation, it is the finest E.E. composition in E Anglia, reminding one of the glories of Salisbury, and certainly related to Ely's prominent W entrance. E Anglians are used to thinking of Perp. builders, as at Melford, who filled their walls with glass. Here E.E. builders did it. If only some of that glass survived, as at Canterbury, and if only most of Ely's Victorian glass were not so inadequate . . .

The south side of the cathedral. We now move to the S side of the cathedral. Here is the best general view of it—for you see the W tower and the twin transept turrets without being conscious of the missing wing. You see the extent of the long Norman nave, clerestoried and so always meant to bear (as now) a timber roof, not a heavy barrel-vault. Finally, you see the full contrast between the smooth vertical cylinders of the W towers and the spiky, angular circumference of the *Corona*. The pinnacles are Gilbert Scott's (1860) based on James Essex's (1760) to give extra weight to the eight piers of the crossing. The originals, like the lead-covered oaks above the inner lantern, seem to have been battlemented, following the twin W transept turrets, and followed by the later 14th-century W tower topping—the very risky, exhibitionist conceit that first greets visitors across the miles of level E Anglia. Still one final diversion before entering—the path from the Porta to the S transept is beset with distractions, most notably *Prior Crauden's chapel* to the left: its buttressed vertical lines and the elaborate window tracery of the first floor chapel illustrate ideally how an eminent 14th-century prior's chapel should look. Crauden was prior when the central tower fell and when the octagon was rebuilding, and there is a natural interest in the private chapel he built himself. But the restoration is unsympathetic and the most remarkable features are the original floor tiles, including a well-known representation of Adam and Eve. Unless there is ample time,

Crauden's chapel may be noticed merely in passing. But a short deviation well worth making is to the right, just into *Infirmary Lane*, leading to the present Deanery. The 12th-century *Infirmary* was built in the form of an aisled nave, nine bays long (to allow for isolation?), and a chancel chapel (now Deanery). Much is converted for use by King's School, as in all this remarkable amount of survival from monastic times. The nave arcading (interrupted) frames the 'lane', still round-arched, but with decoration recalling St Mary's on the green, and so rather hard to date by style. At last we prepare to *enter* the cathedral church. Bricked-up 1501 cloister windows lead to an inconsequential arch with classical mask on keystone. Within the NE fragment of cloister, Humphrey Smith, 1743, is perpetuated for his 'superior ability in draining fenny and marsh lands' of the Isle: John Sanderson's design, carved by Charles Stanley.

The Monks' Doorway. To left, beyond strained metaphor to two men who died in railway accident, 1845, is the arch of *c.*1300 that contained a large wooden book-cupboard, the monks' main *library*. To the right, a 12th-century doorway into the sacristy, almost obliterated by need to strengthen corner pier. The Monks' Doorway straight ahead. Generations of monks passed through here every few hours on their way to and from dormitory, chapter house and cloister. 'Trefoil' effect created by two small projections in each of which an abbot or bishop kneels with crozier, fending off two horrible winged dragons devouring each other in the surrounding arch. A benign tonsured head looks out over all, so we enter. What? All over Christendom churches were founded in honour of the local patriots who identified Christianity with the creation of political allegiances. King Anna of E Anglia (nephew of Raedwald of the Sutton Hoo ship burial) was one of these, slain in 654 by King Penda's heathen Midlanders, and this

Ely Cathedral: Prior Crauden's chapel and the south-west transept

abbey was founded twenty years later by one of Anna's remarkable daughters, Etheldreda (or Audrey): succeeded as abbess by her sister Sexburga, whose daughter Ermenilda in turn succeeded her. The shrines of these holy ladies, E of the high altar, were objects of pilgrimage, patriotism and devotion. Ermenilda had done wonders by marrying Penda's son, converting him and bearing him children—good for East Anglian-Mercian relations, and for Ely's prosperity. On the vigil before her Feast Day, 12 February, in 1323, the monks walked bravely in through this door in procession to Ermenilda's shrine in the far NE corner, behind the high altar and

beyond the Norman central tower, knowing it was on the point of collapse. That February night, the monks had hardly regained their dormitory when, suddenly, the tower fell. The crossing and Norman work E of it were wiped out. Northwold's work and the shrines he had rehoused were 'miraculously' unscathed. The dramatic event gave rise to the astonishing crossing you begin to see from the Monks' Doorway. Beyond that, to the E, you also glimpse the 14th- and 13th-century vaulting of choir and presbytery. To all that we soon return.

The Nave. From this same position, turning left you see sturdy S aisle of Norman nave, tunnelling, with sim-

ple groined vault, through to the W wall, 230 ft away. (E wall even farther.) Before moving, notice old colouring, delicately patterned, in a segment of S aisle vault, also, on other side of nave, in third arch from E. How sympathetically the painted Victorian nave ceiling, especially perhaps the deliberately subdued pattern by Le Strange in the six W panels, relates to the early painting. (Nave ceiling completed by Gambier Parry.) Monks' Doorway in mind, walk W past Owine's Stone (described under Haddenham) and through doorway in S wall: the *Prior's Doorway*, carved in Barnack stone, badly weathered, yet one of the richest works of sculpture of its

(*above and opposite*): Prior's doorway and detail, **Ely**

age (*c*.1135) and packed with details clear on a sunny day. On the tympanum, Christ in Majesty, naturally aloof and all-seeing; something engaging about the two winged archangels holding his mandorla together: they do it with great style and panache. Shapeless lumps at the base of the columns on either side were humans seated on lions, a N Italian conceit. The prior would come this way along the cloister from his grand apartments: he was the head of the monks under the abbot (then, later, under the bishop). In 1109, to reduce the ungainly size of Lincoln diocese, Cambridgeshire acquired its own see, with a bishop seated here, and so the abbey became a cathedral, the abbots bishops. In 1103, the mummified remains of St Audrey and the others

had to be moved to make way for the new Norman building, which shows that the E end of the Anglo-Saxon abbey lay near the E end of the present nave. Edward the Confessor was at school here *c*.1010. Later, *c*.1036, his younger brother was shipped here by opponents, blinded, and buried in the aisle 'near the W tower', probably near the site of the present tower.

The crossing. Back at the main crossing, the S transept retains the earliest Norman work: fine, rather classical line-colouring (mostly blue) in capitals of transept aisles, very high (late medieval) hammer-beam roofs (repainted). Before going farther E, we now begin to appraise *the central lantern*. It is breathtaking enough, before you grasp the detailed plan of construction: as you

look up into central boss in lantern, $152\frac{1}{2}$ ft above the floor, there is an overwhelming sense of space and of supreme architectural virtuosity. For you think of one of those fireworks that bursts into one great star with points down-curving and then into another. Unlike the firework, unlike the firmament, these stars are fixed, and except during major repairs in the past two centuries, have shone down over this place for six centuries. The star-burst analogy helps to illustrate the engineering, the way the weight is distributed across this enormous span of 70 ft. The building began with the clearing away of the entire Norman crossing and working from the next piers out, which is how the ground floor of the octagon was created. Now the complexities start. How did

they even imagine those clusters of eleven ribs fanning out so that, in each cluster, five formed the sill of the upper octagon, the lantern? (In fact those clusters rise to support a perfectly firm floor, hidden from below.) The point at which explanation, and statistics, add to the wonder, is when one learns that the corners of that upper octagon are formed by eight oaks, 63 ft high and over a yard thick, now lead covered and sticking out above the roof, the most successful and impressive feature of the *corona* from outside. For centuries the upper star-vault of the lantern supported a bell-chamber above it, and bells! As it is, some 400 tons of timber and lead are held up there as though weighing no more than fibreglass, and poised above a span of 70 ft! The tower fell in 1323, a year after John Crauden became prior and Alan Walsingham sacrist: men of energy and vision, they had already made a start on a new Lady Chapel when the collapse of the tower deflected their main energies. The bishop, John Hotham, also interested himself, especially in the renewal of the first three bays E of the new crossing. Walsingham's contribution was decisive and fundamental. His imagination created an octagon by widening the crossing one bay in each direction. To prepare the masonry frame for the great timber vaults, he called in John Ramsey, a Norwich master mason. They were ready for the carpenters by 1328. To devise and supervise the detailed timber structure, the supreme achievement of its kind, he brought in William Hurley, Master carpenter to the king. In 1334–5, the great posts went up. By 1342 the job was finished, and Hurley went on to build Edward III a great timber pavilion, 100 ft across, at Windsor. Queen Philippa was a friend of Crauden. He died just before the octagon was finished. Walsingham succeeded him as prior, for twenty years, surviving the Black Death. As you stand below, notice among the masonry details four carved heads on hood-moulds: the two on the SE

△ Detail of the Monks' doorway, **Ely**

Nave and north aisle from crossing, **Ely** ▷

Entrance to Bishop West's chantry, **Ely**

crowned) and Peter (with tonsure, key and church). Both S and N aisles end impressively in very rich screens of the end of the Middle Ages, the frontispieces to two extraordinary E chantry chapels. This S approach brings us to Bishop West's chapel past various memorials. Bishop Peter Gunning (1684) lies thoughtful on his gadrooned shelf, original author of the prayer 'for all sorts and conditions of men' and planter of one of the great planes in the palace garden. Opposite lies John Tiptoft, probably the Lancastrian baron who died in 1443, not the inhuman Humanist who died in 1470. In the E corner, the *chantry chapel of Bishop West*, 1525–33, displays much delicacy of both design and detail. The iron gate with briar rose by an Ipswich smith opens into a majestic parade of pedestals and canopies from which 260 sculptures were ripped out by the Puritans! Remaining details include early Renaissance lettering and cherubs' heads, and blue colouring recalls the Romanesque of the S transept. Fine central bosses and ceiling. In the great E window, Wailes's 1857 glass glows well from afar, but not as you pass to Bishop Alcock's chantry with its delightful glass cock on a ball *in situ* each side of the screen entrance. The chantry was begun in 1488, and then overdone in his lifetime: fanvaulting and much late Gothic confectionery. Retreat to *Bishop Northwold's tomb*, immediately N of the high altar, but originally at St Audrey's feet in the middle of this splendid room he erected in her honour: the foot of his tomb is a good place to appreciate his work. When he was young, Hugh Northwold's election as abbot of St Edmund's at Bury was disputed, and described in gripping detail, over the years 1212–15; and the dispute revealed him, as King Edmund himself had been, the protagonist of local E Anglian patriotism and 'liberty' against external tyranny, Angevin, instead of Danish. From many years later, after his burial here at the feet of King Anna's daughter, Hugh's splendid

arch represent Bishop Hotham and Prior Crauden, and they face on the NW arch Alan Walsingham and a spirited layman—probably John Ramsey, but conceivably William Hurley. These are beautifully carved, and presumably likenesses. Binoculars needed for these, for the near-by small carvings of the foundress's life, and so much else. The painting on the wooden vaults probably represents Master William Shank's 1336 design: if only it had not been totally overpainted at the Victorian restoration!

The Choir. Now, E along the *S choir aisle*. It is always lighter than the N. Here you best see the excellent quality of the grey and lavender marble piers from Purbeck, used to dignify Hotham's 14th-century choir and Northwold's 13th-century presbytery beyond. The 13th-century work is spectacularly fine, from floor level right through to the vault, holding its own with Lincoln. Binoculars reveal three beautiful bosses carved with the church's three patrons: Etheldreda (over the place of her shrine), Mary (being

◁ *pp.136–7*: Under the Lantern, **Ely**

Purbeck marble tomb (ravaged) shows him with his feet on a (leonine) wolf, the legendary protector of Edmund's head after the Danes beheaded him, and, in miniature beneath his feet, a scene showing Edmund, hands bound to an oak tree in front of him, and a Dane shooting an arrow into his back. There now stands propped at Hugh's feet a fine stone throne-arm, carved with a wolf like a Chinese dragon, perhaps a surviving fragment of his own throne. In this N aisle, two more very remarkable marble tombs are those of Hugh's predecessor (Niel, or Nigel, his soul is shown in a napkin), 1133–69, all through the Anarchy, when Ely was twice captured by King Stephen, and Hugh's immediate successor for only a few months, William Kilkenny, looking like a bearded Poseidon in medieval bishop's robes. In the floor, a brass commemorates poor Basevi (holding his plan for ?the Fitzwilliam Museum). Where aisle meets crossing Henry Caesar, Dean 1614–36, kneels, 'a benefactor to the choir and music' less than a decade before Cromwell put an end to the choral service, 'so unedifying and offensive', by marching up the nave with some soldiers and calling out to Mr Hitch, the Precentor, 'Leave off your fooling, and come down, Sir.' Just round the corner, in the *N transept*, Edmund's martyrdom was prominently painted in the vault over his chapel (first on right). The painting, now very faint, seems to go back to the 12th century. The W side of this transept seems to have been the reception area for pilgrims. In the NE corner one approaches the Lady Chapel—also the stairs to the museum of stained glass.

The Lady Chapel. The Lady Chapel, begun the year before the crossing tower fell and had to be rebuilt, is spell-binding, as you would expect from a work of that time of inspiration and virtuosity. Alan Walsingham, as sacrist, inaugurated the building and may well have conceived its design. A monk called John Wisbech supervised the work

The choir from the crossing, **Ely**

(including the fund-raising) for twenty-eight years and thirteen weeks before the Black Death killed him in June 1349. In the 1350s, sculptures and additions such as 'the duke of Lancaster's window' were made, but Wisbech was said to have completed the stonework, E and W windows, the images inside and out and the roof. Creamy clunch carved into an overall rhythm, with 'nodding' canopies over the niches, producing an almost living wave. The general impact of this room, cruelly battered to bits as it has been by the

Puritans, is deeply moving. Just enough colour survives, in stonework at the NE corner, in the roof vaulting and in a few upper window-lights, to enable one to imagine, especially on a day of golden sunlight, a few of the glories of this temple devoted to the life and miracles of the Virgin. So far as the glass is concerned, an excellent way of learning more about it is to climb into the N triforium, overlooking the nave, to an admirable *stained glass museum*. Interesting though the post-medieval work often is, the example here of one of the canopies from the Lady Chapel steals the show both in design and in the combination of light with colour. At the E end of the nave aisle below, a permanent exhibition of *The Stones of Ely* lies rather neglected. With more careful display, relating the stones to the parts of this great church and some of its neighbours, appreciation and enjoyment could be even further increased. A 2-mile foray along the Lynn Road to *Chettisham* is rewarded by one of the best-tended little medieval churches and churchyards in Cambridgeshire. N and W walls late Norman, and suggestions of former impressive Norman chapel. Returning to town, Highflyer's Farm, E of the Lynn Road, is named after famous horse of Richard Tattersall who lived from 1771 where the RAF Hospital now is. A front garden at the corner of Lynton Close, nearer the town, contains an obelisk erected nearby in 1787 to mark a plantation of oaks by James Bentham (p. 128).

Eversden, Great and **Little** [14] formerly Evers*don*, meaning 'boar's hill'. *Mare Way*, meaning 'boundary way', a green lane on the chalk ridge behind, was also probably a prehistoric ridgeway running from Ermine Street to Chapel Hill, Haslingfield. (Four other parishes' boundaries converge here on the site of a maypole: q.v. Harlton.) *Great Eversden*—churchyard shielded on N side by chestnuts. Chalky slopes rise to S. Impressively weatherbeaten tower topped by brief leaded spire and weather-cock. Church struck by lightning 1466, badly burnt and evidently rebuilt. Two steps down into nave, bare, but with good arch-braced tie-beams running also across chancel. Misericords. Small rococo organ in chancel. *The Homestead*, opposite church, a jettied Tudor house. *Little Eversden*—has what it calls a 'High Street' but St Helen's church is beautifully secluded beside Church Farm. Rustic wooden 14th-century S porch. Grotesque stops to 14th-century W window, with haunting faces. Chancel stalls and panelling by Bodley (from Queens' College): W, on Great Eversden boundary, former medieval hall house, with pigeon cote, etc, had its timber-work exposed, then plastered, now stripped, and, alas, looks awful.

Fen Ditton *see* Ditton, Fen

Fen Drayton *see* Drayton, Fen

Fordham [12] Royal manor, like Exning, Soham and Isleham, probably from very early times; so St Peter may have had a church here as early as the 7th century. In the S of the parish, a Gilbertine priory was set up early in the 13th century. Nothing of it remains on the delectable site, which frames a redbrick Georgian house, handsome beside Ely-Newmarket road. Marshy woodland Nature Reserve. Village now large, with printing works, etc. Mill Lane has attractive houses and Congregational chapel with school-room (1844). Good flintwork in the *church*, entered at NW through clunch undercroft beneath remarkable 14th-century Lady Chapel inspired, perhaps, by Ely, and in turn prompting Mildenhall's in Suffolk. E.E. doorway into church painted black in imitation of Alwalton marble. Chancel retains complete scheme of striking Edwardian colouring: 'a token of their timeless love, to Laura Mabel Townsend, and . . . painted by her sisters, Edith and Minnie, 1905'. They frame well Victorian glass in E window.

Fowlmere's [14] name describes its most distinctive possession, a mere of wild fowl, lying W of the village, but recently 'improved' away. Houses multiply in SE. The parish, another sleeve-shaped one, runs SE from the mere across the chalk to edge of clay 'woodland' at Chrishall Grange (redbrick, handsome, *c*.1700, crowned by curved 'Dutch' gables). Its straight SW boundary lies along the *Bran Ditch*, bank and ditch ploughed down but still visible, a W continuation of the *Heydon Ditch* that once barred SW approaches up the Icknield Way (pp. 12–14). Close to two main highways, the inns did well. Pepys 'laid at the Chequers', 1659, which was improved by W.T. (William Thrift), 1675. It catered for post-chaises, the Swan for coaches, the Black Horse for the stage waggons. Fire destroyed half the village, 1634, doubtless taken as a sign of Parson Morden's Laudian iniquities (1610–44). Cruciform *church*, fabric originally Norman, now mostly later work. Interior light and attractive. Screen. Medieval oak door. Monument shows portrait of William Mitchell, 1745, relative of Benets of Babraham (q.v.), being unveiled by allegorical lady perched pensive on his sarcophagus. William Cole brought some friends to see it when he was showing off his new chaise after Christmas, 1769. Memorial to a Chisholm, 'late of city of Sydney, N.S.W., 1845'.

Foxton [14] is familiar to readers of Rowland Parker's life-story of the place, *The Common Stream*, 1975. The village street, with its unusual number of unspoilt, unstripped plastered timber-framed cottages, many still thatched, is built along a stream. Parker believes this was dug by 6th-century villagers. So imaginative a book would have been made more interesting by supply of chapter and verse and a proper index. Parker's most detailed reconstruction shows rebuilding of entire village between 1550 and 1620. If the street seems full today, then remember that over fifty houses and cottages stood there, gable to gable, in the Elizabethan age, much as they do today near post-box and bus-stop at the green. *St Laurence's church* stands back a little from the street, a jolly weather-cock on a spike above the grey early-Tudor belltower. The Perp. clerestory, usually the outward sign of a good roof, does not disappoint. Down three steps into the nave. Broad, beautifully carved roof timbers, with bosses, including well modelled figures of the donors (m. and f.) on the beam immediately W of the (presumable) canopy of honour. Who were they? A hart in a thicket is on the boss W of that, also what looks like a Sacred Heart. Presumably this 'roof-lift' is the result of Bishop Grey's Indulgence, promising in 1456 forgiveness of sins to all who contributed to Foxton's chancel, nave or belltower. Good Tudor pews. Ewan Christian did his work well in the 1881 restoration, making the most of the lovely bare chancel (the piscina almost wholly reconstructed!). Parclose at E end of N aisle. Only the base of the roodscreen is original. The large old font is certainly crude. Parker says 'assuredly Saxon'.

Friday Bridge *see* Elm

Fulbourn [12] 'Wild-fowl stream'. Suburban sprawl and old County Asylum buildings. Boundaries set on Roman roads and Fleam Dyke. Two main manors and two medieval churches in one churchyard until 1766 when one, All Saints', collapsed. The other, part of the manor given by the hero of Maldon (991) to Ely, is dedicated to St Vigor, a 6th-century bishop of Bayeux, who destroyed a great idol there. One wonders if the sharing of this site by two churches may not mean that it, too, replaces a heathen monument. The manor with All Saints' went to Alan of Brittany in 1066, who gave it with Fen Drayton to Bon Repos deep in Brittany. Its manor house, guarded at the gate by splendid stone eagles, has belonged to Mr Townley's family since the 18th century: the core seems to be a century earlier. *St Vigor's*, now a 13th- and 14th-century building, restored in 1869, is mainly interesting for its contents; brasses include effigies of a 1370s patron, William of Fulbourn, chaplain to Edward III, and a 1470s vicar of All Saints'. Late medieval pulpit, traceried with birds, appropriate in this old fowlers' parish. Village centre pleasant, with low almshouse range and new crinkle-crankle wall.

Gamlingay [13] looks SW into Bedfordshire. Last element, -ay, in place-name, is said to be the Anglo-Saxon word for 'island' but Gamlingay is not well watered. The rill running past, behind the SE side of the village, helps to explain siting of medieval manors and the village itself. That it flowed no closer also explains the holocaust of seventy-six houses in 1600. With them apparently went the medieval market—downstream to Potton, and never regained. Yet there was some revival. In 1665, the fine row of almshouses W of the church was built. By *c*.1688, a remarkable sophisticated house at the N end of West Street (at the main corner of the village) was given three plaster ceilings, probably by Henry Doogood, the craftsman of similarly remarkable work in Pembroke College's Old Library and on Market Hill, Cambridge. By then, Sir George Downing had acquired Gamlingay Park. In 1912/13 his grandson, the 3rd Sir George, founder of Downing College, built himself a new house with marvellous gardens there, between the village and Gamlingay Great Heath. The house was soon demolished by the frustrated widow of his heir. (Woodbury Hall, in this parish but somehow consigned to Bedfordshire, was Regency, remodelled by Philip Tilden in 1931 and again by Basil Spence after destruction during Army occupation, 1944.) Local dark brown carstone used (with clunch dressings) in chimney stack of house of *c*.1600, No 18, Dutter End, near *the church*. It is the striking material used in the building of the church, and most notably in the W tower, very impressive. N porch, with clunch-vaulted groined ceiling; 1200-ish font with its Tudor cover; banner-stave locker; Ralph and Elizabeth Lane's multicoloured rococo monument made in Peterborough (1754). Tall, traceried rood-screen of these parts.

Well detailed E window by Morris and Co. Medieval stalls, thought to be *c*.1442. There were four chaplains and chantry priests already in 1406. Absorbed in detail, one sees the force of Pevsner's judgement on the architecture: 'The interior somehow lacks the zest of the exterior.' But how good the details are, and not least in this church the graffiti. On a pillar of the S arcade, close to the floor a small crowned female head, perhaps *c*.1400, is reckoned by Mrs V. Pritchard one of the most beautifully-drawn graffiti in her (richly illustrated) book. A Latin inscription from here was published in the Cambridgeshire Antiquarians' *Proceedings* in 1915, and was therefore known to M.R. James: 'Death is like a shadow which always follows the body.' (One thinks of *Casting the Runes*, even more of Hans Andersen's *The Shadow* which James translated.) Finally there is the simple: '*Hic est sedes* Margaret Tayl..d.' Her husband, Walter Taylard, rebuilt the N transeptal chapel in his lifetime, and died in 1466.

Girton's [11] name conjures up a serious cocoa-coloured Victorian building beside the main road W from Cambridge, a convent of learning in Waterhouse Gothic, austere, and a fairly safe distance from the men's colleges. Not even Waterhouse deterred many of those women intellectually, and now men have been persuaded to join them in the fellowship of their devotions. But Girton is also a medieval parish and village, with an exceptionally interesting Prehistoric and Roman past illustrated in the University Museum. The well-kept unwalled *churchyard* now has a pleasant green suburban setting. The two lower thirds of the W tower are probably 11th-century Norman, judging by the very careful horizontal coursing of the pebble exterior. Another unusual aspect of the tower is that it is rectangular, not square, in plan, with the long axis N–S. The delightful simple interior is whitewashed

Gamlingay: Emplins, stripped of old plaster coat. In 1601, centre of large precinct, back and front

and hung with George III's arms. Two brasses in the chancel commemorate specialists in canon law: licentiate-in-decretals, William Malster, 1492, William Stevyn, 1497. The effigy of Malster is lifelike.

Gransden, Little [11] In the 1880s, the church was all too comprehensively restored by the architect St Aubyn, but a strange graffito of man with sword survives inside the W door. In a churchyard of chestnuts and yews, it stands above thatched cottages and looks across a leafy valley to *Great Gransden* in *Hunts*. Hayley Wood, near Gransden Lodge, is a fragment of ancient natural boulder-clay woodland, open by written permit from Cambs Naturalists' Trust.

Grantchester [11] is rightly remembered for one long, engaging poem written by Rupert Brooke during a visit to Berlin in 1912; it ends with two of the best-known lines in our language. Three years later he died at the Dardanelles and his name follows Baker, Blogg and Bolton on the village war memorial, for he made the Old Vicarage his second home in those years. Confusing place-name. The river name was Granta, and this village began as *Granteseta*, 'the *settlers* by the Granta', which still describes it: 'chester' crept in here by mistake after *c.*1200 and got the place confused with Cambridge itself (p. 12). Fragments of late Saxon interlace carving are now built into the church's S wall. The curved stone churchyard wall on N and E (High Street) is medieval: brick wall W of tower is the Manor Farm's, whose garden provides pleasant extension to churchyard. The church's stucco texture is disagreeable. Extremely virtuoso 1360-ish chancel designed, Pevsner suggests, in the Lady Chapel workshop at Ely, a few fragments of original glass in the frilly window tracery, and certainly the ogival niches either side of the E window are Elyesque. Massive circular font. As to the village, there is an amiable self-consciousness; two pubs within

speaking distance of each other across the village street, gardens full of country flowers, allotments. The RCHM's *Inventory* (1968) says it well: 'a place of recreation and retirement for the students and scholars of the University . . . some of the smaller buildings put up between 1715 and 1850 are not without academic overtones.' Those dates may reasonably be extended to include Balls Grove. The straight flat footpath from Cambridge does not disappoint. And if it is faintly surprising to find the church clock saying only 2.35, the summer's shade around the Old Vicarage is as if time did stop at 1912. 'Oh, is the water sweet and cool,/Gentle and brown, above the pool? . . ./Stands the Church clock at ten to three?/And is there honey still for tea?'

Graveley [10] on the boulder clay sloping up to the border of Hunts., with a church dedicated perhaps very early to the E Anglian saint Botolph. In 986, a thegn left Graveley and Elsworth to his wife, then to Ramsey abbey. Its flinty 15th-century E Anglian-looking tower glows in the setting sun. Four delightful gargoyles (?reset) over the W doorway. The Revd Henry Trotter is deservedly commemorated by J. Dixon's urn and obelisk, 1766. He 'rebuilt and beautified' the present brick chancel (inevitably given Gothic E window and chancel arch 1876). Charming thatched cottage adjacent, once three, brick fronted by 'James Ford, August 1838'.

Guyhirn *see* Wisbech

Great Abington *see* Abington, Great and Little

Great Chishill *see* Chishill, Great and Little

Great Eversden *see* Eversden, Great and Little

Great Shelford *see* Shelford, Great and Little

Guilden Morden *see* Morden, Guilden and Steeple

Haddenham [8] on the W 'shore' of the Isle of Ely occupies a dramatic ridge, with views down N and S to the fens, and two westerly spurs: North Hill (with Hill Row along its S slope) and, leading to Aldreth, the spur known as *Lindon* in 1086, whose fishermen owed Ely 3,333 eels a year. At main village crossroads, pleasant green churchyard with beautifully carved headstones. Walls of large dignified church contain local Lower Greensand ragstone: mainly late 13th/early 14th century, with thorough rebuilding in 1870s. Tower 'rebuilt', and bells rehung, 1876, in public appreciation of the good old earl of Hardwick. Very handsome great 14th-century tower arch contains tall, delicate screenwork. Brasses and matrixes. In S transept, a replica of *Owine's stone* (original is in S aisle of Ely cathedral). His career is mentioned by Bede. When St Etheldreda's first husband died, *c*.655, the Isle of Ely, her dowry, was administered for her by Owine. In 660, when she became Queen of Northumbria, she took him with her. He became a monk and, being no scholar, set the brethren of Lastingham a fine example as a workman with adze and axe. He was Bishop Chad's friend when he founded Lichfield in 669. The presence of this stone suggests that he came back with Etheldreda in 673 to help her found her double monastery at Ely. In use as a horseblock on the far side of the street facing the E front of the church, the stone was taken to the cathedral by James Bentham (1708–94), the historian of Ely and a man of action. It is, of course, the base of Owine's memorial cross. Its inscription in Latin is carved with the Saxon letter E: 'Give thy light and rest to Owine, God. Amen.' Wall monuments in nave aisles have been gilded recently and the heraldry painted, the colour relieving the stonework and white plaster. Two are ardent testimonies of Royalism in this Cromwellian stronghold. A well-engraved window, signed David Peace, 1969, recalls a Head

of the Primary School. Richard Arkenstall founded a school here in 1640. S of the church, the pleasant collegiate-looking building, dated 1863, is now used as County Library, with 'Arkenstall's Centre' added in equally pleasant modern style. The village has several good houses, especially Porch House (with central two-storey porch), dated 1657. A.C. Benson tried living at Hinton Hall, Victorian, *c*.1905–10, but found the silent fen too much for him. *Aldreth* commands the main ancient causeway across the fen from Cambridge to the Isle. Causeway crucial in defence against William the Conqueror. Now almost impassably overgrown, it is drained by a dyke along its W side, and a little way E a parallel road leads to the High Bridge crossing, passable for cars in summer, in winter too rutted by tractors. It was already decayed in Charles I's time. A single street rises fairly steadily from the causeway.

Hardwick [11] In wide, open country, a ridgeway running along the N boundary, the Portway running E–W across the middle—its straight sand-coloured gash through the arable green impressive. Steep roofs of old Blue Lion inn seem more at home than the shallow-pitched new houses just N of Portway. *Church* has brown field-stone fabric and small Midland stone spire. Interior whitewash brings out quality of dark timbering of unusual roof—queen-post structure running through nave and chancel. The other chief medieval exhibit is a formidable iron-bound chest. Prominent, rather fine rood staircase, which seems to have gone up one stage higher than the rood-loft. Iron altar rails.

Harlton [14] village looks N over valley of radio-telescope 'ears', but up the Roman road to Orwell there are views S as well. Here Mare Way crosses, and the boundaries of Barrington, the Eversdens, Orwell and Wimpole meet, and the maypole stood till the 1870s in the trees just

◁ **Hildersham** Cross symbolizing the Trinity, the patron of the church, and probably commemorating Robert Parys and his wife, 1408

145

W of the road at Maypole Farm. Technically in Harlton, it was known as the Orwell maypole, perhaps because the Orwell people were the last to celebrate May Morning. The *parish church* of the Assumption of the Virgin has been restored with tremendous care in memory of Gwen Raverat (1885–1957), whose book *Period Piece* gives perennially amusing insight into the life she remembered in Cambridge. The church surprises and delights. The nave columns of the local clunch are tall and graceful. The Dec. E windows of the aisles and the Perp. N and S windows are admirably traceried: *all* perhaps from the second half of the 14th century. Original door to rood stair. The *clunch screen* has of course been stripped of what must have been a glorious sculptural design. One fine though fragmentary (seated) figure survives, reset over the N doorway (why there?) and gives some idea of the original conception. The arch above was filled with a tympanum—probably a Last Judgement. Graffiti in S arcade. An elaborate and amazingly well-preserved alabaster composition, thought by Mrs Esdaile to be by her remarkable 'discovery' William Wright, is ostensibly a monument to Henry Fryer, who kneels, armoured, between his father, a doctor of medicine, and his mother. His widow reclines on a lower shelf, prayer-book in hand, and presumably promoted the work. Notice especially the noble male supporter dabbing tears from left cheek with hem of garment. Henry had been killed in 1631 in a duel at Calais and his elder brother John, who had been disinherited by their father, 'secreted' Henry's will. It came to light only after his own death in 1672. Who can doubt that he is represented by the male weeper?

Harston [14] has been painfully suburbanized along the A10. The church is approached from the N, pleasantly set against the fine trees of the Manor House to the S. Interior light, whitewashed, pamment-floored. Royal arms hang properly over chancel arch. Medieval screen and pulpit much restored. A slender obelisk on Maggots (short for Margaret's) Mount (a pleasant walk) holds a flame of liberty aloft. It is signed by Charles Bottomley, *c.*1739, and commemorates Gregory Wale. 'He lived an advocate to liberty.'

Haslingfield [14] First syllable pronounced Haze, a large parish including Chapel Hill and its steep fruitful slopes down to the Cam at Harston and the Bourn Brook at Barton and Grantchester. (Chivers grow much fruit here for their jams.) The village is grouped round Manor House and church, where the Mare Way crossed the valley. Grand house built by Thomas Wendy (1500–60), a Renaissance man who studied medicine at Ferrara, attended Henry VIII on his deathbed, and was a friend of Dr Caius. His altar tomb here 'mislaid by the architect' in the 1875 restoration! The low Tudor brick wall skirting the park along N side of High Street is the public reminder of him. When house reduced in early 19th century, Bourn Hall acquired an elaborate chimney-piece from his day. *The church,* early given to St Mary's abbey, York, has a particularly distinguished 15th-century W tower, faced with local clunch ashlar and conceived with beautiful twin belfry louvres; then, at the corners, the square buttresses rise to octagonal turrets under the influence perhaps of Great St Mary's, Cambridge. Interior stonework all starkly whitewashed. By *c.*1250, the Scales family had this manor and presumably presided over the rebuilding of the Norman church, of which only the chancel walls remain. The dog-toothed chancel arch celebrates the transition to Gothic. In the E window of the vestry, visible across the locked ironwork gate, glass with arms of Lord Scales (d.1305) and wife Isabel Burnel. From early 15th century, chapel stood on the ridge and beside Barrington road, with an image of the Virgin that was a scene of Easter pilgrimages till the Reformation. There, a later Lord Scales dedicated his chains in thanksgiving for his release from captivity after he and Talbot and Fastolf had been completely out-soldiered by Joan of Arc. Back in the church, Lord Scales's shield of arms may be seen on boss in S aisle. In the chancel the Wendys, their monuments and their Jacobean painted chancel roof. Henry VIII's doctor's heir, nephew Thomas, was a Puritan, but that did not prevent his son, Sir William, from commemorating parents and sister in effigy, 1619, when the new painted wagon-roof was put in. Sir William's nephew, Sir Thomas, and Danish friend, Ertman, are remembered here, Sir Thomas, 1673, recognizable in white marble. Is it another of Bushnell's works (see Babraham)?

Hatley, East and **Hatley St George** [14] To NW, Buff Wood Nature Reserve has interesting woodland flora. The two medieval churches were over-restored: one is now abandoned. There is a view of a large red-brick early and middle 18th-century house in fine parkland, Hatley Park: built by two branches of the Cotton family.

Hauxton [14] A prehistoric crossing at the watermill: probably the Mare Way heading for Nine Wells, Shelford, then Wandlebury. *Church* 12th century. Interior still very rewarding: a massive, plain, Romanesque chancel arch. A slot in the keystone shows where the base of the later medieval rood was fixed. Screen, tympanum and a large part of the roodloft were removed as lately as 1861! There are remains of transepts just W of this great arch and in the E wall of the nave adjoining the chancel arch. A niche contains a painting of Becket, *c.* 1250—some seventy years after his martyrdom. On opposite side of E end of nave,

Hinxton

a remarkable medieval pulpit springs from a single support-post.

Heydon [14] occupies the SE end of the Bran Ditch where it entered the relative security of the clay woodland. It provides Heydon with almost two miles of E boundary, crossing the line of Icknield Way which it was designed to bar very formidably (p. 14). Behind, on the spur of Anthony Hill, strip lynchets mark the ridges of medieval fields. A bomb wrecked the church in 1940: chancel rebuilt 1952, rest finished 1956. Excellent fabric of new N aisle and clerestory, the local flint laced with single courses of red brick. Cool interior of clean new clunch-work in the original Dec. style gives sense of being in a medieval church when it was newly finished.

Hildersham [15] stretches 2 miles each side of the Linton Cam, with the N boundary on Wool Street (Roman): one manor each side. A great conical Roman burial-mound, like Bartlow's, stood just W of the church in Dovehouse Close and had been used as the site for the *maypole*. It was removed in 1852, when the whole vicinity of the church was receiving its present distinctive Victorian aura. In the churchyard, weeping beeches 60–70ft tall. Across the road, big Victorian 'Tudor' rectory, *c*.1851, built by Robert Goodwin, 1816–99, rector here for fifty-three years. Through his 'zeal and liberality', the church was endowed and restored (later with C.A. Buckler as architect). Interior gloomy, but chancel, which Goodwin insisted on rebuilding '14th-century' to match nave aisles, has complete scheme of painting and redecoration of *c*.1890, restored early 1970s at cost of £3,000 by S. Dykes Bower and Campbell Smith. Paid for by brass-rubbing charges, bringing in £1,000 a year! Fragments of medieval glass reset include Virgin and Child in top light, S window of chancel. Reredos; iron, brass and copperwork; candelabra; screen. Two oak effigies, lately stolen. Font very handsome, trans

E.E./Dec. Those very remunerative brasses include later medieval members of the Parys family.

Hinton, *see* Cherry Hinton

Hinxton [14] Riverside settlement with easy access: parish running E to the Roman road (A11). From A130, double avenue of young beeches leads to Hinxton Grange. Red Lion Square, with pub and substantial house opposite, both oversailing and welcoming; Church Green even more so, with thatched cottages on left leading to W front of church: gracefully tapered leaded spire. Then, within the S porch, surprising moulded 15th-century doorway complete with traceried oak door. Pamment-floored church of powerful character, crowded with dark stripped-pine Victorian pews, entered through low doors. Almost Roman, round Romanesque arch of (blocked) N doorway. Square Norman font. Rood stair tunnels up behind Jacobean pulpit with sounding-board. Remains of tall, darkstained, slender screen. Hatchments in S aisle and chancel. In spacious 13th-century S chapel, brass to Sir Thomas Skelton, 1416, Steward to John of Gaunt's duchy. In chancel, three large marble monuments, one by Edward Stanton (Mrs Esdaile was certain) bears long inscription to Royalist Sir Thomas Dayrell, 1669. Hinxton Hall; research labs, wears curious arrangement of pilasters on E front.

Histon [11] Leafy charm about Abbey Farm House and brook running through village green; ugly shopfronts; traditional thatched cottages. Red-brick Gothic Baptist chapel inaugurated by Mr Chivers, 1899: they started jam-making in a barn in 1870. The gardens of W.J. Unwin, famous seedsmen, are usually open. There were two medieval churches, but St Etheldreda's, a furlong W of St Andrew's, was demolished by Sir Francis Hinde c. 1588 to provide materials for his new N wing at Madingley Hall. At *St Andrew's*, fragments of 12th-century chevron mouldings beside the W doorway, in honey-coloured and buff limestone rag. The Norman building became, only a century later, an early Gothic one:

in the S wall of the transept, E. E. colonettes, and in the E wall lancets are very visible. The 13th-century builders also used a superior free-stone with a tinge of pink: is it an early product of the Weldon quarries? Pevsner says the designer of these splendid transepts 'must have come from the lodge working at that time at St Radegund's Nunnery (Jesus College) and at St John's Hospital (the later college): too many details coincide'. He is thinking of the famous double piscinas, the clunch's softness making possible the extraordinary thinness of the outer mouldings, so that they resemble cane hoops, or even wire; part of a complete scheme of blank arcading, design unlevel. E walls admirably shafted beside the window groups. Richly cusped niche in S transept must have held a St Catherine. S door original. The chancel, by Sir Gilbert Scott, is made wretched by Clayton and Bell's stained glass. Not far N of the church, *Guns Lane*, a pleasant green bridleway, leads to Rampton and was the medieval main road to Ely.

Horningsea [11] Meadows and chalky fields beside Cam, on site of Roman estate and Saxon minster (see Ditton). In 1971, brambles were scrambling over the S aisle of *St Peter's church*, but all now in hand again. Shape of E piers suggested presence of Anglo-Saxon porticus N and S of nave: see plan in church. Chancel mainly clunch. Interior dominated by ghostly Elizabethan pulpit with tester, complete with tasselled cushion. At *Clayhithe*, Bridge Hotel, of white-painted brick, is dominated by tall, rather fine 19th-century house, Dutch-gabled, yellow brick with stone mullions. Dock Lane terminates unforgivably in cubic Rural Council pumping station, enmeshed in emerald chain-links and concrete posts, and connected by barbed wire to the river.

(*left and opposite*): **Ickleton**: 12th-century wall-paintings

Horseheath [15] probably means just that. Fine open country; divided by Wool Street (Roman) from West Wickham; long views SW down to Bartlow. In the churchyard wall, this inscription: 'GEORGE V, R.I. Our King in mellow autumn tide Here viewed a bloodless fray. May duty, love and peace abide to bless him day by day. Army manoeuvres, Sept. 18 1912.' What a vanished age that rejected prayer evokes. The *church* is largely a 14th-century rebuilding, but pieces of chevron moulding outside the vestry wall betoken earlier walls: indeed if similar pieces behind the pulpit are *in situ*, they suggest a prodigious former Norman chancel arch. Very grand large Perp. windows either side of nave. Pleasant memorial in one to a much loved teacher, engraved 1967 by David Peace. Broad, flat 15th-century nave roof like Wilburton's. Remains of delicate wooden screen. The chief interest lies within the chancel: the brass of someone in 14th-century armour, possibly William de Audley, 1365, and two large Alington tombs. They held the manor from 1397 to 1700, made a park after 1446, entertained Elizabeth here in 1578, rebuilt grandly from a design by Sir Roger Pratt, 1663–5, all destroyed and sold up, 1775–7, a deplorable loss. Gates at Cheveley and Cambridge. Pleasant old rectory opposite: rebuilt, and garden laid out, before 1744, by Revd Edward Bassett, LL.D., whom Cole described as 'a worthy facetious man and publisher of some pamphlets. He married a shrew of a wife, a Presbyterian, who would frequently go up to the meeting house when her husband was going to church.'

Ickleton [14] Despite the M11, lies in remote country, all green in high summer, and palest brown in winter. Its sharp leaded broach spire shines white above the trees—a landmark for miles around. This distant view is especially appealing from the great terraces of (possibly) Bronze Age farming (locally known as 'Boadicea's war defences') on Coploe Hill at the S edge of Ickleton parish, where there is a small Nature Reserve, and from a mile further S, in Strethall (Essex), where the Grange that belonged to Tilty Abbey (Essex) retains its medieval timber frame. The lane down from Coploe Hill tees into that branch of the Icknield Way where it forms Ickleton's main street, Abbey Street: quiet and lined with delightful old houses and cottages, timber-framed, thatched, and properly plastered. A modest priory of Benedictine nuns is now represented only by Abbey Farm, mainly 1692, with clunch walls 3 ft thick, off Duxford road. One night in August 1979, a pyromaniac broke into the church and kindled a great fire of books and vestments round the organ. The E end suffered particularly badly, but in June 1981 all was rededicated after a restoration costing £280,000. There was one great bonus: the discovery of a brief, but apparently almost complete, series of 12th-century wall-paintings, true frescoes, unparalleled in England. *St Mary Magdalene's* (originally St Mary's) stands in a green churchyard with shrubs and a handsome old timbered and pargeted house (Mowbrays). Only the small W doorway prepares one a little for the interior. Ceiling of S porch, clunch, is groined and carved with a tree and early 14th-century heads. From inside the S doorway, the nave presents a scene of the most exciting antiquity: its N and S aisles have semi-circular arcades and the splaying edges (voussoirs) are emphasized by alternate pieces of Barnack stone and Roman tile faced with a salmon-pink Roman-brick cement. The arches rest on 'cushion' capitals looking, as Pevsner says, like 6th-century Doric work, supported as they are on sturdy cylindrical pillars several of which are tapered Barnack monoliths, perhaps used in a late Saxon church here and brought from the near-by Roman town of Chesterford. Above the two E arches of the N aisle, the new-found brick-red paintings from Angevin days. Within the main scheme of the upper tier of pictures, the splays of two former windows from the Norman clerestory have long shown painted subjects: in the E one there seem to be a palmer (?St James) and a madonna, and in the W one Christ with three apostles bearing books, the painting of one of the apostles more completely preserved than anything in the recent find. The main series presumably led to splendid Crucifixion and Doom on the Norman E wall, and depicts in four scenes the climax of Christ's life: the Last Supper (Judas helping himself to a fish), the Betrayal, the Flagellation (Christ tied to a column), and Christ carrying the cross. In the three spandrels below, three martyrdoms: Peter crucified feet uppermost, Andrew spread on his saltire cross, and an uncertain one. Underneath, within the arches, notice the decorative *trompe-l'oeil* pattern, like antique coffering. The Norman cushion-capitals give way to a 14th-century Gothic E nave arch, surmounted by newly revealed traces of a contemporary Doom, Mary represented most unusually—baring her breasts in symbolic intercession and supplication for the sinners faintly discernible below. In S transept, the fire scarred the monument showing in low relief St Leger Herbert, killed near Gubat on the Nile in 1885 while taking notes as war correspondent of the *Morning Post*. Bench end carved with St Michael weighing souls, and an angel with Tudor roses. Along the benches, some scores of hassocks of recent needlework and designs include one portraying the inferno of 1979.

Impington [11] More suburban than village feeling now. The Village College (see Sawston) has given Impington a certain fame: its architects in 1938 were Walter Gropius and Maxwell Fry, and Pevsner adjudges it 'one of the best buildings of its date in England, if not the best'. Forty years on, the building looks surprisingly commonplace which is perhaps its best tribute. St Andrew's village *church* still pleases the sightseer most: partly by the surface qualities and colours of its fabric, partly by its modest, well-cared-for interior. Nave's S wall shows the outlines of a tall, blocked ?13th-century window at the W end, then comes the large wood-framed late medieval porch, then two Perp. windows and at the E corner a small carved head and fragments of carved chevron announcing a 12th-century stone building before the Gothic one. Chancel much rebuilt 1878. White plastered interior preserves faded painting. In the tower, brass figures of John and Margaret Burgoyn with children, 1504: he with proud Burgoyn talbot on his coat.

Isleham [9] is still pronounced as it was spelt in 895, *Yselham*, one of a group of early royal manors, which argues the early establishment of a church. The King *c*.950 gave this church to Rochester. Like St Andrew's church, this is a village of exceptional interest, its 'vernacular' buildings of clunch and pebble, ragstone and brick, range from late medieval to the present: very unpretty and un-'Cotswold'. In Sun Street, the Sun Inn stands opposite an almost identical timber-and-plaster dormered house, sensibly modernized. At the corner of Church Street, old Fire Station behind garden wall. Opposite, in a lime hedge, the solid wooden medieval lychgate has supporting struts worn shiny with church-going hands. One may approach this truly splendid building through a churchyard beset by guardian geese, and past the base of a medieval cross. 14th-century ashlared S porch a beauty, one window recess still with original painted plaster and two others with fragments of stained glass. Panelled S door, *c*.1670, with big brass handle. Inside, the first surprise is the scent of incense. Then the width of the nave and the splen-

dour of its roof: can Mildenhall, Lakenheath, Soham or Methwold match it? Binoculars needed. Then the tall arcades, early 14th-century, with 15th-century tracery in the spandrels and tinted shields of the Peyton family alliances: they paid for the great clerestory, and Crystofer in 1495, 'dyd mak thys rof.' They held one of the manors from 1451. A magnificent brass memorial on their tomb (N chancel) asks prayers for Thomas (d. 1484), plated in armour like a lobster, with two wives, Margarets, the one in the marvellous floral dress saying 'Lady, Jhu mercy.' Now one notices the shimmering brass eagle-lectern, with engaging small guardian lions, comparable with that in Christ's College (and that in St Mark's, Venice!); only this one had to be fished out of the fen in the 19th century, whither it had been pitched by the Puritans. Through a wooden parclose, the chantry chapel of St Catherine occupies the S transept: founded by Robert and Margaret Walkfare in 1321, but known unfairly as the Peyton chapel since their tombs predominate. A decade after this, the bishop (Rochester) completed his chancel and came and 'dedicated' everything. New tower followed *c*.1340, but collapsed in 1861. Its replacement by Street found 'crude and insensitive' by Pevsner, but at least he got the materials right. Medieval benches in N transept; 1619 wall monument for Barbary Themilthorpe, a child, 'For all are like to flowers, grass or hay, That this hour springs, next dies and fades away.' Alec Clifton-Taylor's last word on this wonderful building is all too true: 'It is the glass in the E. window that is such a tragedy.' *Chapel of the Priory* of St Margaret of Antioch may be dated, from the remarkable herringbone courses of ragstone, to the first years of the Normans, never extended and little altered. It seems to have been given by the Count of Richmond and Brittany (cf. Fen Drayton and Fulbourn) to an abbey on a Breton promontory, St Jacut de la Mer.

Kennett [12] is one of very few surviving Celtic names in the region. Does that imply the survival of British among the first English colonists hereabouts? The *church* (key next door to PO) is reached down a long wooded track, and stands just above the flood-plain of the Kennett stream, which divides it from the Hall. The churchyard is screened by elms and along its S side effectively moated by deep ponds, as at Snailwell. Inside gloomy. Trans. Norman/E.E. features (some ?due to Cambridge Movement).

Kingston [11] Ancient royal farm, as name implies, running from the Bourn Brook up on to the ridge of the Mare Way and with Porters' Way along the W boundary; E boundary including a bit of Eversden Wood, an old survival. The Old Rectory is a timber-aisled hall with two-storey solar of 13th/early 14th-century stonework. A medieval hall house, partly thatched and clapboarded, stands at the edge of a former green. Church tower of very Cambridge proportions. The chancel has been clunch rendered, with Victorian decoration. Porch W window betrays signs of fire which caused substantial rebuilding of church in 1488. Medieval S door opens to delightful first glimpse of pamment floors, 14th-century base of font, tall aisle arcades, extensive medieval and Elizabethan wall-painting, and black-letter texts. Crucifixion painted above chancel arch displays blank spaces for vanished, three-dimensional cross and Mary and John. Three pairs of angels, painted against red background, wings shaped strangely like trumpets. Rich Elizabethan pulpit. Tall screen: medieval and Jacobean tracery. Chancel 13th-century, its principal treasure, much faded, over the N doorway, is the painted outline of two armed lancers, moving on foot into attack (against the Devil). Monument to Dr Fogge Newton, rector, provost of King's College, d.1612. Primitive and mysterious graffiti.

Kirtling Towers

Kirtling [12] somehow became Cat-
lidge in Tudor times, but has now
reverted. The Conqueror's niece,
Judith, in 1086 had a park here 'for
the beasts of the forest'. From her it
went to the de Tosny lords, founders
of Conches, near Evreux in Nor-

mandy. In 1260, three men were
carrying a cask of wine over the
bridge of *Kirtling castle* when the
bridge broke. N and E sides survive
of the castle's square moat, the most
formidable in the county: the deep
but dry W side is flanked by a

charming grass walk to the church.
Within it, on the castle's platform,
was built a great three-sided brick
Tudor house, perhaps incorporating
Norman hall. At ground level, a turreted gatehouse is all that remains,
now lived in, as *Kirtling Towers*. Be-

Kirtling

house, has ceased in this century to be one of their chief seats and is owned by Lord Fairhaven. It is therefore easier to glance at their lives through their funeral monuments. *Church* approached from W through farmyard at back of the Towers (the former baronial household crossed the great moat from the S). Immense chestnuts and alarming cry of peacocks from Hall Farm. S wall of nave, Norman, and, within the porch, awaits the impressive portal of the days of the de Tosny lords: the tympanum is supported by bearded corbel-heads as at Gt Bradley nearby (Suffolk) and, in a central circular recess, Christ sits in majesty with all-seeing eyes, a zigzag arch representing the heavens. Below, the very ironwork of the door is Norman. Inside, N aisle displays amusing rustic bosses and corbels under wall posts, part of a large-scale refurbishing financed in 1522 by executors of local sheep farmer, Richard Pytches—including painting of Doom and rood (gone), building and glazing of (presumably) heightened clerestory and work on the tower. N transept 13th century, converted after 1555 ?to North family pew: ragged staff in roof marks marriage then to Dudley widow. Raised floor of S aisle and carved shields suggest its construction, through Norman S wall of nave, as Elizabethan household pews. Nave roof Victorian, also the rather fine 'baronial' North Chapel roof, 1872. Church restored since 1978. (In 1877 the last lord built the small RC church near the approach to the Towers: part of stained glass crucifixion of *c*.1530, and Flemish wooden corner font.) A crude 1564 'Dec.' window N of the chancel leads us to consider the North monuments, in their S chapel, for the finest is the 1st Lord North's, of that same year, a black, mottled, marble table-tomb, with delicate Renaissance relief. North may have been remembering his old colleague Audley's monument at Saffron Walden, twenty years earlier. In the chancel, a brass delineates a

hind lies a massive rough grassy mound, the rubble grave of Norman and Tudor buildings. The S front of the Tudor house was approached through the gatehouse and then, very unusually, up a flight of steps to the main entrance. This was flanked by columns dated 1572 and bearing the heraldic dragon-supporters of the Norths—probably the same striking pair now guarding the outer gate. Pictures show the house completely dwarfing the gatehouse, which is an attractive compromise

between Hampton Court's and Leez Priory's: two-storey oriel bow-windows look out above the entrance. Edward North, a successful London lawyer, married *c*. 1526 the widow of Edward Myrfin of London. Her fortune enabled him to buy Kirtling and establish their celebrated dynasty here. He did well out of the monastic lands at the Dissolution, like his colleague Lord Rich, who built Leez and whose daughter married North's son. Kirtling Towers, with adjoining early Victorian

bearded Edward Myrfin who died at 26 in 1553 on his return from a very early Grand Tour; another Renaissance man. I suppose he was North's stepson, and hardly born before they were married. He had gone 'through all the Princes' courts with other famous places of Europe, and likewise of the Isles of Greece, and so to the Turk's court then being in the city of Haleppo, and so returning thro Jury to Jerusalem . . .' Back in the Norths' own chapel, Roger, the 2nd lord, retired to this big solitary six-poster in 1600. In early September 1578, the Queen and Court were here for fifty hours. Apart from improvements to 'the banqueting house' and new kitchens, all that was needed was 'trymming upp of chambers', which indicates a very commodious mansion. Later she made him treasurer of her household. He was a close friend of Leicester's, and at Zutphen behaved with great courage and spirit: wounded in the leg, he engaged the enemy 'one boot on, one boot off'. Here he lies with both feet on a superb dragon. The 3rd Lord North (1581–1665/6, who founded the spa at Tunbridge Wells) inserted his own unhappy epitaph in the E wall 'post varios errores', for there were tensions in the family as the old man lived on here with his heir and the grandchildren, one of whom, Roger (1653–1734), immortalized them all in his *Lives of the Norths*. In SE corner of parish, towards Cowlinge, in Banstead's Farm and Great Wood, the old man cut glades and 'no name would fit the place but Tempe. Here he would convoke his musical family, and songs were made and set for celebrating the joys there, which were performed, and provisions carried up.' The 4th lord's ledger slab in the chancel (1677) says he 'undertook fourteen children'. His fame rests in fathering that remarkable brotherhood, the youngest of whom wrote their *Lives*. Their funeral monuments lie elsewhere. Here are several coloured hatchments. A tablet records the 12th Lord North's only son, 1891–1936, wounded at

Bourlon Wood. *Upend* is an attractive hamlet of old thatched cottages and farmhouses.

Knapwell [11] The eponymous spring, now called the 'Red Well' from an iron content, rises in a boggy patch in remarkable woods just E of church and village. Woods rightly a Nature Reserve, with records of management going back nearly to the Conquest. Best approach through chestnuts down Church Lane, past church (with specimens of crumbling 'Elsworth Rock' in tower) and manor site with great pollard elms and round mound possibly from the 12th-century Anarchy: belonged to Ramsey from c.1040. Path swings S through wood, then W to bottom of village street, sheltered, with pleasant cottages and traces of several former ones.

Kneesworth *see* Bassingbourn

Landbeach [11] J.R. Ravensdale, in *Liable to Floods*, has written the classic story of its development: how that great 'moat' just NE of village was a defence not against humans but against the black fen water, and the present simple 'street-village' pattern emerged from a more complex grid. To the S, at the crossroads, where there had been a common green, a market cross stood till the 18th century. Careful restoration of old cottages, including one by the Cambs Cottage Improvement Society, near the church. The *church* presents a slightly dingy appearance, its cement coat peeling off: a good Midland stone spire. One should not enter it without thinking of Erasmus, who doubtless attended services when he was staying here with friends, the Gunnells, in 1513. The medieval pulpit, brought here from Jesus College in 1787, is the kind the rector of the day mounted to find himself addressing the greatest scholar in Europe. Very good roofs, tie-beam alternating with hammerbeam, survive from Erasmus's time, and indeed two miseri-

cords bear arms of 14th-century bishops. The lectern is said to be part of a Dutch pulpit group brought from New York in 1882. Much of the rectory is a remarkable medieval and early Tudor building, under that pleasant brick exterior.

Landwade [12] is on the Suffolk boundary, W of Snailwell. The church stands in a park beside the Hall, which at first looks 1926, and was remodelled from a 16th-century clunch building, a gable of which one sees from the path to the church. This may have been a farm or dower house, for next to the church is a grand, empty, moated site. Base of medieval cross in churchyard, and church largely of clunch, unfortunately rendered and dotted with stones. Interior well lit, with considerable fragments of 15th-century Norwich-school glass. Set of 15th-century benches in nave and well-preserved five-bay chancel screen, elegant, to rood-beam height. Continuous roof, nave and chancel, 15th-century arched braces and principal rafters disappear behind plaster ceiling. The church is said to have been rebuilt c.1445 by Walter Cotton, who bought the manor in 1431 and founded a dynasty that later moved to Madingley. The good monument to Sir John Cotton (1543–1620) in the S transept says he lies in the S aisle of this church made by himself. Was he matching a N aisle already built? Their only surviving son, John, lies by himself, rather portly in armour with full-bottomed curly wig, 1689. He married Jane Hinde, and with her, Madingley. Their son John and his wife Jane appear in lively profile on a white marble, unsigned, but this most delectable combination of cherubs with medallion is surely Thomas Adye's, c.1714? Other memorials.

Leverington [2] extends W from the Nene bank to Gorefield, the seat of the main medieval manor, but no longer to Parson Drove (q.v.). At Gorefield, Bone's Gote uses Middle

Leverington

English word for watercourse, as in 'gutter'. Road N from Leverington church runs along part of ancient Sea Bank, which bears the sign 'Roman Bank', but is now known to be 10th or 11th century. The Romans had no need of it. Sea Bank marks the line of the W shore of the great funnel-shaped estuary beside which Wisbech stood. Leverington has a *church* of great architectural distinction. Its dedication to St Leonard underlines the early 12th-century origin of this place (unmentioned in Domesday Book). St

Leonard's popularity owed much to Bohémond's thanks for his release from a Moslem jail in 1103. All that remains here of the 12th-century building is a carved capital preserved in the room over the porch. But in the rebuilding that began in the 13th century, St Leonard's monkish head and shoulders beneath the hand of God were carved in the niche over the western portal. Three stages of the tower are E. E., the stone probably from Barnack, with a noble arch into the nave; then its design was changed. The sturdiness

achieved at Elm by crowning the corner buttress with turrets was exchanged here early in the 14th century for a belfry crowned by turrets recessed at the foot of a magnificent spire (162 ft, and superbly rebuilt in 1901). Meanwhile the chancel was being rebuilt at the end of the 13th century: the delicate beginnings of Dec. written in the traceried E window (and its delightful gable light above). How this quickly grew into the more familiar flowing tracery is seen alongside in S chapel's E window. From outside one

scarcely notices the N chapel's Perp. E window, but wait! The main entrance is through a magnificent two-storey S porch, early 14th century, and designed like a large (ragstone) tabernacle or shrine. Inside, great wooden cross-beams have been fixed to hold things steady. But the view of the base of the tower through the W arch, with its very stiff-leafed capitals, restores confidence. So does the 15th-century font. Then attention is captured by deep blues, browns and silvers of a Tree of Jesse window in that 'debased'-looking tracery E of the N aisle: the most famous of family trees got up to look like the most gorgeous Christmas tree. Each figure is framed in oval tracery in the loops of a vine (31 the work of the restorer in 1900). Shimmering, gleaming, it is one of the richest works of art in this county. In chancel, one window filled with six 15th-century disciples and apostles, 'replaced and completed' by T.F. Curtis of Ward and Hughes. Three small groups of 15th-century glass commemorating Sir Lawrence Everard's family, and including a pietà, were reset in 1908 in the S chapel. In this S chapel, much pleasure derives from the way the 18th-century marble memorials have been looked after and the walls whitewashed. The Swaine family monuments include a very pretty one to Spelman Swaine seated beside a pink obelisk, 1803. They lived at Leverington *Hall*, near the church, a beautiful brick house with an Elizabethan core which they improved and remodelled in the 17th and 18th centuries. Mr and Mrs S.L. Thompson show the house *by appointment*. Very large Georgian walled *Rectory*. Leverington *House*, built *c*.1852 seaward of the old sea bank by Mr Peatling, brewer and wine merchant: preserves parts from the lantern of Wisbech Octagon Chapel. *Beechwood*, end of Church Lane, has an exceptionally interesting old dovecote. At *Glendon*, built beside the Sutton road in 1831,

(*left and opposite*): **Leverington**

the row of walnuts was planted by E.B. Crosse at a party in 1851, before sailing his merchantman, the *Violet*, to the Adriatic: captured by Barbary pirates, he died before the year was out. At *Gorefield, St Paul's church*, 1870, dressed in sparkling black flint and wearing a bell-cote, stands in a pleasant churchyard among farms and much new cottage building. Chancel warmly coloured and given a canopy of honour in memory of the first vicar, 1903.

Linton [15] Large, almost a town, straddling the 'Linton' Cam. The village street grew N and S of the bridge, with a regular market and fairs, held from 1246 and finally supplanted by shops *c*.1860—the last surviving market outside Cambridge. Street now mercifully bypassed by A604, maintains hospitable pubs. International Stores preserved Georgian front of (older) No 33. Market Lane leads to the Shepherds' Hall. Here the street broadens and the market was held from the 14th century: a previous market place was E of the church where the lane comes up from Hadstock mill. Off Horn Lane, the old Congregational church is approached through avenue of large stone tombs. In Church Street, a secluded lane with its own crossing of the duck-dabbled rill, the *church* is grouped with a timber-caged guildhall that was being completed in 1523, and a charmingly plastered and thatched cottage: churchyard cared for. Church seems a shade less so: there was a drastic restoration *c*.1870. John Millecent and his wife, with brass coat of arms, 1577, might not be displeased: this lord of the Barham manor was zealous protestant, Thomas Cromwell's servant, and nearly lynched in the Lincs rising, 1536. His grandson's wife Douglas, 1653, has a monument deservedly concealed by the organ. Yet three memorials in particular deserve the sort of care one finds at Leverington: Wilton's monument to Elizabeth Bacon and her brother, Peter Standly, 1782, with life-size

figures of Hope and Faith and a portrait of the brother who left £1,000 for its making, and two wall tablets to George Flack and Susanna Green, 1693, with portrait busts. W.M. Palmer, most admirable Cambridgeshire antiquary, physician here 1900–25, died here 1939.

Litlington [14] parish slopes down the chalk below the Icknield Way. *Ashwell Street*, flanked by a single line of beeches, duplicates the Icknield Way just above the Spring Line for the benefit of those travellers who preferred the shelter of the woods and the nearness of water: a 'summer road' perhaps as old as the Way itself. At SW edge of village was a 4th-century villa, in area 500 by 300 ft: at least thirty rooms ranged round all sides of a courtyard, and with a walled cemetery in a field known 'from time immemorial' (Sir Cyril Fox) as 'Heaven's Walls'. *Limlow Hill* was marked out for a hillfort, never made. Very unpolished village centre. *Church* unendearing. Lively head of a scold, in bridle, carved *c*.1330 as head-stop to moulded arch in N arcade. Old bosses retained in roof and picked out in gilt: they include a particularly moving crucifix. Medieval pulpit and tall, graceful rood screen.

Little Abington *see* Abington, Great and Little

Little Chishill *see* Chishill, Great and Little

Little Eversden *see* Eversden, Great and Little

Little Gransden *see* Gransden, Little

Little Ouse *see* Littleport

Littleport [9] Over 15,000 acres of Fenland solitude, reaching the Norfolk borders at Rack Fen in the N and Burnt Fen in the E, that name going back traditionally to Hereward's 'scorched earth' strategy. E of the Ouse, the parish's long S bound-

ary traces the meanderings and roddons of the Brandon river's original course. Beside its present bank, St John's church at *Little Ouse* was built of flint in 1869. Littleport *church* has a noble E Anglian tower, late 15th century like all else except the two N aisles, 1857, which give the interior great breadth and capacity. Gravestones lately displaced, yet one still hears the clatter and smash of furniture and china from the vicarage as it was hurled against them in the night of 22 May 1816. The men of Littleport, goaded by starvation and by an odious farmer called Henry Martin, were brought together by the sound of the horn normally blown by the lightermen taking pleasure parties to Downham Market Fair. The vicar tried to defend the vicarage with a loaded pistol, then fled with his half-clad family on foot all the way to Ely for help. Thence a lawyer rode through the night to Bury St Edmunds and returned with a corporal's guard of sixteen dragoons to Ely, where the rioters had arrived and got rather out of hand. Next afternoon the dragoons advanced to Littleport with old Sir Henry Bate Dudley, prebendary of Ely, in his element at their head, charging at a hand-gallop down Mill Street. They found the rioters behind some benches in the George and Dragon and soon secured them. In June the judges arrived and five of the ringleaders were hanged. They are commemorated on St Mary's church tower, Ely. They are not forgotten here.

Little Shelford *see* Shelford, Great and Little

Little Thetford *see* Thetford, Little

Lode [12] A medieval word for waterway, here applies to the hamlet (promoted to parish, 1894) that formed the N fenland, part of the ancient sleeve-shaped parish of Bottisham (q.v.). Church built 1853. The lode itself is likely to be a Roman canal and drain. A whiteboarded watermill at the far end of the hamlet provides an eye-catcher from the spectacularly fine gardens of *Anglesey Abbey* (National Trust), the layout and adornment of which are reminiscent of a latter-day Roman villa. Its name seems to be a corruption of Angersale, meaning 'grassy nook', appropriate enough. About 1212, and probably earlier, a hospital was endowed here. In 1217, the rectory of Chesterton (q.v.) was given to canons regular near Turin, and Master Laurence of St Nicholas came over as their first rector. By the time he died at Anglesey *c.*1236 he had established a priory of canons regular here and at his 'own expense, care and industry' built 'almost the entire fabric of church, cloister, refectory, dormitory and prior's lodging'. The *prior's lodging* appears to be what survives. You arrive, in the shade of *Ulmus montana pendula* and a superb *Tilia petiolaris*, at a large grey-white L-shaped building of clunch and limestone rubble, roofed with local tiles, and with 'Jacobean' red-brick chimney-shafts. The N (right-hand) wing is the original 13th-century under-croft with what one assumes was the *prior's chamber* over, modified in the 14th century (and extended to N and W in our own). The S wing, at right angles, essentially of the same period but more altered, was probably the *hall* of the prior or his guests. The church and cloister presumably lay to the S and SW of this surviving building, but no serious investigation has been made. The priory went to the Hyndes at the Dissolution, who neglected it in favour of Madingley (q.v.). The surviving buildings were given their secular domestic character in Jacobean times; then, most of all between 1926 and 1958 by Lord Fairhaven. The official guide, indispensable for a full enjoyment of the astonishing garden, says: 'While perhaps not everyone will respond with the same enthusiasm to the rich eclecticism of the interior, it is impossible to be in two minds about the garden.' One example of the endearing eclecticism: Lord Fairhaven collected 250

oils and watercolours depicting Windsor Castle (and 500 prints), including a remarkable view of castle and town in James I's time, a very interesting and pretty view by Tillemans, and a glorious one by J.B. Pyne. There are also two breathtaking Claudes. Of local topography, the one remarkable painting shows Landwade Hall and church—beautifully. But what a garden! It has rightly been classed with Sissinghurst and Hidcote among notable accessible gardens of the 20th century, and, furthermore, claimed that 'by AD 2050, they will constitute the only major layout of the sort in this country which is not past maturity.' Like Sissinghurst, it calls for at least two visits a year—in spring, and summer. There are not just emperors in the Emperors' Walk: half-way along, there is a most moving group of feminine graces from the Temple of Concord at Stowe. There are great marble vases from Wanstead, by Schee-makers and by Laurent Delvaux. Ten Corinthian columns from Chesterfield House form a circular temple guarded by Jan Van Nost the Elder's lions. Do not neglect the older setting, the canons' fishponds and the inscrutable, unruffled, authentic Roman lode.

Lolworth [11] The church is perched on a ridge above the Cambridge-Huntingdon road and approached from a small green past the Old Rectory: in June, old roses in Old Rectory's front garden. The church walls display much ginger limestone rubble (?carstone). Both aisles gone. Interior parquet floored. The Stations of the Cross, moulded apparently in inedible toffee, were presented in 1930 by Father Dredge. The aisles seem to have been lost in a late 14th-century storm and fire, and the church rededicated in 1406, according to Thomas of Walsingham. Brass, 1610.

Longstanton [11] usually one word. Village street a mile long. Elms. *All Saints'*, at the crossroads,

sprawls comfortable behind the stump of a churchyard cross: two aisles, a *very* flowing-traceried S transept, *c.*1340, and W tower holding aloft an E Midland stone spire. General Dec. feel inside: S aisle curves in unusually to meet transept with window to light pulpit. S aisle contains beautifully designed and carved tomb of Sir Thomas Hatton, Kt. and Bt. (d. 1658), whose father was first cousin of Sir Christopher, Elizabeth's I's friend. Sir Thomas married an Alington of Horseheath: wears skullcap, fine ringlets, expressive face. His wife has just put down her scriptural reading for the last time. *St Michael's* still maintains its impressive nave roof of reed-thatch, sweeping down over low support-walls. Under a chestnut in the church-yard, a sunken bricked well-head suggests an ancient holy well. Within, in the rebuilt chancel (1884), one of those double piscinas as at Arrington and Histon and Jesus College.

Longstowe [11] As at Longstanton, a mile-long street but thinly inhabited, and interrupted by the former Cambridge-Bedford railway. The street is, as Layer wrote before 1640, 'a town unhappy for the want of good water': it stands on a boulder-clay watershed. However, a stream flowing N into the Bourn Brook springs in time to feed the fishponds that now provide a string of ornamental lakes through woods. These shade Hall and church, and may be the area settled by those Earningas (*see* Arrington) whose 'stow' (it often meant 'holy place') gave its name to a medieval Hundred. Well-kept churchyard. Church contains dramatic memorial of Sir Ralph Bovey, 1679: as a deluge falls in the background, he raises his naked torso out of the flood and reaches out for anchor offered by God. A mutilated monument below relates to Anthony Cage (d. 1603), whose Elizabethan house provides the core of the *Hall*. It was extended *c.*1880 and largely rebuilt in an impressive, sympathetic 'Jaco-

Lode: Anglesey Abbey gates

bean' way *c*.1897–1914: Flemish panelling, views of water and woodland.

Madingley [11] The steady slope from Cambridge is remembered by thousands of readers of Forster's *The Longest Journey* who never made the climb. It is well worth making. If one stays on the St Neots road, the crumpled outline of the post windmill prepares one psychologically for its neighbour on the ridge, the tall mast flying the stars and stripes for almost 9,000 American dead in our common cause in World War II. From the flag to the chapel a long wall of Portland stone bears the names of over 5,000 on air or sea missions whose bodies were never identified—starting with Frank J. Abbadessa of New Jersey and ending with Leonard C. Zieleniewski, the young men Elma Dean had in mind when she wrote: 'Give swing

bands, not gold harps, to these our boys./Let them love, Peter—they had no time.' The graves of the rest are marked by Italian white marble, fanning out radially down the slope. Opposite the Three Horseshoes, a terrace by Tayler and Green, 1967, almost alone among recent English architects in understanding how to design for villages (mostly in Norfolk). Farther on, the red-brick lump of Madingley Hall displays its E front with features of a 'prospect house'. This front is largely the building of a successful lawyer, Sir John Hynde, about the end of Henry VIII's reign. Then, in the 1590s, a splendid wing was created along the N front by the demolisher of St Audrey's, Histon. It originally came much farther E of the E front: along the N, it paraded an attractive-looking loggia of eleven round Italian arches, but facing N! In the 1720s, John Hinde Cotton, 3rd Bt., nephew

of Jane who kneels at the back of the church, married the Craggs heiress, added a block behind the original E range, and created the very fine saloon in the old great hall. Then, in 1754, the beautiful late 15th-century ornamental stone gateway of the Old Schools in Cambridge was dismantled to make way for the University Library and its materials were brought to this omnivorous house; they became the Gothick gateway to the stable court, most probably to the design of the admirable James Essex. The old stone façade at this point of arrival is the most attractive single feature of the house, which was bought in 1948 by Cambridge University for use mainly by its valuable Board of Extra-Mural Studies, for weekend conferences, etc. It was hired for a year, 1861, for the Prince of Wales while he was an undergraduate. A plaque recalls that his father spent a night here trying to redeem the boy and, so doing, in poor health, precipitated the Queen's widowhood. The *church*, beside the park entrance, is full of interest but presents an unattractive (N) face to the park—the usual approach. Enter and the outside is forgotten. You are in a N aisle arcaded by beautiful columns, each a cluster of four round shafts, more or less quatrefoil in plan, soon after 1300. Just inside the door stands a very peculiar Norman font, which just might have come from St Audrey's, Histon, when that provided the building materials for the N wing of the Hall here. Chancel shortened in 18th century: the communion rails, with fine barley-sugar balusters, are said to come from Great St Mary's, Cambridge. The three E lancets presumably replace a Georgian window; a S window has good remains of medieval glass. Hanging in the tower, ten emaciated wooden angels from the roof ('fourteen cherubims in wood to be taken down'—Dowsing, the official Cromwellian smasher) might be taken for expressions of art in our own melancholy time. Six framed painted panels came in the 18th century from the Hall: they represent six apostles, Flemish, c.1600, striking, see St Andrew. Among the monuments, perhaps the most touching is a comfortably swaddled child in alabaster. Jane Hinde, 1692, head on elbow and eyes swivelled towards heaven in the manner of Osbert Lancaster, is the heiress whose marriage to Sir John Cotton of Landwade (q.v.) brought him all this. Their spinster daughter Jane, aged 59, is shown kneeling in 1707 with a book, in a spirited work, hard to see with the light of a W window behind her. George III arms apparently Coade stone. Park outside just recognizably by Capability Brown.

Manea [8] rhymes with brainy, seems to mean 'island common', and was a hamlet of Coveney till the cutting of the Old and New Bedford rivers in the 17th century made them 16 miles apart by road. The new rivers rendered obsolete Darcey Lode, Manea's old winding W boundary waterway that had drained ineffectually in the Wisbech Ouse. The church is a total rebuilding of 1875 in the same dreary stone as Wimblington's. *Public hides*, 'The Ouse Washes' at *Purls Bridge* and *Welches Dam*. RSPB with Cambridge and Isle of Ely Naturalist Trust own 2,000 acres of Washland (the great strip of regularly flooded grazing marshland between the two Bedford rivers). There are numbers of the rare ruff, and the black-tailed godwit, and occasionally black tern. Immense numbers of wildfowl winter on the marshes. Access strictly by permit from The Lodge, Sandy, Beds.

March [5] means boundary: of what? In Domesday Book it was merely an outlying grange of the abbot of Ely's manor at Doddington, though the abbot of Bury also had a small holding: the conjunction here of the two major E Anglian religious magnates points back to St Wendred's association with the place. Her connection with the E Anglian royal house, and possibly

Madingley Hall

with St Audrey herself, is suggested by the survival of St Wendred's Well at Exning, near Newmarket, one of their halls. Here she has remained patron of the superb church that perhaps stands where her shrine was. But what *boundary* was here? This takes us back beyond Wendred to the Romans. The *Fen Causeway*, their road crossing the fen from Denver to Whittlesey and the N Midlands runs through March. Here, lengths of causeway supporting the road, and to the E the roddon of a silted canal it ran beside, are still impressive. To Wendred's contemporaries they probably suggested a boundary, as indeed they do to some modern archaeologists. Grandford House, 2 miles N along the A141, is one place where the causeway rampart is visible: S of the house, W of the road, and here running almost parallel with it. Incidentally, aerial photography has

shown areas of remarkably dense Roman settlement and cultivation across this N side of the town—immediately N of Grandford House, and even more in the fields E to the Twenty Foot River from *Flaggrass Hill Farm*. This N side of March is generally known as a key point for sorting and remarshalling railway wagons. Advanced technical improvements of 1929 and 1933 resulted in 50 miles of track in the sidings and about 2,000 railway jobs. This aspect of the town is echoed in ornamental cast-iron porches such as Wade's Hotel's, in Station Road, and in the Coronation Fountain, 1911, in Broad Street, one of the markets. In 1888, when the Isle became one of the new administrative counties, it sensibly established March as its county town, equally convenient for both Wisbech and Ely. Now, the main attraction remains St Wendred's church, to the

March: St Wendred's church (*above and opposite*)

S, rich and rewarding even among the best of the local medieval churches. It has suffered a recent indignity, the reduction of its churchyard to the vulgar euphemism of a garden of rest, dotted with a handful of lobelia-framed tombs. But what a glorious church: a most attractive mixture of honey-coloured ragstone, silver-grey ashlar for the buttresses and the battlements that crown one of those features that specially delight E Anglians and their visitors—a clerestory, adorned by flint-and-brick flushwork, and designed to light a remarkable roof. St Wendred's roof is worth a very long journey over the fen. A double hammerbeam roof, it seems almost alive with three tiers of wide-winged angels, the lowest ranged along the wall posts between the clerestory windows, then upon each of the hammerbeams. A heavenly host, if ever one materialized! Two memorial brasses are worth a moment, for those commemorated surely contributed to this great work.

Melbourn [14] A rural and suburban village. Its High Street, built on a delightful curve, is ruined by weight and press of A10 through-traffic. This is a very big parish, with a S boundary along the Icknield Way and a W boundary at the edge of Royston. To the S, Goffer's Knoll, a beech-capped spur, is a landmark for miles around. Composition of W front of church, closely comparable with Haslingfield's, excellent Perp., but inside, the main structure, including the aisle arcades, is, as so often in these parts, 13th-century. Nave roof is dated c.1500 by rebus of Bishop Alcock of Ely on tie-beam. (Bury Manor given to Ely bishop in 970.) Hitch family, here three more centuries, gave the richly traceried rood-screen in 1505. Stalls.

Meldreth [14] apparently named from the mill-stream, the boundary with Melbourn. All sorts of housing and new building, including the well-grouped but painted-brick

Spastics School (Architects' Co-partnership). Stocks, at crossroads under spreading chestnut, might be reserved for people who paint good brickwork. S of them, some dignified Edwardian houses, and The Court, 1773 and 1891. At the church, the 13th-century arcading of the tower takes the eye, as at Orwell. Fine lofty interior, with Perp. S aisle arcade of five bays, tall, delicate rood-screen and original nave roof—very similar to Barrington's. Two large brass candelabra in nave, one Georgian, one Victorian. Ropes of eight bells hang in ringing chamber. Early Victorian 'Perp.' pulpit. The narrow Norman chancel, distempered cream, has three tall Norman windows and a thin Dec. one: in it, a delightful ruby-red and silver light displays a small monk, perhaps a donor, kneeling before the lamb of God. There are traces of medieval red wall-paint, and remains of oak medieval stalls in the chancel. A Romano-British coffin, AD 300–400, lies in the nave.

Mepal [8] is divided from its fen by the Bedford rivers and interrupted by the thoroughfare traffic of Ireton's Way. Picturesqueness lost in fire of 1860s, yet there is Octagon House, an early 19th-century oddity, and beside the Three Pickerels an unspoilt stone farmhouse, and the *church* stands pleasantly in meadows near-by. Whitewashed interior retains old feel, despite many restorations. A memorial on W wall relates to the draining of the Bedford Level and the building of Fortrey Hall, now reduced to a modest farmhouse beside the Old River and very evidently decaying in 1981. 'To James Fortrey, descended from ancient stock in Brabant which took an asylum in England from the persecution of the Spaniards in the reign of Queen Elizabeth. He was 3rd son of Samuel Fortrey, esq., who, upon undertaking the draining of the Bedford Level, erected a commodious habitation in Byal Fen . . . Having lived a favourite of four princes, he . . . passed the remainder

of his days in retirement between Portugal and Byal Fen.' He died here 18 August 1719 in his 63rd year. At Kew, his father Samuel had built the remarkable Dutch house, Kew Palace, in 1631.

Milton [11] is now 'in-filled' with suburban and even urban housing, yet in Fen Road, Milton House looks much as it did in 1770 when the Revd William Cole moved in from Waterbeach. The late Dr W.M. Palmer, the best of authorities, described Cole as 'the most industrious antiquary that Cambridgeshire has ever had or is ever likely to have'. He felt under an obligation to his friend James Essex, the first Georgian architect who properly understood Gothic structures, for redesigning the cottage, 'for which he would take nothing'. Their main external alterations were the service end and brewhouse projected towards the road (with inevitable bits of masonry 'rescued' by Cole). He also filled his Gothick sash windows with medieval glass. Not for nothing was he Horace Walpole's lifelong friend and earnest correspondent. (Full description, *Monumental Inscriptions and Coats of Arms from Cambridgeshire*, Bowes and Bowes, 1932.) Here he compiled his hundred folio-size volumes, now in the British Library, and dispensed hospitality. Near by, Queen Anne Lodge is the best example I know in Cambridgeshire of unspoilt ornamental parge-work. It should be compulsory viewing for all interested in the conservation of old Cambridgeshire houses. Milton Hall, c.1790, has been attributed to Soanes's published designs, and the layout of the grounds to Repton: now Eastern Electricity Board. The *church* has an attractive interior, whitewashed, very simple Norman chancel arch, early 14th-century arcades and other detail, nave roof plaster-ceiled, tie-beams with 17th-century pendants, handsome 17th-century communion rails from King's College, and a well-made monumental brass c.1553. Francis

Jeep's Farm College is built of pleasant gault brick on the edge of the cultivated fen.

Morden, Guilden and Steeple

[14] In fresh, unspoilt open country, well tree'd, two long strip-shaped parishes with feet on the Icknield Way, crossed by Ashwell street below the ridge, stretch N to the stream of the Ashwell Cam. Originally Mor*don*, meaning marsh-hill, the strip was laid out to combine river-meadows with the drier hill slopes. *Guilden Morden*, beautiful in the view from Tadlow but rather a dull village, has successfully raised the money for repair of chancel, spire, etc. recently. (Both have steeples.) Inside, the medieval rood-screen with altar-enclosures became pews either side of the chancel entrance. In its painted panels, SS Erkenwald (7th-century bishop of London and E Saxons) and Edward alone survive, much redaubed. Twenty-three villagers drowned on way to America, 1845. The church bell was remembered to have tolled unaccountably at the time of the shipwreck. *Morden Hall*, yellow-plastered and many-gabled, is 'one of the best preserved moated sites in the county'. House in main enclosure may go back to rebuilding after destruction in 1381 revolt. At Hooks Mill, watermill and (derelict) tower windmill side by side. *Steeple Morden*, chancel flattened when the old steeple fell in 1633. New steeple, 1866, shingled; top half of tower hung with pink and yellow tiles. S aisle ashlar faced, rest downland flint.

Newton

[14] near Cambridge ('new' at least by *c*.1050). Clunch garden walls, with graffiti. 'Town Street' lined by beeches and limes, leads to Hall and church in small churchyard set deep in great chestnuts as in a forest glade. There, hidden among wildly overgrown box and yew hedges, lurks a semicircular stone mausoleum, 'Ionic', by Ambrose Poynter, 1922, for the Waldsteins. Inside the little church

has great atmosphere, partly through having its walls almost full of memorials, chiefly white marbles, and partly for its beaten (repoussé) brasswork of the *art nouveau* period, made by a Newton craftsman called Prime. Of the marbles, M. Noble's to Lt-Col Christopher Peach Pemberton, of the Scots Fusiliers, is best, with standing allegoric figure. He was killed at Sedan, 1 September 1870, while observing and recording the Franco-Prussian war. He fell while advancing with the staff of the Crown Prince of Saxony. Massive font, comparable with Shepreth's. Transepts. Awful glass. The *Hall*, now used by National Seed Development Organization, is enormous. From mid 18th century, two rear wings survive. A great neo-Queen Anne House, Swithland slated, was built across the S front, 1909, for Sir Charles Waldstein (1st Lord Walston), second Director of the Fitzwilliam Museum, and makes a grand impression.

Newton in the Isle

[2] was 'new' at least by *c*. 972. Like Leverington, flanks the Nene outflow on the E side, and has made much marshland in what used to be a large inlet of the Wash. Churchyard full of well-carved headstones. Church emptied of atmosphere; but well kept. Broad nave with arcades of late Norman round columns, and aisles widened in 14th century, with interesting window tracery. William Cole, in the 18th, found 'the pillars painted like marble. The pulpit was curiously painted and gilt with a fine gilt canopy.' John Lumpkin, churchwarden in those cheerful days, 1711–62, lived in a beautiful house (now two cottages) next to the church. Since his day, the medieval glass of the Colvilles has gone from the N aisle, where the E window is signed by Easton, 1931. Dreadful Victorian glass.

Oakington

[11] Crowland abbey owned the manor: now the RAF presides. Manor house flanked by scanner on airfield. Rather standard fawn-coloured church with regular

Perp. aisle windows has above the tower parapet, on stalks like artificial flowers, small red warning lights to remind low-flying aircraft. Chancel walls contain rust-coloured puddingstone, distinctly friable. S doorway leads into surprisingly attractive Children's Corner, and Norman font with triple arcades irregular as in Bayeux Tapestry. S nave arcade looks as if carved out of solid Norman walls. Restoration by parishioners themselves: four bells rehung and last wall repointed 1980. *Westwick*, originally an outlying dairy farm.

Orwell

[14] The maypole that stood just across Harlton's boundary was known as the Orwell maypole. The path to its site climbs N above the church, past the old clunch-pit on Toot Hill, the Old English word for 'look-out hill': worth climbing for view S over Ashwell Cam. The chancel's height and great early Perp., window areas proclaim its inner grandeur. Built *c*.1398 by the rector as a memorial to Sir Simon Burley, lord of the manor, a brave companion of the Black Prince and one of the tutors of his son, Richard II; he was beheaded, after impeachment by the Merciless Parliament, 1388, for his pupil's failure to learn how to govern. Now that the medieval glass is gone, the finest feature is the roof, wagon-shaped in five slopes and with alternate bosses and shields carved at the intersection of sixty-six square panels. In the ridge, four larger bosses contain specially interesting but unidentified secular figures, with traces of original colour and with hands arranged as though originally holding standards: probably members of Burley's family, but perhaps Anlaby's, the loyal rector's, as well. There was a Georgian reconstruction, possibly as a result of William Cole's visit in 1743. There was also a restoration in 1883 when Trinity College, the patrons, had the temerity to substitute six modern coats of arms, including their own, for originals! To build the school across

the road, c.1883, a mound was levelled, conceivably a motte on the ancient manorial site. Next to it springs the stream that gave Orwell its name. No. 30 High Street's garden wall is thatched, and there are old houses and 'cottage gothic' cottages. There are extensive moats and traces of a church at *Malton*.

Outwell *see* Upwell

Over [11] means river-bank. The large and developing village has been set round by orchards since the middle of the 19th century, when the railway reached Swavesey and the Ouse declined as chief means of transport. The manor was one of those given to Ramsey by Eadnoth II, bishop of Dorchester 1034–49. The very fine effect of church and spire is marred by disagreeable rendering, except on S front of S porch: yet the fabric is reckoned to be built with Barnack stone. The early 14th-century work signalled by ball-flower ornament and two patterns of window tracery is identical all round the N and S nave aisles. No one should enter the building without first saluting its patron, the Blessed Virgin Mary, carved at the end of the Middle Ages and now in dire need of the most expert attention, above the W portal (cf. St Leonard's, at Leverington). Here she is at her Assumption in a remarkable mandorla, a glory or sunburst, with two angels on either side, rolling back the clouds. The Perp. work of the chancel *relates* to the Dec. work: that is to say it is based on the design principle of arcades in outer walls (as at Wilburton, etc.), the windows set within the arcades. (Incidentally, the chancel is said to have been rebuilt in 1840 and again from 1856 on.) The carved heads in the early Perp. capitals of the nave columns are extremely rustic, lively and amusing. There is a patch of medieval wall-painting. Several blocks of stone have never been carved—remain waiting for the sculptor. Stone seating right round nave. Chancel stalls

Over

with carved misericords, *said* to have come from Ramsey. Jacobean pulpit with onion-domed sounding-board. Scenes of pleasure craft and pleasure through the reeds and across the Ouse to the Hunts. bank at *Overcote*.

Pampisford [15] Locally pronounced Panser; the -ford was -worth till the 17th century. Quiet seclusion, partly the effect of so many trees, not just about the Hall and its park, which is famous for them. Neat thatched houses and cottages in the little High Street and in Beech Lane N of the church. From here, *St John's church* with its spiky spire looks quite Victorian across a playing-field (again beauti-

fully tree'd). But it has a remarkable Norman feature and is probably on an earlier site. The Norman feature is an enchanting tympanum, carved with a pictorial life of John the Baptist in a style very like modern child art. Here, as at Leverington and Over, the main portal displays unforgettably the patron of the parish. Fanning out round the tympanium, ten toy Romanesque arches read from right to left. (1) A font symbolizes the Baptist's function, while (2) his father Zacharias bows before (3) an angel. In (4) a dancing, dishevelled Salome holds the attention of (5) her father Herod. At the top of the tympanum and mid point of the sequence (6) St John, winged like an angel, is the one

Pampisford: St John the Baptist's church. Tympanum showing his beginning and end

figure facing the villagers as they arrive. (7) is occupied only by the block and (8) by the head newly severed by (9) the executioner. (10) is devoted solely to the head, this time apparently floating up to heaven like a child's kite or balloon. Several windows look like Kempe's work but only one is signed by him (W end, N aisle). The font, properly enough, is Norman. *Brent Ditch* is sometimes called *Pampisford Ditch*, and from early times was known locally as 'the green ditch', which may signify some prehistoric water scheme. *Pampisford Hall* and *Park* are the creation of the Parker Hamond family, whose 1830s house was enlarged and richly decorated in the French and Italian Renaissance fashions in the 1870s. The formal gardens were by G. Marnock and the parkland trees were already celebrated in Victorian times. Since their purchase by the present owner's family in 1893, the park has further matured and includes, for instance, over a thousand foreign species of conifer and a herd of revered historic cattle—Old English Longhorns.

Papworth Everard and **Papworth St Agnes** [11] Evrard de Beche (1155–75) has left his name with the

S parish, Agnes de Papeworth (*c*.1160) with the other, where the church adopted her patron saint. Motor traffic pours through *Papworth Everard*, the church an ugly Victorian rebuilding W of the main road. A valley slopes down steeply below the W wall, so tower set on N side. Public footpath to Yelling (Hunts.) leads W. Remains of medieval settlement in valley to S. *The Hall* (G. Byfield *c*.1809), roughcast all over, is now world famous: office of successful heart transplant hospital. The hospital's history is illustrated on two tapestries by K.L. Borne, 1943–5. Bust of founder in entrance hall amid chocolate-coloured scagliola columns. *Papworth St Agnes* Manor Farm is approached from Graveley road by a beautiful winding tree-shaded lane. It is part of a group of remarkable buildings on the brink of decay. The house, Elizabethan and Jacobean, its E front built of re-used stone, contains good plaster ceilings and original garderobe. Approach to church gloomy, across a green lined with derelict thatched cottages and a disused communal bakehouse, yellow brick, 1850. At the instigation of the rector, J.H. Sperling, whose descendant still lives in the Old Rectory, the *church* was rebuilt, 1848–54, in a

very effective chequerboard pattern of freestone (dominant) and flint and brown pebble. It is at once reminiscent of Sawston Hall and Lord Darcy's tower at St Osyth. The Friends of Friendless Churches have happily taken up the challenge to conserve it. The Mallory family were here from early 15th to early 17th century: no connection with Sir Thomas Malory, author of *Morte d'Arthur*.

Parson Drove [2] Beautiful medieval *church* in danger (1972) of being taken over by the birds; happily in 1975 vested in the Redundant Churches Fund, and since then very well restored. Noble arcading, and a superb stone-panelled tower arch framing a tall vault with at least one very well carved boss. Chancel gone: said to have been washed away in the floods of 1613. At W end of Parson Drove a long green, at right angles to main line of street, is planted with oaks, including a spreading one, and has old village Cage (later fire-engine shed) surmounted by Victorian Jubilee clock. The Emmanuel church *Southea*, is a good brick building of 1872, like Christchurch, Upwell. High Church. Wesleyan chapel 1838 reminded Pevsner of New England. Immediately W of Parson

Rampton

Drove and Cloughs Cross an area of remarkably intensive Roman farming revealed by aerial photography. A planned *drove*-boundary marks its W edge.

Prickwillow [9] Carved in 1878 from several neighbours. Cam-Ouse formerly ran out to E from Ely, meandering as far as Prickwillow before swerving W to Littleport. This eastward meander from Ely silted up and formed a roddon on which the N side of the village street, and the street itself, perches fairly securely: the channel on to Little-

port stayed open, for it is joined by the Lark from Brandon, brought here in a straight stretch thought by experts to be Roman: familiar to holiday waterway cruisers. St Peter's *church*, 1868, was built on piles. Bell, 1691, from the cathedral, as is the fine font of 1693: white marble, with strings of pearls issuing from their (scallop) shells and winding themselves round the necks of jolly winged cherubs. The dead must go to Ely, so high is the watertable. *Shippea Hill* Farm, Railway Halt and Inn are within these bounds now, though Plantation

Farm, Peacock's Farm and Flanders Farm lie just N. Plantation and Peacock's Farms are the scenes of the archaeological digs in the 1930s that established not only the Roman but also three earlier levels of prehistoric human occupation. Here, S of road near Flanders Farm, and at first house as you turn S on B1382 for Prickwillow, you get very clear sightings of the roddon that represents the early natural channel of the Little Ouse on its wanderings from Thetford.

Pyemore *see* Downham

Quy *see* Stow

Rampton [11] Giants Hill, willow screened, in a cow-pasture seems to have been part of early medieval strategy for getting over to the Isle. E of church, strongly moated and reminiscent of Burwell: being unfinished, it seemed to C.W. Phillips likely to be another of the forts ordered by Stephen and made redundant in 1144 by the arrow that killed Mandeville. Small triangular green with chestnuts, village pump and foot of stone cross beneath fine plane trees. Attractive small manor house alongside green just in Church End: large Dutch-looking shaped gables. *Church*: rustic flowing tracery in chancel window. Broad, low red-brick 18th-century porch. Inside, view across reeling little S aisle at once recalls Claydon. Here the nave is bigger and the eye goes straight to the well-preserved Elizabethan pulpit, complete with tester, set against piers of (former) Norman chancel arch, replaced by 14th-century arch. Fragments of medieval paintings on N wall. Chancel paved with old pamments. Several fragments of late Anglo-Saxon stone coffin lids in E wall. Rather eroded stone figure of 14th-century Delisle lies grasping his sword, shield on shoulder, probably the builder of the chancel.

Reach [12] Name may be a reference to the way the Devil's Dyke left the shortest course across the open

Rampton

Rampton manor house

country in order to connect with the end of Reach Lode—a canal that itself reaches inland from the Cam to a (disused) quay or hythe at this point. Since the Devil's Dyke is late Roman or Early English the lode is generally accepted as Roman. As you stand on the NW tip of the great rampart looking down towards the quay, the line of houses (including fragments of a chapel) on the right was Burwell's trading post: the larger collection of houses, including two former inns, running parallel with the Dyke but also at right angles along to Delver End, was Swaffham Prior's. The disused hythe is worth walking to see: a ton-

gue of rammed chalk protruding between two narrow waterways, each leading to small basins at the back of the various trading houses. There was considerable sea-going traffic. Coal was still coming in here in the 19th century, but the port at last stopped trading after 1884 when the Mildenhall-Cambridge railway line came through; itself now only a scar across the land. Annual fair still opened by the mayor of Cambridge.

Sawston [14] occupies the triangle at the confluence of Cam and Linton Cam: these drove its paper-mills, and the lime in them contri-

buted to the parchment and the leather businesses that have shaped Sawston as a large industrial village since the mid-19th century. (At Dernford Mill, papermaking began in the 17th century.) Mary Tudor made her mark on Sawston when she stayed a night with the Huddlestons at the Hall in 1553, at the dangerous moment of her accession. It was burnt down either by Protestant Cambridge townsfolk or by soldiers of the desperate Northumberland. She gave the family leave to use stone from Cambridge castle in the rebuilding, which is dated in the central quadrangle 1557 and 1584. They remained loyal to the old

Sawston Hall

Catholic faith and their descendants still own the house. It is large, and hard to find a modern use for: very little altered in essentials since Tudor times (a front walled courtyard has gone). An impressive and most attractive aspect of the N front is its decorative colour and texture: much of the structure is of clunch, but the projecting three-storey entrance porch, and the front of the (ground floor) great hall are engagingly chequered with alternate squares of mellow red-brick and ashlar (perhaps from Cambridge castle). There is of course a chapel and a most memorable priest-hole, very cunningly hidden in a most unlikely position at the top of the newel stairs (indeed there are two other hiding-holes, indispensable to Recusants in times of crisis, and there are well-contrived garderobes). In the *church*, near-by, the three bays of lofty, aisled Norman nave were extended E by two bays in the 13th century, presumably over the site of the earlier chancel, whose early 12th-century doorway is reset in the later S wall. N aisle column bears graffito, apparently 12th century, of a man in Phrygian cap. Larger graffito seems to show pagan man brandishing pagan sword: T.C. Lethbridge thought it was inspired by one of the hill figures he had bared on the Gog Magog Hills, visible from here. Tombchest, 1423. Arms of William IV, attractive ironwork.

Shelford, Great and Little [14] connected by 'shallow ford'. Motor traffic ravages *Great Shelford*'s delightful village street. The N boundary of the parish is aligned on a prehistoric track from the major ford at Hauxton Mill. By the river, King's Mill (beautifully converted by Sir Leslie Martin for his own home), the wistaria'd mill-house and clapboarded range of cottages (Owldom and Water Meadow), form an idyllic backwater. Battlemented, flintpebbled *church*: square tower, the crowning octagon adopted here by the rebuilders only after two 18thcentury collapses. Tall interior, apparently the work of *c.*1400 promoted by Thomas Patesley, vicar. The beautiful remains of the brass memorial of a priest, presumably Patesley, are beside the high altar, with the three crowns of Ely, patrons of the living, and a chevron between three crosses crosslet. Good remains of a hammerbeam roof. Tone and atmosphere are set by the uncoloured oak of the delicate roodscreen, by the parclose screen in the N aisle and the pulpit with tester. Above the screen, a vision of the Last Judgement, a Doom, was planned as part of the framing of the chancel arch, and drawn in delightful detail with rich browns and golds. Over God's right shoulder the sun blazes, and on that sunny side below, a simple cross stands and people march smugly into heavenly mansions. Over his left shoulder, the pale moon, with its face of the man imprisoned, glimmers while the damned are enchained by horned devils. In *Little Shelford* the threestoreyed, five-bay, yellow-brick *Manor House* built *c.*1750 'by an opulent ironmonger of Cambridge' has lost its small glazing-bars, but is well framed by trees and a walled garden. Just E of the church, a distinguished Victorian Gothic house with windows of clustered lancets is called '*Priesthaus*'. The large Perp. S chapel is the most prominent feature of the *church*. Tomb and effigy of John

Snailwell

de Freville, 1312, probably rebuilder of chancel: Frevilles here four centuries (brasses in S chapel). Pulpit, formerly three-decker in middle of N wall of nave, still has tester. Wale family monuments include General Sir Charles Wale, Col of HM 33rd Regt. of Foot, a younger son: 'In February 1810, at the head of his brigade the Royal York Rangers, he decided the capture of the island of Guadeloupe from the French.' Little Shelford's boundaries meet those of Newton, Harston and Hauxton at the foot of Obelisk Hill, or Maggots Mount (Harston); and in 1920 Little Shelford people still spoke of walking that way as 'going up the maypole'. Other maypoles stood at Orwell and Hildersham, not far off.

Shepreth [14] John Layer (c.1586–1641), an early historian of this county living here as lay rector and squire, noted that it was 'environed on all sides except the south-east with rivers and brooks, and has a pleasant sweet brook besides running through the middle of the town': -reth is Old English for brook, and they perhaps used the one running through the middle of the village for sheep-dipping, much as that running through adjoining Meldreth was used for milling. Both, indeed, had mills by 1086. Shepreth Riverside Walk has lately been established as a countryside amenity in the meadows by the Ashwell Cam. Layer's ground-floor study retains heavily moulded beams and a well-carved bracket with a cock, rebus of Bishop Alcock of Ely (1486–1500): Ely owned Chatteris nunnery which owned the little manor here of which Layer was squire. One of the other four Shepreth manors took the name Docwra's in the 16th century: its house, N of the church, L-shaped and going back to the 16th century, was remodelled and given a truly 'prettie' brick front soon after 1743 by Joseph Woodham, whose initial is in the wrought-iron front gates. The Woodhams lived at Tyrells Hall, Georgian, where their ornamental

Soham: mill at Downfield

buildings included one now a motel. Massy W church tower of clunch is still rough-keyed for lime plaster. Tall N doorway, Norman and 13th century. The aisle arcade is built of clunch, so are the unusual recesses, one either side of the simple, handsome Norman chancel arch: one

Perp. traceried, the other Dec. traceried, going through to the chancel like a window.

Shingay-cum Wendy [14] both originally ended in -ay, meaning island, and both are still watery in willow-framed meadows. Landscape seems uninhabited except by a few horses and cattle. This emptiness goes back far into the Middle Ages. The symbol of it is the extensive moated site beside Manor Farm. In the 1150s, the manor became one of the earliest preceptories of the *Knights of the Hospital of St John of Jerusalem.* Jerusalem was a Christian kingdom 1099–1187 and, even after the Christian forces were ejected from Acre in 1291 and the Templars were disbanded in 1308, the Hospitallers continued to furnish from their preceptories all over England money, arms, cloth, 'medical comforts for the troops', in the struggle against the Muslim. An experienced multi-national society, they seem to have been skilful farmers. Shingay's great moated site stands for the efficient medieval Enclosure that enabled the Shingay preceptory, with Wendy and estates in adjacent Croydon and Arrington, to come fourth wealthiest in England and Wales. In 1540, they had property in forty-two Cambridgeshire parishes. A century later, John Layer of Shepreth recalled how people executed in Cambridge were fetched for burial at Shingay. Wendy's churchyard, beside large sunny house with Gothick windows, pleasant on sunny mornings : churchyard wall rebuilt to commemorate the Queen's coronation, 1953.

Shippea *see* Prickwillow

Shudy Camps *see* Camps

Silverley *see* Ashley-cum-Silverley

Snailwell [12] means 'slow stream' but at the approach from Newmarket the swift racehorse is worshipped in effigy: first Hyperion, 1930–60, then, at Snailwell Stud on ridge, Chamossaire, 1942–64. Descend into lush valley of the Snail, with nestling village. The church, with its Norman round tower and hunched nave roof almost as high as the tower, is beautifully embowered. S across lane Church Farm is white

Soham

pargeted in the middle, between darkstained barn and early 19th-century brick. W of this, the blissfully plastered and ochred Old Rectory. W of the tower, a deep pond, 'the old waste well', then four ponds beyond and the source of the Snail. Bees, bantams, mares and foals. Inside, the *church* is rather gloomy, all much restored, but worth entering to see the nave roof—Suffolk type, arch braced to collar-beam, and then hammerbeams with large human figures (half length). Light flooded into the church in 1848.

Every window was thereafter filled with Victorian coloured glass of no artistic, nor the least doctrinal, merit.

Soham's [9] name denotes a lakeside settlement. Here, till two centuries ago, the reedy mere (*sae*) spread W from the Soham Lode right over to Fen Side in Wicken— covering thirteen or fourteen hundred acres: hard to think of 18th-century farmers being capsized by squalls as they tried to sail across. In Domesday Book, Soham is entered first among the Cambridgeshire manors William took over direct from the Old English kings. It marked the W edge of the upland, or mainland, of the old E Anglian kingdom. Not till the early 12th century was Soham Causeway built—to Stuntney, and thence across to Ely. That Soham was thought of in the 7th century as a sort of west coast Dunwich was neatly demonstrated by St Felix, the first bishop of E Anglia. He died at Dunwich, but here they brought him to be buried. In Canute's time, the remains of Felix were removed to Ramsey. The medieval tradition at Ramsey spoke of a boat race on Soham Mere between the monks of Ely and Ramsey with the bones of St Felix as prize! The present churchyard is on the site of a pagan E Anglian cemetery, yielding an elaborate heathen cruciform brooch in the type assigned to the half-century immediately before Felix's. So perhaps this early sacred place was chosen for Felix's minster, where the chancel of the present impressive cruciform building stands, its great W belltower of c.1500 proclaiming its allegiance to E Anglia by the beautiful flushwork patterns round the embattled parapet. The earliest visible feature in the church is the outline, in the outside of the S chancel wall, of one side of a fairly primitive Romanesque priest's doorway, set at a lower ground level than the present. After the tower, the most impressive external feature is a pair of beautifully ashlared pinnacles flanking the N transept, each capped by a monkey: they greet the townspeople at one of the two main approaches from the town's enormously long main street. Inside, four graceful late-Norman arcades of the nave aisles. Elaborately beautiful pointed chancel arch (trans Norman to E.E., the dog-tooth ornament used to great advantage). Massive pillars of 12th-century crossing. Great 14th-century E window (full of 1874 glass). Figure of sainted bishop, perhaps Felix, painted on N wall of chancel. W of

this, but still E of the crossing, a fine 15th-century chapel has preserved its screen, mainly red and gold. The roof is a splendid structure, hammerbeams alternating with tie-beams, intended to compete with neighbouring roofs: binoculars desirable. Fine carvings in spandrels of S aisle roof. Two sets of misericords, now at W end. Tablet in N aisle commemorates Fireman Nightall and Driver Gimbert, whose courage in detaching a blazing wagon from an ammunition train in June 1944 saved Soham from disaster. Down by the station, Mere Side is a long cottage settlement, perhaps aboriginal. E of the church, down White Hart Lane, St Felix House has swags on its Regency doorcase. The Fountain Inn, partly burnt down in 1900, retains Justices Room with a fireplace of 1583. Attached to the back of the inn, the 17th-century steelyard, for weighing the wagonloads as they left market: overhauled in 1929, it was found accurate to two ounces. Soham's lands reach N almost to Prickwillow and W to include *Barway*. The road to Barway passes Hainey Farm, already in 1086 a small arable island, named 'bird-isle'. Barway, 'hill-isle', is worth visiting for views along Soham Lode and to the cathedral. Little medieval church, transformed into agreeable house, font in hall. W of Barway and NW of Old Fordey Farm, remains have been found of a late Bronze Age causeway leading across the Cam to Little Thetford.

Southea *see* Parson Drove

Stanton *see* Longstanton

Stapleford [14] Suburbanized village by former ford. Lutyens designed Middlefield. *Church* has 12th-century chancel arch and (stored at the W end) some late Anglo-Saxon work: also brass of William Lee, vicar forty-three years, to 1617. Its parish reaches N over the Gog Magog Hills to form a boundary on Wool Street (Roman), and so includes Worm-

wood Hill and *Wandlebury*, the most impressive Iron Age hill-fort in the region. John Layer, in the early 17th century, 'could never learn how these hills came to be called Gogmagog hills, unless it were from a high and mighty portraiture of a giant which the scholars of Cambridge cut upon the turf within the trench (i.e. the hill-fort), but is now of late discontinued'. The cutting was resumed and William Cole remembered it c.1724. The antiquity of this creature seems to be corroborated by a graffito in Sawston church (q.v.). *Wandlebury* was formidable in the Iron Age, almost a thousand feet in diameter, encircled by concentric ditches and ramparts, with long views in all directions and an absolute dominance of the eastward approaches from the Cam valley bottom. It was acquired by the Godolphins, devoted to the Newmarket turf, who built a house here, now gone: in the making of offices and plantations, the entire inner rampart was destroyed. A raised lawn marks the house site: great barrack-like stables with a cupola (1708) remain, now lived in. Beneath the cupola, the famous Godolphin Arabian was buried in 1753, one of three original Arab stallions at the head of so many successful racehorse pedigrees. Now that the site belongs to the Cambridge Preservation Society and is open to the public, the main natural history lies in the delightful plantations of trees. The Godolphins spoilt any serious chance of recovering the story of the hill fort. As to its views down over Cambridge, they too have been spoilt, by the twin chimneys of the new Addenbrooke's Hospital.

Steeple Morden *see* Morden, Guilden and Steeple

Stetchworth [12] One of the (6-mile) long sleeve-shaped parishes stretching from the clay woods to Newmarket Heath. Newmarket accounts for the main recent story: trees in shelter belts and clumps, a

Stretham Old Engine (*above and opposite*)

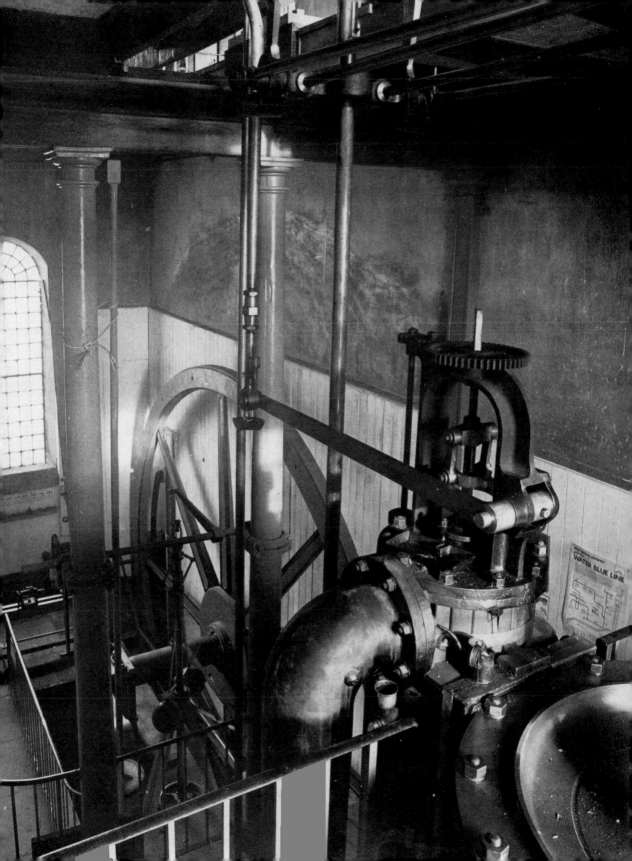

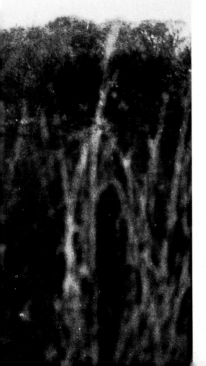

big riding school, the National Stud. Stetchworth Park, smart, 1796, was bought by Lord Ellesmere in 1883. In 1891 Egerton House was built for him and in 1905 he had the White Horse Inn designed by Voysey: now a private house, at the chestnut-shaded junction of village street and Church Lane. Here was the medieval 'camping-close' and a maypole. Old cottages well cared for. *Church* approached through avenue of beeches. Interior a pleasant tie-beamed tunnel, dark despite white-wash. Torch needed to see elaborate graffiti on clunch columns of 15th-century nave arcade, e.g. caricatures of lady and owl, each in elaborate head-dress. 15th-century brass. Two melancholy monuments, each commemorating a youth of 19: one melodramatic, put up by sorrowing sister to Ashton Benyon, 1856: the other, attributed to Abram Storey, occupying whole E end N aisle, to Henry Gorges, *c*.1674. His father Richard, Lord Gorges, managed the Corporation for draining the Bedford Level from 1656: his walled gardens and sum-merhouse survive: house rebuilt in 1796.

Stonea *see* Wimblington

Stow-cum-Quy [12] Stow's church stood well, on a gravel-capped spur projecting S over the former Fulbourn Fen, but spur site obscured by old and new A45s. Quy's church down since Middle Ages. Stow-cum-Quy Fen, to the NW, is a Nature Reserve open to the public. *St Mary's, Stow*, in old red-brick-walled churchyard, shows signs of 1879 restoration outside and in, but not too much. Inside, unusually handsome details: Victorian oak benches and framed and painted Hanoverian arms over chancel arch. Early 15th-century choir screen. The pulpit stair leads up from the fine brass effigy of John Ansty with great sword, four daughters and twelve small sons. He built Quy Hall *c*.1465. (The present Elizabethan house seems to have

made use of four of his roof-trusses. It was given its curious ornamental brick casing in 1868–70.) 12th-century church aisleless, 13th-century dog-tooth ornament in E arch of S arcade, 14th-century window tracery in nave aisles, and arcading in chancel. Victorian arms carved in clunch of S aisle window-jambs. Poor hammerbeam roof.

Stretham [9] takes its name from the Roman road N from Cambridge, though that was submerged from the 4th century to the 17th. Its replacement, turnpiked in 1763, entered the parish at the Royal Oak, now in a lay-by beside a bridge over the Ouse (Old West River), the site of Stretham Ferry for centuries. Market place, a quiet triangle since the village's recent by-pass. A slender stone market-cross has survived, surprisingly, since the early 15th century. W side of market presided over by church and Old Rectory, whose Georgian sash windows mask ranges of the 14th and 16th centuries. *Church*, with tall 14th-century Midland spire, has an unappealing surface from the Victorian restoration. Inside, too, one feels the 'reverent care' of Hugh Pigot, rector 1869–84. Rector's son, Innes Stitt, 19, missing near Arras in March 1918, knew, as a poet, his chances. Good new local brick housing, 1981. A mile S, on the bank of the Old West River, *Stretham Old Engine* demonstrates memorably one process of draining the water from the ever-shrinking peat fen into a river flowing 4 ft above it (12 feet above it in time of flood). A great wooden scoop-wheel, over 37 ft in diameter, is turned by an engine of 1831 (naturally much renewed before diesel replaced it in 1925). Near-by stood a Roman villa, very rare in the fen itself.

Stuntney [9] 'Stunt' means 'steep' in the Fens, as in Lincs., so this isle rose abruptly from the fen. Prosperous eel-fishery in 1086. Hall now earthworks. Shiny renewed black flint walls of *St Cross church* and neo-

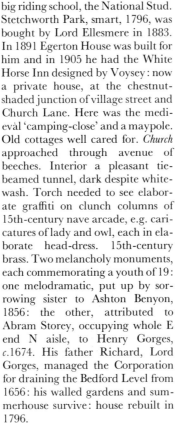

◁ **Stretham** (*top*)
  Sutton from the fen (*left*)

Sutton

Norman details lead to surprises: small Barnack S doorway with lively Norman zig-zag arch and, inside, the font bowl on its 12th-century pedestal is fluted. The Norman zig-zag chancel arch has absurdly been turned 90° to form opening to organ chamber. In 1903, the Victorianized nave was reduced to the present attractive proportions by W.D. Caroe; W Windows commemorate the 1903 benefactor.

Sutton [8] on ridge at SW edge of Isle of Ely, looks S to surprisingly eminent smooth spur of Haddenham's North Hill. Sutton presents an even better view than she enjoys—her 14th-century church tower rises like a monument on the ridge, tall, square above the belfry, then suddenly moulded into two octagons, a sturdy one holding up a delicate corona in tribute to the glorious lantern set above the mother church at Ely earlier in that century.

The predominant material of *St Andrew's church* is sparkling flint and pebble, but there is much grey freestone. The window tracery is another reminder of the cathedral: the 1370-ish form of the E window is if anything more graceful than that added to Ely's Lady Chapel about the same time under Bishop Barnet (1366–73). Here at Sutton, the grand two-storeyed, vaulted, S porch bears on its bosses the arms of Barnet and his successor, Thomas Arundel, Bishop of Ely at 21, Richard II's Chancellor, translated to York in 1388, and then helped Henry IV to power in the revolution of 1399. One point of the story is that the inclusion of the arms of York in this porch makes its building a little later than 1388, rounds off the entire magnificent church in perhaps two decades: another is that the heads of king and bishop carved in the porch must represent Richard II and Arundel. Inside, the late Dec. window tracery is beautiful, on the brink of Perp. Stone seats run all round the aisle walls. Each of the great aisle windows is set in a larger blank arcade, to look as if *double* aisles were intended: this enhances the sense of space and light. Mutilated stone figure of the Virgin. Tablet below tower recalls 'a respectable collar and harness maker of this parish'. The park of Sutton House (25 acres) at present contributes a valuable green calm to this E end of the village. N of the village, the Burystead farmhouse retains the (secularized) 14th-century chapel used by the prior's tenant. Beautiful mounds of newly-fired pink and yellow field drain pipes at brickworks on Ely road. To the W of the village, Sutton's fen spread well beyond the Old and New Bedford Rivers, where, at Sutton Gault (nothing to do with gault clay) Tracked Hovercraft Ltd. briefly established an experimental station.

Swaffham Bulbeck [12] has a doubly romantic name, which shows that it began as a farm of settlers from *Swabia*, then, soon after 1066, the bulk of it became the estate of

◁ *p.184*: (*top*) **Swaffham Prior**; (*bottom*) **Swaffham Bulbeck**, Burgh Hall
p.185: **Swaffham Prior** street (medieval house behind Georgian fronts) and Baldwin Manor

Hugh of *Bolbec*, inland from Harfleur. Proust adjusted that name to Balbec, to evoke all his sense of the Norman coast. Their house here is probably represented by Burgh Hall, now an attractive Wealden house of *c*.1500 within remains of main moat 40–50 ft wide. Broad, aisled *church* largely of clunch, 13th century, much rebuilt in later 14th. Much original timbering in 15th-century nave roof. Thirty-six medieval carved benches, coarse by Suffolk standards, give character to the building. 15th-century N Italian vestment chest of cypress wood serves as S aisle altar. Opposite, a 15th-century house had its open hall divided horizontally in early 16th century. N past the turning to Lode, at a corner Lordship Cottage faces S over a green, and only two front buttresses give a hint of its 13th-century date (improved by good Jacobean carpentry): history obscure. Further N, attractive hamlet *Commercial End* is as big as the parent village. Connected via Swaffham Lode to the Fenland waterways, it flourished by the traffic of heavy goods from the 17th century. Presumably the Lode had earlier fed the old village direct. The Merchant's House is late 17th century, red and buff brick. Opposite, the maltings' kiln, with tiled conical roof, incorporated in pleasant house. To the N again, a vaulted undercroft of *c*.1300 survives from small priory of Benedictine nuns founded by the Bolbecs. The walls of clunch and notably early black flush-flintwork are embodied in an early Georgian brick house; the site of a Roman settlement adjoins. Prehistoric round barrows and ring ditches at the SE end of parish. There the remains of rectangular earthwork round Hare Park mark a hare-warren set up *c*.1605 in aid of royal coursing.

Swaffham Prior [12] Both Swaffhams run in 7-mile strips from near the Icknield Way to the Cam. White Droveway, which supplies the straight boundary between the fens of the two parishes, may well be Roman. This great broad, ditched causeway provides (from Upware) the most impressive approach to Swaffham Prior village. Whereas the Bolbecs held three-quarters of Swaffham Bulbeck, the Prior of Ely held only a third of Swaffham Prior in 1086: another third was held by Hardwin de Scalers, and the last third by 'three of Count Alan of Brittany's Knights'. I see here the explanation of Swaffham Prior's twin churches, by no means identical but set most spectacularly in one churchyard on the 50-ft ridge rising immediately E of the village street. I suppose the first, St Mary's, belonged to Ely, the second, SS Cyriac and Julitta, to the three knights (perhaps also to Scalers but he was based elsewhere). The rare dedication supports this idea. Cyriac, or Cyr, was a child, martyred *c*.304 with his mother Julitta. His cult spread most strongly in the Near East and in France. His best known dedication is that of the school at Versailles which became the St Cyr military academy. The Elizabethan chalice is inscribed 'Soffame Prire othr wyse called Sant Serres.' Not only the grouping, but the architecture of these two churches is unforgettable, and after grave vicissitudes both look very well again. (Parishes united, 1667.) *St Cyr's* suffered most. In ruins in 1805, all but the tower was rebuilt next year in pale-yellow brick by a pupil of Wyatt. Falling into ruin again in the 1970s and open to the Fenland winds, it has been maintained since 1976 by the Redundant Churches Fund. But the 1490s tower is the thing. Round the octagon, a most original pilastered effect is created by corner buttresses rising from carved corbels to pinnacles above the flushwork parapet. The tower and church of St Cyr, delightful in themselves, become so much more so in relation to their

very exciting Norman neighbour, *St Mary's*. Her (most unfeminine) church is entered beneath a truly monumental tower, and here you see what St Cyriac's parishioners had in mind to copy and in their way outdo. The sturdy, square Norman first stage is transformed into an *octagonal Norman second stage*. This most agreeable local form, the octagon tower, which we are apt to attribute to Ely's marvellous example, is already here at Swaffham in the 12th century and may possibly itself have got the idea from the central 'clerestory' of the Round Church in Cambridge. At Swaffham, anyway, we have a Norman octagon and more: in the 13th century, third and fourth stages were added, both sixteen-sided. What a building: like a glorious Roman lighthouse! Well, a Romanesque lighthouse of a Christian kind was intended. In the 14th century, this tower was capped by a large commonplace E Midland stone spire, struck by discriminating lightning in 1767, damaging the nave and leading to the late 18th-century scene in which both churches languished as picturesque ruins. As you enter the superbly refurbished tower of St Mary's now, look right up into the interior: the floors of the upper stages never rebuilt. Then the great broad Romanesque tower archway into the (earlier) Norman nave: 15th-century aisle arcades, weatherworn from the years when all lay open and St Cyr's was used. Since 1979, a practical screen of plain glass fills the tower arch. Brasses include an effigy in wide kneeboots and spurs, 1638. The Allix family, at Swaffham Prior House from 1751, commissioned the blue, green and gold series of windows depicting, as in a family album, Wicken Fen, a World War I trench, etc.: made by Ward and Hughes, designed by T.F. Curtis, Edward VII acceding in SW, Great War ends in NE. View down from among clipped yews of churchyard to white gables of Anglesey House in village street. Manor house sites along the W side, the fen side, of the

Bench ends at **Swavesey** ▷

street. Swaffham Prior House probably succeeds to the manor of 'Baldwins, alias Lees, and Knights', a reference perhaps to those three knights of the Norman Conquest. A house of 1736, opposite the Village Hall, is called Knights Hall. Edwin Muir's cottage faced the churches.

Swavesey [11] *St Andrew's church*'s grandeur, beauty and interest are sensed at once from outside. Inside the very fine S doorway (five architectural orders, early 14th century), first impression is of elegance—the panelled bowl of Perp. font on a tall curved panelled pedestal, and the six bays of tall arches dividing the nave from the N aisle and the great S aisle are deeply impressive. Then comes the extraordinary clue to the long story of this church's magnificence. In S chancel chapel, what was the outer SE corner of the nave before the aisles were added, has stones laid in the 'long-and-short' manner that invariably proclaims pre-Conquest masonry. Traces of similar quoins may be seen at the NE corner of the nave. This sets out the very large proportions of the Saxon nave of what was probably a minster. Swavesey was one of those royal manors belonging to Edith the Fair, mother of Harold's children, which passed to Count Alan of Brittany and Richmond (see Fen Drayton, etc.). Count Alan gave this ?minster church to be a cell of the abbey of SS Sergius and Bacchus (in France, Serge et Bach) in Angers. St Serge, with its incomparably fine 13th-century Gothic choir, seems to have maintained two or three monks here and a prior-vicar. The names of the late 13th- and early 14th-century priors are invariably French and suggest unsuspected links between Swavesey and Angers. We look with renewed interest at the church. In the S wall of the S chancel chapel, notice remains of a 13th-century attached shaft and arch of piscina or sedilia at a much lower level than that of the Perp. one that replaced it. Here is proof of the great width of the 13th-century S aisle

before all the transitional E.E.-Dec. work replaced it—the handsome tall S aisle windows. 14th-century sedilia and rich armrests and misericords in ?early 15th-century stalls; bench ends; roofs. In S chancel chapel, monument of great distinction, by Edward Marshall (and possibly Nicholas Stone), *c.*1631. Elizabethan Manor House near by retains hall screen. To the S, surprising vestiges of a seigneurial borough were first demonstrated in J.R. Ravensdale's admirable *History on your doorstep* (BBC, 1982). In 1230, the Zouches got Swavesey and in 1244 a grant of market and fair. Market Street widens out as market place; it ends in a vanished dock such as supplied heavy goods in so many fen-edge villages before the railways. What distinguishes Swavesey is that The Old Market House physically represents the control of the market from an actual castle, slender remains of which lie to W.

Tadlow [14] Approached up a steep grass path, St Giles's church sustained its present character from Butterfield in 1860. Tudor plank-and-muntin granary at Tadlow Towers rebuilt at Wandlebury by Cambs Preservation Society, since 1971.

Teversham [12] church, beside a small green, has view over meadows to towers and spires of Cambridge. Bold stiff flowers and foliage capitals of E.E. S doorway gives a foretaste of one great delight of the interior: nave arcades with capitals by the same carver—stylized flowers and stems in a manner that returned in *art nouveau*. Finely carved Elizabethan alabaster tomb. Remains of colour in panelled painted ceiling behind tall tower arch. Lacey roodscreen, *c.* 1400, with traces of colour. There are also traces of an earlier stone screen. In the chancel, two rewards: delicate fragments of sedilia, and the rhythmically-panelled Victorian roof, very ingeniously arranged. Bold frieze of angels with banner inscriptions. Choir stalls, ?Edwardian, well carved, with iron

candlesticks, perhaps by local blacksmith, his forge just E of church. Jacobean pulpit bought in 1891 from Cherry Hinton church, next parish.

Thetford, Little [9] 'Thiutford' *c.*972 and already 'Liteltedford' in 1086. 'Tedford' implies a major river-crossing, a sort of trunk-ford. This may refer to a crossing of the Cam before it was joined, *below* the ford, by the Old West river. That river was almost certainly brought here artificially, at an undiscovered time: Thetford's name suggests a piece of medieval rather than Roman engineering, which rendered the ford impassable and created this village's charming 'backwater' character. In a pleasant small churchyard beside the village street, a sunny buff-coloured ragstone church, towerless, has 14th-century nave window tracery. Stone and brick rectory retains two 14th-century rooms. A peculiar *round house* of dark red brick and thatch, said to be Georgian, looks older. No 31 well designed: local gault brick.

Thorney's [5] 10th-century name, 'isle of thorns', explains its irresistible appeal to early Christian ascetics. The blueprint for the first monastic establishment here was adopted during the speeches after the consecration of Peterborough vividly described in the *Anglo-Saxon Chronicle* for 656. Thorney's earliest name, *Ancarig*, means 'isle of the anchorite'; clearly, it had already found its vocation. The site was granted, and soon Thorney had its own saints, the alliterative anchorites Tancred, martyr, Torhtred, confessor, and their sister Tova. Such golden age saints were venerated when an abbey was resurrected here in 972, a whole century after its obliteration by the Danes. The great bishop Ethelwold of Winchester now took the lead in establishing a regular Benedictine abbey, equipping it with the relics of these local saints, including Huna of Chatteris.

Thorney Abbey, west front ▷

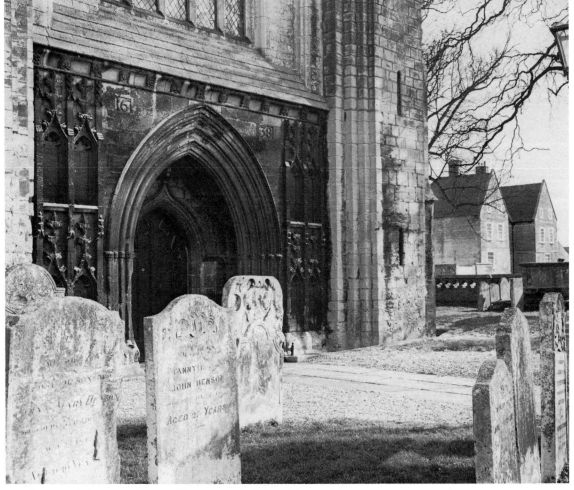

Thorney Abbey, west doorway. House occupies E side of former cloister

Three altars Ethelwold consecrated at Thorney: at the E end to St Mary, at the N porch to St Benedict, 'patron of all monks', and the western altar in the nave for the use of 'the lay clergy and the people', to St Peter. So, at the Dissolution here at Thorney, it was the people's nave that survived. What was destroyed and dispersed can hardly be imagined. Altered and reduced as it is, the W front is still deeply impressive. The nave is the rebuilding by abbot Gontier, of Le Mans and Battle, who completed it with W towers and stair-turrets in 1109. It may originally have had three great round W triumphal arches such as Lincoln already had and as Peter-borough acquired much later in the century. The flanking arches came down with the aisles. The surviving middle arch has, from the 15th century, a gigantic Perp. W window, walled up and fitted with a more modest 'Perp.' window of 1638. The tops of the two Norman stair-turrets were beautifully remodelled in the 15th century, crowned by parapeted and panelled octagons—again that powerful Ely motif! The octagons are linked by a very handsome horizontal screen of nine niches, each containing a well-preserved stone figure from—probably—a selection of founding fathers and patron saints. Inside, one misses the aisles acutely: without them, the lovely sturdy Norman arcades of Barnack seem pointless. In 1579 146 tons of stone from here were shipped off from Guyhirne for the new chapel of Corpus Christi, Cambridge, itself now replaced. The 1841 'Norman' transepts are of stone from Wansford, its brown contrasting with the Barnack. The very dominant E window is a copy of the 13th-century Canterbury glass. Six pleasant panels of Swiss glass, various Huguenot memorials, and a floor-stone commemorating Mr George Smith, Steward to the Earl of Bedford, 1651, remind us of Thorney's central role in the creation of the great Bedford Level. To the S of the church, a square close with round lawn marks the site of the cloister and, behind the wall on the W side, the large stone house—Elizabethan and mid 17-century—was the Bedfords' *pied-à-terre* here, 1550–1910. Now National Trust property in two private tenancies, it may be seen by written request. Its quoins are of re-used abbey stone and its beautiful roofs of ?Collyweston stone slates show up the Welsh-blue slate roofs of the good stone houses opposite. The blue slate enhances the yellow-ish brick of many of the Victorian Bedford Estate cottages, whose de-sign and variety still throw an un-favourable light on so much of our rural housing design. The Victorian duke was proud of his claim—no tenant evicted, excellent public health, minimal crime, no pauper-ism: the historian of Victorian England called it 'the most successful experiment in social organisation that England had so far seen' (G.M. Young).

Thriplow's [14] last syllable means 'burial-mound', perhaps a reference to the *Tumulus* marked on OS maps just SE of the church, barely dis-cernible now. The village below is known to have been occupied in the Iron Age, and to the S the parish rises again to Thriplow Heath, where thirteen more barrows are also probably of that period. Here, on Thursday 10 June, 1647, another Iron Age scene is more fully recorded. After a 'Day of Fasting and Humiliation', Cromwell's army of 21,000 men assembled on this Heath, was consulted regiment by regiment about its own future, and so came into being as the political force dictating to City, Parliament and Crown: 'The remarkablest Army that ever wore steel in this world', Carlyle called it. That after-noon, they moved off along the Ick-nield Way, to the alarm of London. They were too busy to bother with the *church*, which still had several windows full of painted glass till Victorian times. It is a cruciform, largely 13th-century building, redo-lent of Sir Gilbert Scott (1877).

Thorney Abbey, church interior

What is left of the screen is worth noting, for it was the pattern pre-scribed for the new screen of Great St Mary's, Cambridge, in 1518. Pleasant wall monument to Edward Lucas and family, 1601, of Bassets, a 16th-century jettied house, with carved bressumers and (inhabited) dovehouse in rear: beautifully kept and gardened, one of the best exam-ples of its kind in Cambridgeshire. Pantiled stone smithy on the green. *Townsend Springs* was designed for Lord Walston by Sir Leslie Martin in attractive landscape.

Toft's [11] village centre is strung along lanes laid out in a grid, some of it attractive. The church is gloomy and largely rebuilt, alabas-ter figures; dreadful Victorian glass.

Trumpington's [11] old village as-pect is retained as one approaches the church past Old House, red-brick, step-gabled, string-coursed and 'Dutch'. Big, impressive church, severely restored by Butter-field, has rust-coloured cladding of Bath stone. Interior at once noble and delicate, but Butterfield has imposed Victorian urban feel. Side chapels N and S of nave aisles. Earl-iest parts of all this are *c.*1200. Then the main work was done a century later, presumably before the death of Sir Roger de Trumpington II, in 1326, whose tomb, with famous

brass effigy, is incorporated in the E bay of the N chapel. The brass has been shown (1971) to have been made for Sir Giles, who survived his son (Roger II) and altered it in his honour. Untidy monumental insertions on S side of Sir Roger's tomb-chest add effectively to sense of antiquity so much reduced by Butterfield; so does the fine array of four 13th-century stone coffin lids. The chancel, 13th century, is of smooth clunch with groined and embossed roof, very crudely daubed with colour; E window tracery filled with a visually disastrous combination of jumbled medieval glass and red opaque plain glass: too bright. If only the decorative grisaille of the chancel's SW window were copied. A N chancel window contains 14th-century figures of Peter and Paul: the triangular panel, a three-bodied leopard in a tracery light, is ascribed to Edmund Crouchback, Earl of Lancaster, 1245–96. Tablet set on four medieval corbels commemorates benefaction for poor boys, 1681. Opposite, Francis Pemberton, 1697, with flowing draperies and cherubs' heads; Pemberton hatchment; monument, with mean frame, to F.P.C. Pemberton, d. 1914 in Belgium, is an early work of Eric Gill, who later did reliefs on village war memorial cross. N side of churchyard, base of medieval cross: on S side, *Cedrus atlantica* and two 14th-century clunch windows removed by Butterfield. Large red-brick Georgian vicarage to the E, seen in group with church from courtyard of *Anstey Hall*. Distinguished late 17th-century house (earlier core) takes name from Georgian owners; Victorian expansion, and now government offices. Little Lodge houses RCHM offices, to which this book owes much. To the W, at the bridge, a public footpath leads to *Byron's Pool*. Woodland walk includes in winter jarring industrial views E to a Plant-Breeding Station. River itself delightful, but at Byron's

Tydd St Giles

Pool the weir has been supplied, unbelievably, with bent-necked concrete posts and chain-link fencing. The poet's swimming prowess included three miles under Blackfriars and Westminster bridges.

Tydd St Giles [2] marches with Lincolnshire to W and N, with Norfolk to the E. The W boundary, Lady Nunn's Old Eau, takes its name from Lady Noon, whose husband was commissioner of sewers in 1391. This is part of the Shire Drain, which has separated two counties and two dioceses since Anglo-Saxon times, when it may earlier have separated two kingdoms. It also separates Tydd St Giles from Tydd St Mary (Lincs.) which was probably the original nucleus. The hamlet of *Four Gotes* took its (Elizabethan) name from the meeting there of four main drains: 'gote' is Old English for watercourse, as is the 'Ea' which was Frenchified to 'Eau.' What Tydd means, no one knows. Near the hamlet of *Tydd Gote*, Hannath Hall, Elizabethan, the best-looking house in the parish, takes its name from its owners *c*.1800. Another Elizabethan house, Hornfield, stands to W. In the main village, Kirkgate House, essentially Tudor, gables ivyclad, suffered from fall of tree: home of several generations of Fishers from 1320. In 1868, rector rebuilt rectory from design by brother, Gilbert Scott, who clean removed the Georgian *chancel*, and reroofed and reseated the *nave* and its aisles, which are remarkable. A few good headstones survive including e.g. Sarah Lambert's signed Walton Wisbech, 1864. The *church's* W façade and entrance are a delightful mid-14th-century composition. Inside, unusually spindly Romanesque columns in the aisle arcades, Richard I's time, or John's: the W bay is a little later, and may indicate replacement of a Norman W tower. 13th-century cross-slab commemorates Sir John Fysuer of the Kirkgate family. He may have had a hand in rebuilding of tower 16 yards to SE of nave, presumably on sounder

footings (cf. W. Walton, Long Sutton, etc. near by). Inscription on a nave column in 14th-century French records that Richard, First Priest, began this 'piler', the general rebuilding of 'the pile' then: 14th-century tracery makes one miss the glass recorded here before the Civil War. Carvings on font, allegedly sloth and gluttony emerging from leaves. First two stages of tower, 13th-century, stone, well buttressed and top stage late Perp. of pink gault bricks: ground stage open-arched (but filled in on two sides). Views from top.

Upwell and **Outwell** [6] Their cottages and houses face each other across two parallel roads that wind along opposite banks of a sluggish river: they do this continuously for over 4 miles. This waterway is the source of their name and of their history. In Anglo-Saxon times it and its villages were called *Welle*, 'stream', and early in the Middle Ages, *Upwell* was used for the upstream (southerly) village and parish, *Outwell* for the outflow end. But what river do we see? The OS map shows that the 'Old Croft River' meandered N from Littleport to Welney and thereafter provided the county boundary through Upwell, Outwell and Elm to the edge of Wisbech itself. This 'Old Croft River' is the Old Ouse, worming its way round from Ely. Having the county boundary in the middle of the river has not simplified Upwell and Outwell's story. Their impressive medieval churches, for instance, both stand firmly on the Norfolk side. Cambridgeshire has about half of Upwell's 17,000 acres, and of Outwell's 3,000, mostly fen, but drained and scored by other waterways that explain the presence of these communities. The 'Old Nene' also comes into the picture. From at least the 13th century, and conceivably in Roman times, a way of keeping the Fens drained *and* of providing waterways deep enough for ships to trade inland as far as Northamptonshire seemed to be to deflect

the S branch of the Nene *eastward* from Peterborough, to pick up the Ouse and so gain volume and momentum to reach the sea at Lynn instead of Wisbech. These were early experiments, leading haltingly towards Vermuyden's bold creation of the parallel 'Bedford' rivers in the 17th century, and they tended to pivot on Upwell and Outwell. The Old Nene was steered across through Ramsey, Benwick and March to Upwell, and then at Outwell it was deflected E and S again, through Well Creek (on the line of the modern A1122) to Nordelph, Denver, then on to Wiggenhall and Lynn, then on to this. This sounds a devious enough route, but in the early 14th century it was clearly regarded as very direct and a great improvement on the alternative route from Upwell, then *back* up the Old Croft river to Welney and Littleport, and thence to Lynn. By 1549, both alternatives were still in use, but increasingly silted: the more 'direct' route, Outwell-Nordelph, was blamed for the yearly drowning in Upwell and Outwell of 8,000 acres of marsh and pasture and great damage to their fields. Already there was a hankering after a return to the ancient Wisbech outfall, but by now the sea had withdrawn from Wisbech, except for occasional terrifying visitations. The digging of Popham's Eau in 1609, due E and W from the bottom of Plaw Field, did much to relieve Upwell and Outwell. Vermuyden did the rest. Where the Old Nene meets B1412, Marmont Priory Farm occupies the site of a priory, or chantry, of three Gilbertine canons, founded in 1204: named after Marmande, beside the river Garonne.

Many seemly and substantial houses line the old river, now sluggish and weedy: several have plain Georgian fronts, and Georgian or older rears, but they seem to have seen better days. To the S, Euximoor Fen was Yekeswellemoor in the 15th century: 'the marsh by the cuckoo's stream'. See also *Christchurch*.

Waterbeach: Denny Abbey from NW, showing W doorway and blocked clerestory of 12th-century nave

Waterbeach [12] was originally just 'beche', a 'valley', a reference to the adjacent Cam. The 'Water-' was added to distinguish it from its drier progeny, which became Land-beach. Ravensdale's *Liable to Floods* (1974) shows medieval Waterbeach as a 'small fen archipelago' reaching from S end of the Roman 'Car Dyke' canal some five miles N to Stretham, including the former monastic islands of Denny and Elmeney. Much occupied by airfield to N. Broad green at village centre once formed middle of E side of a triangular green four of five times larger. The simple ungothic brick Baptist chapel beside the rowan tree had its foundation stone laid in 1863 by Charles Spurgeon. At 18, he became pastor here, 1852–4, in a little thatched chapel, drawing people to hear him and baptizing them in the river: soon the most popular preacher in England. The *church* has sturdy late-Norman aisle piers. E of the church opposite The Star, lay

the medieval dock. Only earthworks remain of an abbey of 'Poor Clares'—well-to-do female Franciscans vowed to poverty. Founded with four Sisters from France in 1294, it was moved to Denny in 1351. *Denny Abbey*, in the care of the Department of the Environment, is open April–September inclusive 9.30–7: mostly embodied in a Tudor and Georgian farmhouse, the details of which have been largely sacrificed in the interests of recovering the medieval remains. They reflect a very unusual story, beginning *c*.1160 with the chamberlain of the Brittany-Richmonds (q.v., Swavesey). He founded a cell of Ely on *Elmeney*, the little island N. of Denny. The monks found the floodwaters distracting and moved to the safer island of Denny. They built enough nave to buttress crossing of church; then *c*.1170, Ely handed the place over to the *Knights Templars*. These brethren put in the W doorway and made an infirmary

for old Templars. At their suppression in 1308, Sir John Creke (*see* Westley Waterless) took charge, and soon Denny was made over to the Countess of Pembroke who remodelled the buildings to receive the *Poor Clares* from their small abbey S of the parish church. The old apsidal chancel was replaced by a large new church, destroyed in the Dissolution. Upper chambers were created in the old crossing, transepts and nave, and a first-floor hall built W of the S transept—all serving presumably as suitable lodging for Lady Pembroke and her successors as abbess, and forming the later country house. She moved the cloister away to the E of her new church: along its N walk her new refectory, with its pulpit-alcove, like a porch, survived as a barn—mainly clunch, but an intelligible ruin. By 1379 there were forty-one nuns here, comparable with about forty-six monks at Ely. High religious tone. The most notable post-Dissolution addition to

the fabric is the great chimney-stack
on the S gable beside the 14th-cen-
tury newel stair: limestone and red
brick in chequer-pattern like Sawston's. Great E arch of the 12th-cen-
tury crossing is the dominant feature
of the E front of the house. Pleasant
mixture of old building stone. In
Chittering, a medieval hamlet on the
A10, not much of a place, a section
of the metalled Roman Akeman
Street runs under an orchard, and
the shapes of their irregular fields
are still visible in the fen.

Wendy *see* Shingay

Wentworth's [8] *St Peter's church*,
largely rebuilt in 1868, but a piece
of Anglo-Saxon carved interlace (?
from a cross) is embodied in the outside S wall of nave. More notable,
in N wall of sanctuary, a bold early
12th-century carving of the patron,
St Peter, with key and book and that
original tonsure. An abbreviated
'PETROS' is inscribed behind his
head, but lately no one seems to
have noticed who he is.

Westley Waterless [12] is one of
the long sleeve-shaped parishes of
Radfield Hundred. It was 'west-
leah', west-clearing in the clay
woodland already *c.*1045: as a settlement and parish it was early
carved from Burrough Green, which
is what it lies 'west' of. 'Waterless'
was added in the later Middle Ages
and implies not drought but 'water-
leys', water-meadows. Where they
were is hard to see: just E of the
church? And the eleven vines,
whose production of clusters is
recorded in graffiti with arabic nu-
merals early in the 14th century in
one of the S window surrounds:
were they churchyard growths to
supply *vino sacro*? Round belltower
fell in 1855. Beautiful brass memorial to Sir John de Creke and his wife
Alyne, identifiable by his small
shield: 'on a fesse, three lozenges
vair'.

◁ **Wentworth**: St Peter in his church
Westley Waterless: the De Creke ▷
brasses

Weston Colville [15] began probably as the farm 'west' of Carlton: both are recorded in the late 10th century. The Colvilles' male line had it *c.*1200–1369: their moat $\frac{1}{4}$ mile NE of church, at edge of Covens Wood. Another manor, Leverers, based perhaps on Pound Farm, is represented in church by Sir Richard Leverer's brass memorial, 1428, showing him in his plate-armour, with wheel-spurs, standing in his flower garden, with wife and priest-son. Present Hall, early Georgian. Pleasant view of church and village from W. Church, recorded *c.*1044, recased in beautiful flint *c.*1825, with odd vertical panelling in cream-coloured brick on chancel, tower and E wall of nave. Base of medieval cross S of chancel, beside 13th-century coffin-lid; headstones organized; bare barnlike nave within. J.R. Withers, 'the Cambridgeshire poet', born here and moved to Fordham: published 1856–69.

Westwick [11] Small parish with pub, stream and orchards, Hall with earthworks opposite, but no church. Name shows original 'dairy-farm', 'west' of Cottenham: by 1086 there were two farms, mainly arable. E boundary along green bridleway, once the Cambridge-Ely highway, crosses Oakington-Cottenham road at Lamb's Cross.

West Wickham *see* Wickham, West

West Wratting *see* Wratting, West

Whaddon [14] Pleasantly watered, its outer bounds include the Ashwell Cam and its Bassingbourn tributary with the S end of the great Wimpole avenue, including The Octagon, a large pool. 'Whaddon organs' are edible frogs (otherwise 'Cambridgeshire nightingales'). Old Rectory at foot of W tower of *church*. Late-Dec. early-Perp. nave (? *c.*1375): great grace and nobility within. Chancel arch has E.E. dog-tooth ornament. Remains of Perp. traceried wood screen. Tomb-chest of John d'Eschallers, last of Norman family

◁ **Whittlesey**: St Mary's

△ **Whittlesey** market place

Whittlesey. The best approach: from the north, along Delph Dyke ▽

here four centuries. 3rd Earl of Hardwick's hatchment, 1834, served as inn sign at Arrington, then hung over Melbourne paper shop till brought here.

Whittlesey [5] A little town on a long fen 'island' (3 miles by ½ mile), one of Ely's 'off-shore islands', but in full view of Peterborough, and crossed S-N by the Ramsey to Thorney and Crowland road. From late Saxon times, Ely had the royal rights here, but manorial rights over only the St Andrew's manor: Thorney had the other manor, St Mary's, with one of the most perfectly designed towers and spires in Christendom. Just S of it, the manor house retains a medieval chimney-stack. Forty much more prominent chimneys signal the brickworks fed by an Oxford Clay outlier, and contribute to the Fletton scent of sulphur oxides in the westerly wind. The mysterious Roman Fen Causeway runs E-W across the N side of the 'isle', along Low Road, then on a gravel causeway E over the dark peat to Eastrey, Coates (with its great green), Eldernell and beyond. A square street-pattern may represent ramparted early defences: Wallcroft on the W, Stonald and Bassenhally roads to N, Inham's Lane in the E, and the King's Dike, etc. to the S. Despite closeness to Peterborough, a very jolly market continues on Friday mornings. As at Thorney, there are substantial houses of 'Lower Lincolnshire' limestone and an unmistakable Northamptonshire look. The charming market cross has in its stone columns a pink blush it might have acquired in a Ketton quarry. *St Mary's* tower and spire, overlooking the market (and all else for miles around) is one of the sights of England and is best approached by the walled footpath from the W. Only two blemishes mar its perfection : the recent dismissal of the old familiar headstones from the great churchyard to the skirting walls, where they are meaningless, and the siting

of the old church clock so as to conceal the arches of the belfry-louvres, instead of resting it on the base-line of those openings. All else is superlatively good, right up to the proudest and most endearing of weathercocks. I wonder that no one has observed the quiet tribute paid by the designer of this masterpiece, built on a Thorney manor, to Ely's best known tower-motif; by offsetting at 45° the top stages of the corner buttresses on which the corner pinnacles rest, he has created the definite suggestion of an octagon. This is fundamental to the effect of the tower—to its irresistible combination of shapeliness with strength. It is sometimes compared with Oundle and Kettering, but has not their massive squareness. It is nearest to, yet an improvement on, Rushden in Northamptonshire. The material is Jurassic stone, apparently from two quarries or, at least, two seams: a sandy-buff colour to the top of the three niches, then silver grey through the belfry to the top of the spire. The colour change is gentle, helped perhaps by weathering : it imparts an air of something like natural growth. Much of the interior seems to follow a fire of 1244. In 1862, Gilbert Scott restored the chancel aisle—it became 'Sir Harry's chapel' in honour of Sir Harry Smith, one of thirteen children of a Whittlesey surgeon and among the most engaging of Wellington's soldiers. G.G. Adams's lively bust of him is based on one he did in 1849. His birthplace in London Street is named Aliwal House, after a headlong charge against the Sikhs beside the Sutlej river, a very long way from the Nene. London Street and Paradise Lane are on the way to *St Andrew's church*. Churchyard green but with headstones tidied away, pointless. Interior creamwashed all over, which reduces the effect of the stone structure—graceful tall Perp. aisle colonnades. Georgian wall monuments. Richard Mason, vicar of both churches, was commemorated in a friendly way in 1703.

Whittlesford [14] A flourishing village with small industries, commuting, and pleasant riverside features. *St Andrew's church* among meadows is down a lane and past a *cottage orneé*, thatched and with charming window-lights. Overgrown moat of vanished medieval manor house E of church, and mill beyond that. Just outside E end of churchyard, a lovely hot-air balloon of a stone urn commemorates 'young' Mr Ebenezer Hollick, who died aged 87 in 1828. The Hollicks had the mill and were Baptists, which is why they would not be buried quite inside the churchyard. Old Ebenezer built the very handsome mill house in 1763. Four years later, about forty people were dipped near the mill. The *church*, of warm buff rubblestone, was plastered at one time: Norman nave, crossing and lower part of central tower, heavily stone-battlemented chancel, and now unbattlemented S aisle. Broad Perp. belfry openings chop off lower ?lancet-windows, and the tower is finished by a small, relatively recent lead spire. The stonework round the Norman S tower window is carved with what has been identified as a *sheila-na-gig*: a human-headed male animal and encouraging naked lady : set too high to influence churchgoers. Extremely rustic, reeling S porch, timbered, given by Henry Cyprian *c*.1350. Interior of great interest and delight. The S chapel seems to have been John the Baptist's: a 14th-century guild in his honour raised money for church repairs and his *guildhall* survives at the crossroads in the village—a jettied early Tudor house, over-restored. From his S chapel, a collection of sharply-carved fragments has been preserved from an alabaster altar, with traces of gilding and red and green paint: now in nave wall. Either side of crossing, the Ten Commandments framed in charming rustic rocaille. Amid the later medieval arcading of the crossing there are traces of Norman stone-carving, also graffiti, including a fine archer with drawn bow in base of attached N column. Plaque recalls a Cambridge grocer of 37, 1723, 'an encourager of Charity-Schools' in Cambridge and here. Superb iron-bound chest lies in vestry. Approach to *Mill House* past a large green with attractive play area for children under beech-trees, etc. Large fine 18th- and 19th-century mill buildings of lovely red brick on W side, misguidedly painted over on stream side.

Whittlesford Bridge *see* Duxford

Wicken [12]
In the village street, opposite the end of Chapel Lane, an old tree-shaded house, with low thatch warm round its dormers and stout gault chimneys, is numbered 45. It was James Wentworth-Day's home. No one who has done so will forget opening his *History of the Fens* and reading his description of their indefinable smell coming through the window at night as he lay under that roof-thatch: 'the scent of reeds and peaty waters, of sallows and meadowsweet, of rotten lily-pads—and of fish: it belonged to an untamed, undrained England'. Wicken (the name means 'dairy-farms') occupies a strip of land slightly above the level of Soham's (vanished) mere to the N and Burwell's (now vanished) Adventurers' Fen to the S. To their great good fortune (and ours), Wentworth-Day and the neighbouring Burwell doctor, the late Eric Ennion, were born in the early years of this century just in time to enjoy and record the reclaiming of Adventurers' Fen by the waters during the farming slump of the 1920s and '30s, and before its 'final' expensive rescue in the wartime interests of sugar-beet. Such experiences as theirs led to the steady acquisition, from 1899 onward, of parts of *Wicken Fen* by the National Trust. It now owns 730 acres, one of the best known nature reserves in the kingdom to both amateur and professional naturalists. Its ecological development is at once studied and presented to the general public, and it is good to see sedge and reed being cut, as of old, and shipped out along Wicken Lode for use by craftsmen. But visitors must not come expecting to see 'spreading meres and pike-haunted pools' and the bitterns creeping through the reeds 'like brown ghosts'. For unluckily, Wicken is not a true fen: it stands higher than the surrounding peat fen, and its 'Mere' (just over the Burwell boundary in Adventurers' Fen) has had to be dug and watered artificially. But that mere and its bird life are still worth watching from the Tower Hide. The last forlorn survivor of the many thousand drainage wind-pumps of Cambridgeshire was re-assembled here from Adventurers' Fen in 1956. In the *village*, the older part of the yellow-brick Maid's Head is neatly thatched with reed and given a decorative cap of the harder-wearing sedge: good 'plug' for Wicken Fen. Derelict smock grain-mill speaks for itself. Cross Green is reminder of market, granted 1331, with three-day fair of St Laurence whose *parish church* was built surprisingly near the fen edge, perhaps for the convenience of getting the stone delivered across Soham Mere and up the canal still visible behind the cemetery. Anyway, the N aisle has leant outwards so much that the piers have had to be buttressed, and the Perp. roof replaced by new pine. Two delightful small brasses to Peytons; the burial here of Cromwell's able fourth son, Henry, his Lord Deputy in Ireland, brings us to Spinney 'Abbey' and Wicken's manor. *Spinney 'Abbey'* is yet another of the monastic foundations Cambridgeshire owed to the household and family of the Count of Brittany: in the early 13th century, manor and church went to endow a small priory of Austin canons at the W end of the village. By 1301 there were seven canons, two to say mass daily in the parish church, and an alms-house for seven poor old men. Hall replaced by present farmhouse by B. Taylor in 1775: name and date carved in beautiful stone re-used to front the S and E sides. Pleasant site with garden, orchard and paddock sloping down to Wicken Fen. *Upware*'s great drainage pump is now electrified. In the 1850s, a celebrated donnish club known as the Upware Republic was established in the homely old 'Five Miles From Anywhere—No Hurry' riverside inn. In 1980, a new road-housey 'Five Miles' inn—with restaurant and marina has replaced it.

Wickham, West [15]
is a broad arable parish of gentle clay slopes. Three pre-Conquest nuclei have very old English names: Wickham itself, Streetly Hall and Yen Hall. Yen Hall was *eanheale*, 'lambs' corner', in 974. *Wickham church* looks austere among beautiful tall limes and beeches: gravely restored 1898, being cheerfully refurbished 1975. Well-proportioned square tower, tall nave and choir. Four-bay tie-beam roof being stripped of dark stainer. Elaborately carved arms of Queen Anne.

Wilbraham, Great and Little [12]
in open country, are crossed by Icknield Way and Street Way, and Little Wilbraham has one of the extraordinary series of long straight boundaries laid out, very early, at right-angles to those prehistoric tracks. The Temple in *Great Wilbraham* marks the dairy and sheep farm run here by the Templars (then after 1308 by the Hospitallers): present house Elizabethan. Village charming; modest infilling, and the old cottages well preserved—for instance, Lufters and Whitethorn near the church. Old man mowing church-yard grass and boys playing football in field over the wall. Fine early Gothic features of the *church* in tune with general French influences in 13th century, focused here by French Templars, Malauney, Peyte-vyn, Thomas Toulouse, etc. Approach through young lime avenue. Outside, N wall shows where Norman nave and chancel received E.E. extension to chancel, and transepts at the junction. The addition of a W tower in 15th century deflects

thought of possible central tower until one gets inside and sees, after the dignified Norman font, impressive E.E. crossing arches, with remains of red decoration and painted shields. Beyond, triple E lancets full of Kempe glass of 1900. In tower arch, Tudor panelled oak screen. Ward monuments, Strawberry Hill Gothick. *Little Wilbraham* stands on slight rise above stream. Old Rectory, red brick, glazed pantiles, handsome, 1770: crinkle-crankle wall round kitchen garden. Near S porch of *church*, monumental base of churchyard cross, and minute Norman window beside large Perp. one; 15th-century S door carved with shields of local grandees—Burgh, two Lisles, Bourchier. Interior bare. Three carved oak figures from late 14th-century roof carry a book, a lute, a shawm. The composer Christopher Tye held this living in the 1560s (q.v., Doddington). Brass. Spirited royal arms. *Six Mile Bottom* is a hollow 6 miles from Newmarket, to which 6-mile races were run: 8-mile races began at Fleam Dyke, and there were also 4-mile races. 1933 Italianate mortuary church with views of pine-gridded downs.

Wilburton [8] stands just E of Haddenham on its ridge, with fen running S to the river and N, now that it has the 1,800 acres of Grunty Fen that it shared with six neighbours. *The Burystead*, the old manor house, is a late Elizabethan brick house, thoroughly renovated since 1974. Splendid brick-gabled barn. To the N a new manor house built *c.*1650 was replaced by Pugin, *c.*1850, in brick with stone window tracery, now a school. The *church*, St Peter's, occupies an unusual position in the middle of the village, the main street dividing to leave it on a quiet, tree-shaded traffic island. The view of it from the E is particularly pleasant: honey-coloured ragstone from the local Lower Greensand outlier (with septaria and other erratics) framing the broad late 15th-century E window, stepped buttresses, S porch, tower and small lead spire; and to

the right, sharing the shade, Bell-gables on Church Lane, with tall red-brick bell-shaped gable-end, elegant white sash windows and cornice. (All this at present marred by a poor lychgate and a piffling concrete lamp-standard bearing a No Entry sign.) Other notable houses. The S porch, with room over and brick floor, leads into a delightful broad nave. Two roof bosses are carved with the arms of Bishop Alcock (1486–1500), and the beams arch-braced by spandrels carved with cocks on globes. A wooden cock on a globe is actually hanging from the centre boss, in case anyone doubts under whose aegis the roof was made. S and N walls are delicately arcaded to suggest (perhaps on the Sutton model) the greater width of aisles. The beautiful Perp. chancel, too, has windows set in arcaded walls. Each side of the E window, a canopied niche bears a shield: in the N side, that of Alcock. The bishop, rather than St Peter the patron, is plainly symbolized, too, by cocks looking more like eagles, in place of cusps on the central arch of the wooden chancel screen. On the chancel wall are fixed some panels of an altar tomb and a magnificent brass, 1477, also effigies of early Tudor families. Two faded bishops painted on nave wall represent St Blaise, patron of wool-combers, and St Leger, a 7th-century political victim. Next to them, a brilliant war-memorial window—golds, crimsons, blues—is signed by rebus, M. Rose 1921.

Willingham [11] is a large, curiously M-shaped fenside village, unselfconscious, with pleasant Georgian and older houses among the others. Two objects of special interest: Belsar's Hill and the church. Belsar's Hill, an inconspicuous oval earthwork, 880 ft at its broadest, lies athwart the main medieval approach from Cambridge to Aldreth Causeway and Ely. It may be the remains of an Iron Age fort, echoing Arbury's function at the Cambridge end. It seems likely that it was used in the

Conqueror's attack on Hereward (q.v., Cottenham, Haddenham). In 1221 its name was *Bellasise*, 'lovely seat', a sample of Norman-French irony. Between 996 and 1001 someone gave Willingham (and land at Cottenham) to Ely, and with it this awkward military problem: how to defend it, an outpost beyond Aldreth Causeway? In that role, Belsar's Hill could be the 'Aldreth Castle' referred to in Stephen's reign: there seems to be no sign of any such thing in Aldreth itself. Naturally, Ely's long ownership affected the building of Willingham *church*, though not directly the design of the spire, a grey ashlar Hunts. type of landmark—a 14th-century beacon eagerly looked for on the adventure S through the fen from Ely. (The five bells date only from 1775, but there were earlier ones.) The high quality of the interior certainly suggests the episcopal connection. (Key at Post Office.) First, elaborate fragments of Romanesque stone carving, now built into porch, suggest a showy Norman building. The S door opens on to a colourful interior: a sort of Etruscan red *trompe-l'oeil* cusping over an arch of the aisle arcade and the same red in the wooden S parclose screen, and then a painted pattern in the recess of a W lancet window. The aisles are broad, $6\frac{1}{2}$ yards to the nave's 7, and well roofed, and the 14th-century wooden parclose in the N aisle has its original pattern of pretty green popinjays. The chancel is of collegiate proportions: presumably, from the sedilia, a 13th-century extension of the Norman one. Fifteen fairly simple wooden clergy-stalls, set on original stone plinths, need explanation, which seems to lie in records, after 1340, of large ordination services held here by the bishops (very partial to their near-by estates just across the county and diocesan boundary): at a single service, 293 men were ordained into the various orders of priesthood. Here too probably lies the explanation of the extraordinary sacristy N of the chancel, about which some mystery has gathered. It is a small building, shrine-shaped, with walls and steep roof entirely of freestone, braced with simple, pierced stonework, slender like traceried wood-spandrels and resting on small comic corbels. Apart from the stone mullions, the two small windows were iron-barred—presumably to protect valuables for these episcopal solemnities. In chancel and aisle walls, remains of monuments, and in the floor the matrix of the large canopied brass of an ecclesiastic, also attest 14th-century glories. Roof corbels in the chancel depict the late-Victorian patrons and the architect (R.H. Carpenter, NW corner) of the careful restoration. Finally, the oppressively rich timbering of the nave roof, double hammerbeamed, but looking too steep-pitched, as though squeezed into too narrow a nave. The hammerbeam trusses seem too close to each other, as though made for a large nave, but all re-used by carpenters determined not to waste any. One sees how Cole, the 18th-century antiquary, believed this was a second-hand roof, brought from Barnwell Priory, Cambridge, at its dissolution in 1538. Look at the way the pitch changes to a mini-mansard near the ridge, and the way the ridge-runner's carved decoration looks nearer a 1540 style than the rest, which is earlier. Then notice the smallness of the clerestory lights, only three a side. A church commissioning a roof of this richness almost invariably commissioned a grand clerestory to show it off. They did run a debased Perp. window in the E gable slap through the painted Christ in Judgment, itself thoroughly Perp. Yet Carpenter and Ingelow, in their report at the 1891 general restoration, said they saw no sign that this roof had been reset!

Wimblington [5] as a medieval hamlet of Doddington, had two guildhalls and a chapel. In 1874 it acquired a parish church, a building in shelly ragstone, weathered grey outside and with horizontal rust-coloured stripes. One pleasant window, 1938. Two or three Georgian houses. *Stonea*, an 'off-shore' gravel island to the E, was first recorded *c.*955. A large *Camp* on its SW promontory seems to have been strongly fortified by the Iceni, rather far from their Breckland homelands. This seems to have become the Roman administrative centre of the Fenland. Remains of a tall masonry tower suggest a monument marking the scene of a victory (as at Richborough and La Turbie).

Wimpole [14] the stateliest home in Cambridgeshire, was a home until 1976 when Mrs Bambridge, Kipling's daughter, died and left it with 3,000 acres to the National Trust. Now it is one of the great showpieces of the region, as exciting as any secular building in Cambridge itself: indeed Gibbs went on to do the Senate House and the King's building after working for Harley here. The story of the house begins *c.*1640, but older aspects of the setting need a word or two. The old pronunciation is 'wimple': the 'pool' implicit in the name probably lay N of the house and was transformed into fishponds, then a string of lakes, by the sequence of distinguished landscape-gardeners employed here. The more formal of these gardeners competed, in the grandeur and the straightness of their avenues, with Ermine Street, which supplied the W parish boundary and also the main road link with London (and the north). The strategic importance of this road makes it seem likely that the large mound in the park, 500 yards NW of the house, was a 12th-century castle motte (as at Knapwell). A post-mill stood on it in the 17th century. The ruined Gothick Tower devised by Sanderson Miller and built further N is not an improbable fantasy. It is the first thing seen (straight through the house) as you reach the front door: it will not be the first forgotten, even in this palace of surprises. Whether your first view of the big façade is oblique, approaching through green beeches from the church, or full-frontal up the broad gravel walk, you will be struck by its cheerfulness: it faces S into the full sun, and its sparkle and character derive from the ruddiness of its brickwork and the whiteness of its Portland stone dressings—in particular the vertical lines of the quoins marking the central block and, within that, the slight three-bay forward projection under the pediment. This centrepiece provides the keynote to the whole building—the five-bay ranges Gibbs added on either side are a storey lower, and his Harleian library building further left and the 'offices' further right, still more subservient, in the Palladian way. It is all more or less as the architect Flitcroft left it in the 1740s: in general character a subtle mixture of 17th-century Dutch with Palladian English. The central block is in fact the creation of its owner, the young Royalist Sir Thomas Chicheley, to whom Wimpole had come down from the great-nephew of Henry V's Archbishop Chicheley. Sir Thomas, whose rather insolent portrait, in his armour, is now in the Gallery, was building this 'curious neat house' in 1641, in the Anglo-Netherlandish brick-builders' manner of the time. Facing the front, you can easily imagine the original vertical feature that Flitcroft ironed out: it was really a three-storey projecting porch, surmounted by a 'Dutch' gable, with scrolly sides. Flitcroft retained the essential mass of this middle block. Nor did he alter the red and white effect of the building materials, the other strand in its Dutchness: after all, Flitcroft's father was William III's gardener at Hampton Court. Humphry Repton made the ignorant and immoral proposal to paint the house white all over. His watercolour demonstration of the effect this would have was surprisingly chosen for the cover of the National Trust's otherwise excellent *Guidebook*. Chicheley overspent, and the Earl of Radnor lived here for a time. He is thought to

have employed Hampton Court gardeners: by 1701 Wimpole's gardens were 'worth riding 20 miles out of the way to see'. Soon after 1710, the house came to Edward Harley, 2nd Earl of Oxford, who in London brought Oxford, Harley and Wimpole Streets into being. For him, Gibbs added the W wing (interiors ? by Flitcroft), E wing (1723–4) with famous chapel painted in *trompe-l'oeil* by Thornhill, whose masterpiece it is sometimes considered; then *the Great Staircase*, and behind the W wing, approached through small museum-cabinets to house Harley's coins, bustos, etc., *the Library*: 6,000 of his 50,000 volumes: he kept in London the marvellous manuscript collections that became the nucleus of those in the British Library (British Museum).

◁ **Wimpole** Hall: the South Front
View from North Front to Gothick
▽ Tower

Bridgman was extending the gardens with avenues and what not, to N and S, and Wootton was painting, and Pope, Swift and Prior talking and writing. Oxford lived like a prince, like Chicheley overdid it, and in 1740 sold to Philip Yorke, Lord Chancellor and 1st Earl of Hardwicke. The Hardwickes had the house longest—till the 5th earl, Edward VII's friend 'Champagne Charlie', also went broke and sold in 1894. For the 1st earl, Flitcroft's refurbishing included the great staircase, but the cove with its bold plasterwork, reminiscent of Wilton and Coleshill, remains Chicheley's. The 2nd earl transformed park and gardens, de-formalizing them under Capability Brown, who built Sanderson Miller's 'castle'. The 3rd earl, who succeeded in 1790, made three marvellous contributions with the aid of his friend Soane, devising the Yellow Drawing-room, the Plunge Bath and the doubling of the book-room at the threshold of the library. These designs show Soane at his most original. He altered the great staircase again: with its gaslantern, it remains a most remarkable feature. There were large extensions by H.E. Kendall in the 1840s for the good old 4th earl, most of them quite sensibly removed since 1943. Kendall introduced new and excellent ceilings into some of the old rooms and the balustrade to the front of the central block. Captain and Mrs George Bambridge bought Wimpole in 1938. She set about restoring and refurnishing the house in the most enlightened way. Her study and bedroom are properly kept as she lived in them, the last lady of Wimpole. The *church* should not be skipped. Rebuilt by Flitcroft in 1749, it retains a 14th-century N chapel as a mausoleum. Three noble late monuments by Scheemakers and one by Sir Richard Westmacott cannot suppress the question: why was one original 14th-century window kept, complete with what seems to be its (reset) original glass? The theme is not religious, but heraldic, like the great armorial at Butley

Priory, Suffolk. The shields represent leading local magnates—Bassingbourn for instance, who held one of the five Wimpole manors. Three shields on the left define the puzzle: they represent the De Ufford Earl of Suffolk, who had no territorial connection at all with these parts. The clue to the enigma is contained in the middle light: a fugitive nobleman heavily disguised, with wallet over shoulder. The rebels of 1381 planned to take Robert Ufford hostage (his royal connections are also celebrated in this window) and swear he was their leader, but he slipped through, 'disguised with a wallet on his shoulder', to join the king. There was particular reason to celebrate here in Wimpole the crushing of the revolt: a local rebel, Geoffrey Cobb, held one of the manors. He was pardoned, and perhaps put up this glass in expiation. In front of the window lies the tabletomb of Sir Thomas Chicheley, 1616, who died when his son, the first builder of the present house, was two years old. Two of Scheemakers's sculptures frame the window: on the left, Charles, the Lord Chancellor's son and Montesquieu's friend, who died in 1770 on the next day after he, too, became Lord Chancellor. To the right, movingly beautiful memorial to Charles's first wife, who died at 22. This and the big monument to the Lord Chancellor 'who transformed equity into a system' (the putti playing below with the mace), Scheemakers carved from designs by Athenian Stuart. Canova's pupil, Sir Richard Westmacott, was responsible for the memorial to the Lord Chancellor's fourth son, John, combining Greek design (indeed the Greek noses caricatured) with great tenderness of feeling. Other works, by Thomas Banks, John Bacon, etc. Flitcroft's building much Victorianized.

Wisbech [2] was an early outpost of Ely abbey at the mouth of the former Ouse, and so was fortified by a castle from Norman times. As a capital of these northern Cambridge-

shire fens, Wisbech is braving not merely the agelong assault of the tides but also the formidable erosions caused by the needs of the 20th century. At the Reformation, Edward VI chartered the corporation. The town owes many of its most handsome features to a small oil bonanza following the 17th-century fen drainage: fields of yellow coleseed (or rape) were grown, then crushed in tall tower-windmills and exported. Other prosperous features it owes to Kinderley's Cut, a major improvement in the river's outfall, proposed in 1723 and foolishly postponed till the 1770s: it enabled the sea to be repulsed from its position 4 miles from the town to its present distance—12 miles—with improved river access. No small English town better deserved our admiration: none has suffered worse damage, *since* World War II, through our general ignorance of values in architecture and traffic-planning and despite the sturdy efforts of the Wisbech Society, founded by Alec Penrose just before that war. In January 1978, the implacable sea added injury to insult. A gale forced a great tide into the swollen river. It flooded 2 square miles of the N part of the town and damaged 700 homes: stern reminder of even worse advances—in 1236, for instance, when the shore stood less than a mile off, and the sea rose and drowned castle as well as town; and in 1613, and so on. Not the least powerful element in Wisbech's beauty is a sense of the precariousness of its survival. Till *c*.1290, the complex great Ouse came up here through Outwell, its left bank forming Wisbech's E boundary, dividing (till 1933 boundary changes) Wisbech from ancient Walsoken and Norfolk. This was the river that gave Wisbech its name ('Ouse-valley'), and into it flowed a stream now called the Nene. Medieval references to the 'great bridge' in Wisbech always meant the bridge across the Ouse into Walsoken, even though that river declined after *c*.1290, and though its tributary 'the Nene' increased, particularly after c.1480. By the 1580s the Nene had the 'great bridge', and by the 1790s the old main river had so shrunk that it was straightened and canalized. In the 1960s, this old river-bed, the source of Wisbech's name and original character, was ruthlessly bulldozed into oblivion to make way for Churchill Road and Freedom Bridge, two facilities for motor traffic. *The Castle* occupied the convenient angle between the Ouse and its tributary, controlling not only entry into the rivers but lateral movement round the Wash: King John stayed in it at the time the treasure was lost. Thomas de Braunstone, 'former Constable of the Castle', is shown on an impressive brass of c.1401 in the chancel of St Peter's church. Later, the bishops built themselves a palace on the site. It served as prison for recusants, and was again rebuilt, looking like Thorpe Hall, Peterborough, for Cromwell's intelligence chief, Thurloe. Through all that, the sketchy outlines of Norman motte-and-bailey seem to have survived. In 1793 Joseph Medworth, a Wisbech man, bought the estate, redeveloped it agreeably and in 1816 remodelled the house for himself, removing top floor, keeping Thurloe panelling and old brick wall (? on line of oval mound). Outside that he designed a 'circus', the S half of which, The Crescent, 1808–16, red brick, is wholly delightful. The garden front of his new Wisbech Castle has Gothick glazing. The house is now an Educational Museum, open by appointment. From behind Thurloe's gatepiers it faces Museum Square. On one side of Museum Square, Wisbech Museum was designed for the job in 1847 by J.C. Buckler, with proper Tuscan entrance and poor foundations, for it stands over the filled-in 40 ft-wide moat. *St Peter's church*, a few steps from Museum Square, probably also suffered from being too near the moat: its 12th-century W tower (standing to the E against the present W wall of the church) fell early in the 16th century, and its successor, c.1525–38, was sensibly placed on the N side of the building and used as a grand porch. This ashlared, dignified, well-pinnacled tower is only 96 ft high, but a valuable landmark: at belfry level, it lost some of its carvings when Victorian clockfaces were installed. The other distinguished external feature of the church is the Trinity guild-chapel of the same early-Tudor period. Inside, the parts do not relate to an overall plan, indeed the nave scarcely relates to the long tunnel of the 14th-century chancel: the five Romanesque arches of the N aisle, heading into the space beneath the chancel arch, at first look like some free-standing arcade preserved from Roman times. To S, tall, slender Perp. columns frame an aisle as broad as the nave, and another aisle beyond. E end of S aisle houses large organ of fine tone. Splendidly carved and coloured Royal Arms emblazoned, 1605, by R. Barkstone. *Church monuments.* Apart from the 1401 Constable's brass, the chancel contains a lifelike pair of kneeling figures. Thomas and Awdrey Parke, 1630, probably by Gerard Christmas. Equally splendid, but heavier, Matthias and Jane Taylor, 1633. He was 'a linninge draper whose honesty gained him a fair estate. He had the Constableship of the Castle conferred on him: VERTUE EXCELLS EVERY ESCUCHION.' Two Edward Southwells have two of the richest Georgian memorials, 1743 and (by Nollekens) 1787: Southwells leased castle and manor for over a century until it was sold to Medworth, and they may have built Bank House (now Peckover House, q.v.). Among the headstones outside, look for James Smith's, 1835, typical of the good work of c.1801–40 by Samuel Andrews of Wisbech. From the church, there is no longer need to walk S. The *Market Place* has lost much of its old quality, but there are interesting details. It originally spread over the whole area from Nene bridge to Hill Street. (Just across the Nene bridge, the Old Market, 'old' by 1221, also began at the quayside, probably before the Normans came: we come to it later.) In Hill Street, the Conservative Club uses the Old Grammar School, with step gable dating from about the time of the town's incorporation, 1549, and with an Elizabethan rear wing. The Revd John Clarkson (1711–66) was Headmaster here and Lecturer at St Peter's church when his son Thomas was born: 'the Liberator' of the slaves, whose tall 'Dec' memorial by Gilbert Scott stands near the bridge. From the Market Place, Rose and Crown runs through to Nene Quay. Medworth's developments began with York Row, 1793: all round here is evidence of his enterprise. A rather solemn new County Library building, 1975, supplants, with requisite curve, Ely Place Baptist church. Before turning to South Brink, notice, a short way up Alexandra Road, the simple theatre building, seating 120, a really remarkable survival from 1793, restored and reopened as the Angles Theatre in 1978. A short way out on the Lynn Road, enthusiasts, with Wisbech Society support, are restoring to its original grandeur one of the eight-sailed tower-windmills. Nearby, *St Augustine's church*, 1869. Now for *the Brinks*, on which Wisbech's wide fame rests, two of the most handsome Georgian-fronted ribbon-developments in England. The North Brink and South Brink face each other across two parallel roads following the gentle curve of the Nene, much as at Upwell and Outwell on the other river. But here, particularly on North Brink, the elegance starts one thinking of the banks of the Liffey and then, since this is E Anglia, of canal fronts in the Netherlands, *South Brink* is briefer and more vulnerable. It finds itself part of the A47, from Birmingham through to Lynn, Norwich and Yarmouth. Since the 1978 flood, brick barrier walls are finally making the very word 'brink' inappropriate. 'Tho' much is taken, much abides.' Nos 7 and 8 South Brink, one house

△ **Wisbech** warehouses before 1978 flood: the two on the left survived

of *c.*1720 and refronted, was built for Charles Vavazor — Receiver-General of the county's land-tax. In 1838 Octavia Hill was born in No 7, which bears a plaque saying so: admirable pioneer in housing reform and co-founder of the National Trust. It is a nice coincidence that the Trust was able to acquire Peckover House within sight of her birthplace, and that the memorial to another great reformer, Clarkson, stands just along the same Brink. No 12 South Brink is a house with distinguished improvements of, again, the 1720s. It has lately become the Queen's Hotel. Staircase and landing very comparable with Peckover House. A lawyer family here from 1820s: people still remember their coach and pair clattering out from the stable-yard. Then Ede's Terrace, very agreeable late Georgian, to which our age has added a display of downpipes. *North Brink* faces the sun and is grander: at the bridge end, three tall storeys and an attic, and there are Georgian stone fronts among the delectably graded colours of the brick ones. No 7 has one of the more sophisticated fronts, with 'rusticated' ground floor and panelled interior, but instead of a

Wisbech: St Peter's church, Royal Arms

central front doorcase, a side door that originally led to business premises, in 1704 as oil mill and granary. Similarly, Peckover House was from the 1780s a banking house, though its earlier owners, the Southwells, held the manor: whether it was they who built it in 1722 is not clear. It is altogether desirable. Victorian garden, equally pleasant, with greenhouses full of begonias, etc., and three central fruiting orange-trees. Outside, a maidenhair (gingko) tree, one of the oldest in England, and pollarded after recent gales; it overhangs, in a wall, a mar-

ble boy with dog, 1843. An *Alnus glutinosa incisa* shelters a small cemetery of Edwardian cats. Next door, No 19, with a corner pavilion facing the Brink, marks one of the welcome variants in the series of grand fronts. Where Chapel Road joins, 'The Low' is a delightful corner, and farther up-river are Harecroft House (school), Sybald's Holme and Brewery House with brewery buildings. Back at the bridge, to the left is the *Old Market*, three-cornered, and with the usual handsome Wisbech Georgian fronts. Here stood the jolly Octagon, an 1820s

Anglican chapel designed in tribute to the central glory of the cathedral: it was structurally and acoustically not very sound, got worse and came down in 1952. Between Old Market and river, a range of five large old warehouses were picturesque enough to make people think of Venice, even, and Lübeck. They suffered badly in the 1978 flood: three of the five came down soon after, and now there is talk of gardens. The Old Market is a reminder: on this side of the river, from Anglo-Saxon times, Wisbech stretched eight miles to the SW,

marching with Thorney and including Guyhirn and, now, some of the richest market-gardens in the kingdom. Worship in those outlying lands centred on *Wisbech St Mary*, which became a parish only in Victorian times, but was a chapelry of St Peter's early in the Middle Ages. It is a High Church living, like Coveney's. The fabric is low and long, mostly late 14th century, early Perp., with aisles, broad nave, and very broad E window—the greens, reds and silver of which (it is a 1919 memorial) set the church's main tone. This is enriched by baroque gilt, in candlesticks and chairs, and by many bits and pieces of foreign woodcarving and glass—mostly German. All this warmth and colour recalls the priesthood of Canon Mowbray Smith, 1914–51, depicted life size in brass in the baptistry. *Guyhirn*'s name, 'guide-corner', may indicate a critical junction of tides and freshwaters. A chantry chapel founded here in the 14th century presumably decayed at the Dissolution. Sir Gilbert Scott's yellow-brick church, 1878, was built on its site. Meanwhile, half a mile NE, a small chapel-of-ease of simple beauty was built, bearing its date, 1660, and the initials RP. It is ashlar faced on S and E, mostly brick for the rest. A bell (1637) occupies a pretty bellcote. Inside, old pegs (for those high hats), farmhouse brick floor, plain window-glass, narrow benches and (cut-down) pulpit declare this the local Puritan 'church' version of Little Gidding and Leighton Bromswold (Hunts.).

Witcham [8] village stands out of the fen on S-facing slope like contiguous Wentworth, and like contiguous Witchford takes its name from nothing more sinister than wych-elms: none now visible in view across playing field to church, Hall, and Yew Tree House, which has old yews, and box, and rich brown-

Wisbech: North Brink behind flood wall

Wisbech: Peckover House, garden front

brick old house-front, early Stuart, renewed. Witcham Hall, rebuilt 18th century, stuccoed and heavily crenellated in early 19th: Georgian gates. The *church*, unVictorianized, displays a warm mixture of building materials, though it may read like a hotch-potch. S aisle wall is red brick, English bond, so is S front of porch. W half of 13th-century tower rebuilt, 1691, in deep red brick. Clerestory, with Dec. window tracery, is of honey-coloured shelly limestone rag, like Cottenham's: fine 14th-century cross over E gable. S porch and aisles paved with pamments: aisle has old timber roof. Inside, narrow S aisle with font and large 15th-century clunch pulpit set in original position in arch facing nave. Font *c.*1300: angel censing,

two human heads, two dragons and an eagle! Slender rood-screen rises to loft parapet: no remains of loft itself, nor of paintings lately over pulpit. Dec. E window, replacing lancets, contains well-designed glass by G. Webb, 1946. Lovely irregular-corkscrew altar rails. Memorials include Mr Richard, only child of Parson Taylor: 'cropt by a Fever 1 August 1719, when near the 13 year of his age, one of the fairest Flowers that time has produced.'

Witchford [9] looks S over willows and levels of Grunty Fen, whose N-flowing drain is *forded* by the early medieval main road from Ely to Cambridge via Aldreth. Here, at the Ely boundary, the Hundred of Witchford's court met every third

Tuesday—one of two such local administrative councils in the medieval Isle. The *church* was rendered wholly uninteresting in a late-Victorian restoration. Its reconsecration in 1376 leads to natural assumptions that it had been lately rebuilt. The 'early' 14th-century tracery is disconcerting to all of us who assume a datable conformity of change in gothic styles. Other evidence round here leads to wariness, e.g. about when 'Perp.' arrived.

Wood Ditton *see* Ditton, Wood

Wratting, West [15]—to avoid confusion with the Suffolk Wrattings, settled at the same period and planned in much the same way. One of the 6-mile-long parishes, it tapers

Wisbech: Peckover House, drawing-room chimneypiece ▷

Farm landscapes: (*above*) north of **Wisbech**; (*left, above*) near **Westley Waterless**; (*below*) west of **Wisbech**

from the clay woodlands near the village at the E end to chalk downs nuzzling in behind Fleam Dyke. Parts of boundary as described *c.*990, when an estate here went to Ely. Sir John Jacob, Bt., who built the main range of *W. Wratting Park c.*1730 (the wings are later), also repaired nave and chancel of *church* with freestone, and redecorated the interior so that William Cole said (1746) 'it may vie with any church in the kingdom for elegancy and neatness, being entirely fitted up à la moderne with stucco.' Jacob's son, Hildebrand (1693–1739) was something of a poet, and his son a Hebrew scholar. The Frosts, their successors here 1809–1920s, included E.P. Frost (d. 1922), a remarkable pioneer of flying-machines and President of the Royal Aeronautical Soc. Unluckily, in 1896, they had the church restored to gothic; the architect, Howard Gaye, incorrectly named. Faint out- lines of beautiful plaster panelling in the chancel survive, also a graceful marble font, standing on its head N of the altar. Broad nave roof, Horse- heath type. Successful ironwork screen, 1922. *W. Wratting Hall*, Georgian. Village a bit suburban. Michael Dalton, Jacobean legal writer, at Brook Farm, near World War II bomber airfield. Leys mill, a black-boarded smockmill with white cap and sails, is a cheerful landmark for miles around.

Index

EXPLANATORY NOTE

Access Point.

A2	Motorways
A612	Dual Carriageways
B4541	Trunk Roads
	'A' Roads
	'B' Roads
	Other Serviceable Roads
	Railways
	County Boundaries
	Old Boundaries
+	Churches
·275	Heights in Feet
▲	Summits

Tunnel
Level Crossing

STATUTE MILES

0   1   2   3   4   5

10 miles to 2.1 inches

© — John Bartholomew & Son, Ltd., Edinburgh

G156